CAPTAIN CARTER

WOMAN OUT OF TIME

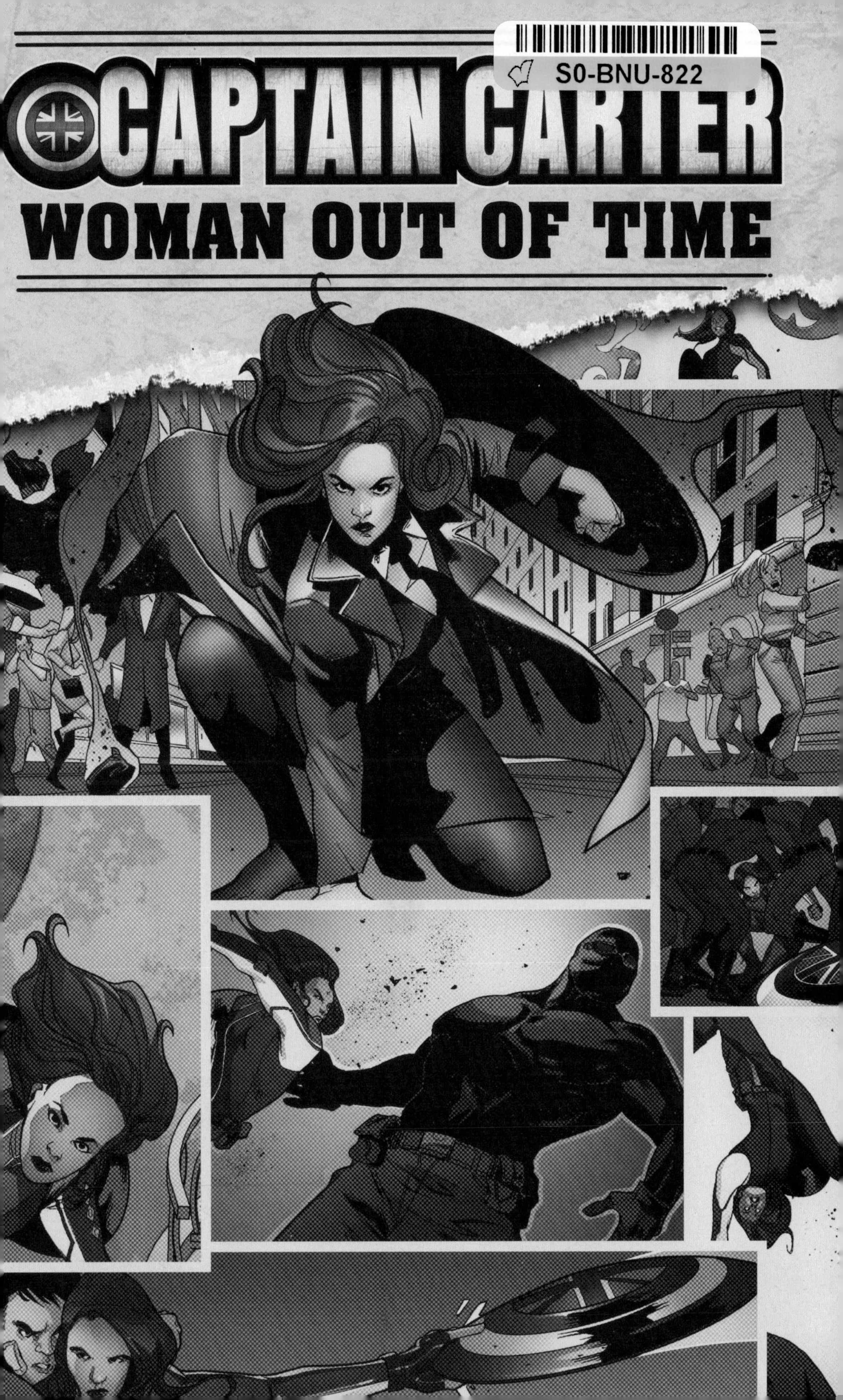

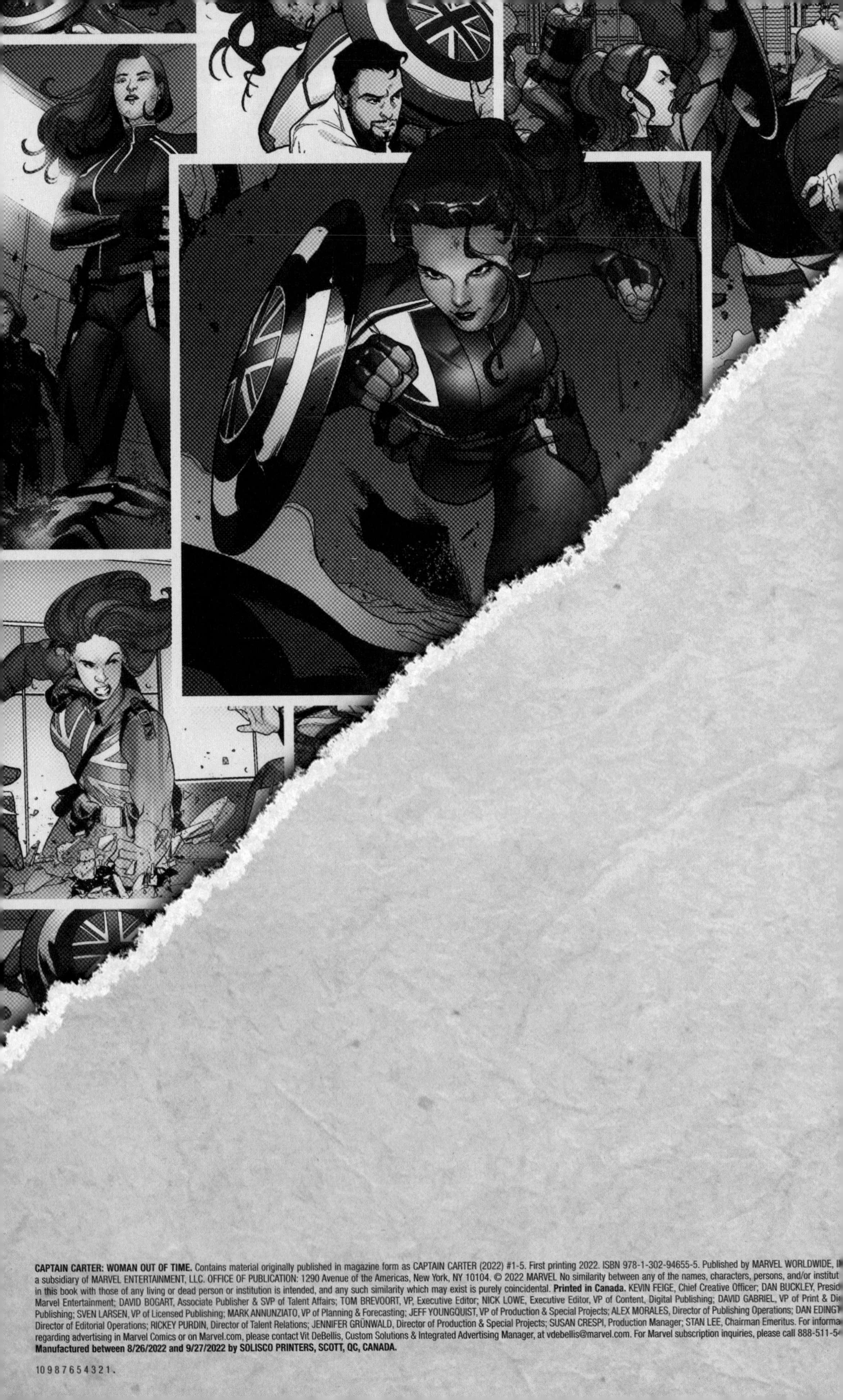

CAPTAIN CARTER: WOMAN OUT OF TIME. Contains material originally published in magazine form as CAPTAIN CARTER (2022) #1-5. First printing 2022. ISBN 978-1-302-94655-5. Published by MARVEL WORLDWIDE, I a subsidiary of MARVEL ENTERTAINMENT, LLC. OFFICE OF PUBLICATION: 1290 Avenue of the Americas, New York, NY 10104. © 2022 MARVEL No similarity between any of the names, characters, persons, and/or institut in this book with those of any living or dead person or institution is intended, and any such similarity which may exist is purely coincidental. **Printed in Canada.** KEVIN FEIGE, Chief Creative Officer; DAN BUCKLEY, Presid Marvel Entertainment; DAVID BOGART, Associate Publisher & SVP of Talent Affairs; TOM BREVOORT, VP, Executive Editor; NICK LOWE, Executive Editor, VP of Content, Digital Publishing; DAVID GABRIEL, VP of Print & Di Publishing; SVEN LARSEN, VP of Licensed Publishing; MARK ANNUNZIATO, VP of Planning & Forecasting; JEFF YOUNGQUIST, VP of Production & Special Projects; ALEX MORALES, Director of Publishing Operations; DAN EDINGT Director of Editorial Operations; RICKEY PURDIN, Director of Talent Relations; JENNIFER GRÜNWALD, Director of Production & Special Projects; SUSAN CRESPI, Production Manager; STAN LEE, Chairman Emeritus. For informa regarding advertising in Marvel Comics or on Marvel.com, please contact Vit DeBellis, Custom Solutions & Integrated Advertising Manager, at vdebellis@marvel.com. For Marvel subscription inquiries, please call 888-511-5
Manufactured between 8/26/2022 and 9/27/2022 by SOLISCO PRINTERS, SCOTT, QC, CANADA.

10 9 8 7 6 5 4 3 2 1

CAPTAIN CARTER
WOMAN OUT OF TIME

JAMIE McKELVIE
WRITER

MARIKA CRESTA
ARTIST

ERICK ARCINIEGA (#1-2) & **MATT MILLA** (#3-5)
COLOR ARTISTS

VC's CLAYTON COWLES
LETTERER

JAMIE McKELVIE
COVER ARTIST/NEWSPAPER DESIGN

STACIE ZUCKER
LOGO AND BOOK DESIGN

KAITLYN LINDTVEDT
ASSISTANT EDITOR

ALANNA SMITH
EDITOR

JENNIFER GRÜNWALD
COLLECTION EDITOR

DANIEL KIRCHHOFFER
ASSISTANT EDITOR

MAIA LOY
ASSISTANT MANAGING EDITOR

LISA MONTALBANO
ASSOCIATE MANAGER, TALENT RELATIONS

JEFF YOUNGQUIST
VP PRODUCTION & SPECIAL PROJECTS

ADAM DEL RE
SENIOR DESIGNER

DAVID GABRIEL
SVP PRINT, SALES & MARKETING

C.B. CEBULSKI
EDITOR IN CHIEF

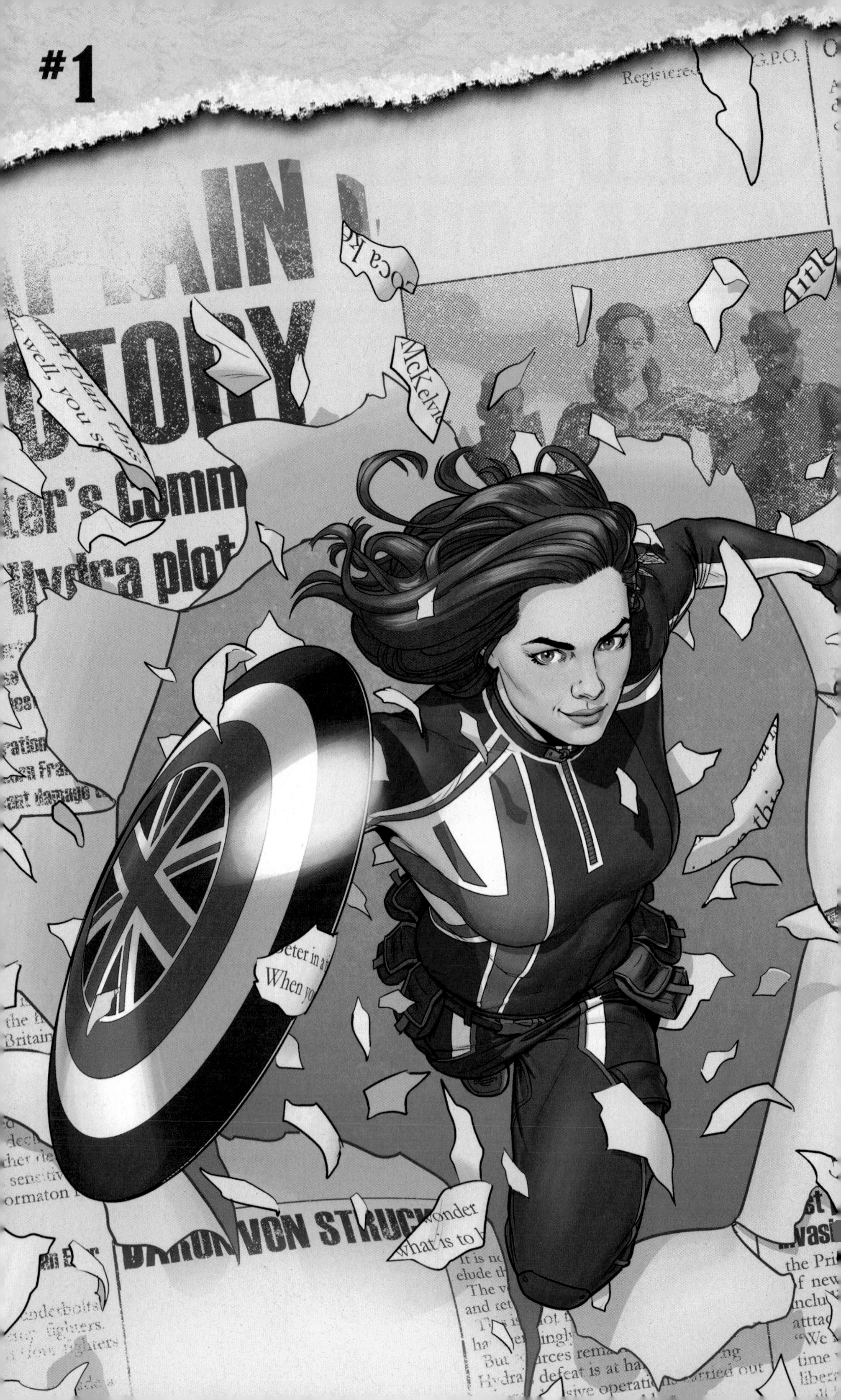
#1
G.P.O.
Hydra plot
VON STRUCK
wonder
what is to
The
But
Britain
the Pri

BRITISH WOMAN MARGARET CARTER NAMED AS MYSTERY HERO

FOR KING AND EMPIRE

WEDNESDAY, JUNE 23, 1943

LLIED SCIENTISTS CREATE
ERFECT SOLDIER

rong, fast, resilient and British--but 'Super-
dier' is unconventional choice

STARK
ELECTRIC APPLIANCES

Morning Chronicle

**CARTER'S
COMMANDOS
IN DECISIVE
OW AGAINST
RA FORC**
Strucker's
The Ropes

Navy Rout
Off

NAZI SCIENTIST
THREAT GROWS

**HYDRA DIVISION LED BY
FUEHRER'S TOP MAN**
N VON STRUCKER'S NAZI
ERS DEVELOP NEW
S OF WAR

DAILY STAN
No. 21,538   Threehalfpence   AN ORPINGTON-SMYTHE
WEDNESDAY FEBRUARY 7 1945

BARON VON STRUCKER DEFEATED IN DARING G

Carter Sacrifice Sav
the United States

**HERO STOPS PLANE CARF
MEANS TO KILL MILLIO**

Search For Body Continue

IN the early hours of Monday morning, Captain Margaret "P
gave her life to prevent Baron Von Strucker from delivering
of highly advanced bombs intended to destroy the Eastern Seab
United States of America.

Captain Carter led her crack unit, popularly known as "Carter's Commandos," in
last remaining Hydra stronghold. The base, located in the Swiss Alps, was the secret testi
of warfare. Carter and her men began the assault to destroy the technology on-site, wi
shortly after from nearby Allied armed forces.

While the attack is reported to have
the prototype

Echo EXTRA
LIGHTING UP TIME: 10.19 pm   Price 1½d.

BLOOD AND FIRE
COMPLAINT

ERMANY'S FUTURE
LIN: CRIMEA CONFERENCE

Victoria Cross
Awarded To
Fallen Hero

CAPTAIN Margaret "Peggy" Ca
is to be posthumously awarded
the V.C., it was announced yesterday.
She is the first woman to receive the
highest honour awarded by the King
Carter's valour in the prese
enemy will be he
private

Daily News   MAY 8

VE-DAY
IT'S   OVER   IN   EURO

ANNOUNCE
BE MAD

70p

SUNDAY, FEBRUARY 5, 1995

ON THE 50th ANNIVERSARY OF CAPTAIN PEGGY CARTER'S HEROIC LAST ACT
A NATION REMEMBERS

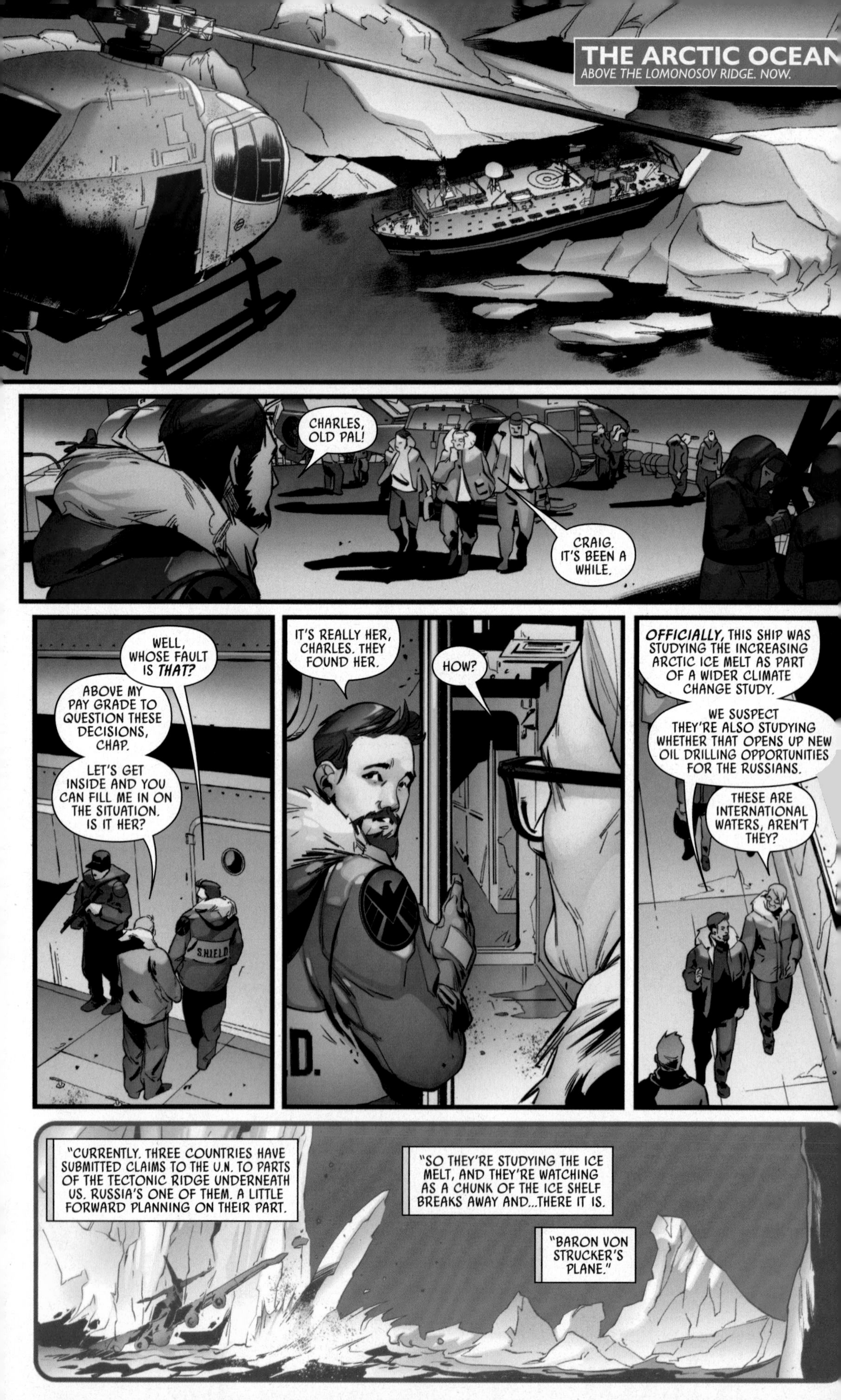

THE ARCTIC OCEAN
ABOVE THE LOMONOSOV RIDGE. NOW.
CHARLES, OLD PAL!
CRAIG. IT'S BEEN A WHILE.
WELL, WHOSE FAULT IS *THAT?*
ABOVE MY PAY GRADE TO QUESTION THESE DECISIONS, CHAP.
LET'S GET INSIDE AND YOU CAN FILL ME IN ON THE SITUATION. IS IT HER?
S.H.I.E.L.D.
IT'S REALLY HER, CHARLES. THEY FOUND HER.
HOW?
OFFICIALLY, THIS SHIP WAS STUDYING THE INCREASING ARCTIC ICE MELT AS PART OF A WIDER CLIMATE CHANGE STUDY.
WE SUSPECT THEY'RE ALSO STUDYING WHETHER THAT OPENS UP NEW OIL DRILLING OPPORTUNITIES FOR THE RUSSIANS.
THESE ARE INTERNATIONAL WATERS, AREN'T THEY?
"CURRENTLY, THREE COUNTRIES HAVE SUBMITTED CLAIMS TO THE U.N. TO PARTS OF THE TECTONIC RIDGE UNDERNEATH US. RUSSIA'S ONE OF THEM. A LITTLE FORWARD PLANNING ON THEIR PART.
"SO THEY'RE STUDYING THE ICE MELT, AND THEY'RE WATCHING AS A CHUNK OF THE ICE SHELF BREAKS AWAY AND...THERE IT IS.
"BARON VON STRUCKER'S PLANE."

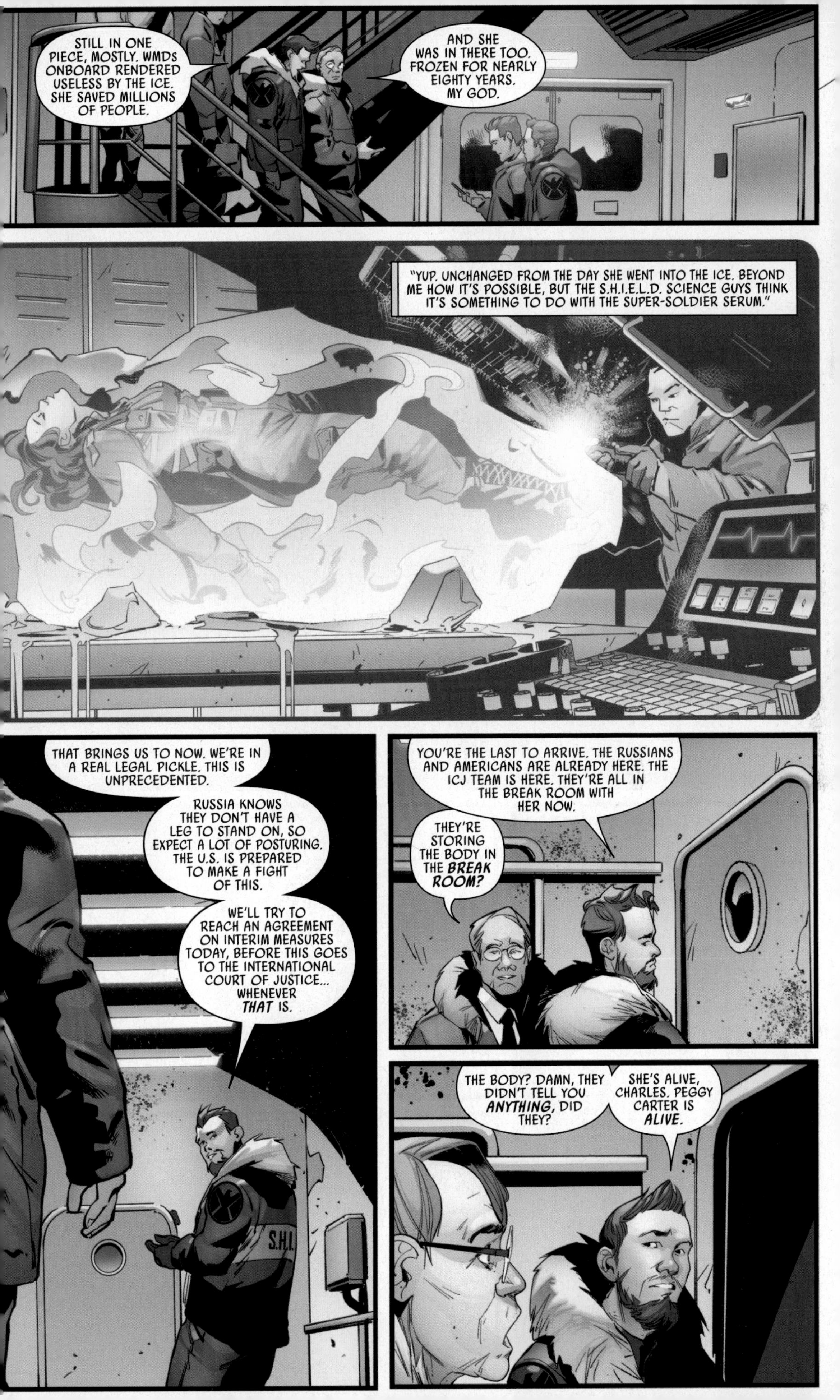
STILL IN ONE PIECE, MOSTLY. WMDS ONBOARD RENDERED USELESS BY THE ICE. SHE SAVED MILLIONS OF PEOPLE.
AND SHE WAS IN THERE TOO. FROZEN FOR NEARLY EIGHTY YEARS. MY GOD.
"YUP. UNCHANGED FROM THE DAY SHE WENT INTO THE ICE. BEYOND ME HOW IT'S POSSIBLE, BUT THE S.H.I.E.L.D. SCIENCE GUYS THINK IT'S SOMETHING TO DO WITH THE SUPER-SOLDIER SERUM."
THAT BRINGS US TO NOW. WE'RE IN A REAL LEGAL PICKLE. THIS IS UNPRECEDENTED.
RUSSIA KNOWS THEY DON'T HAVE A LEG TO STAND ON, SO EXPECT A LOT OF POSTURING. THE U.S. IS PREPARED TO MAKE A FIGHT OF THIS.
WE'LL TRY TO REACH AN AGREEMENT ON INTERIM MEASURES TODAY, BEFORE THIS GOES TO THE INTERNATIONAL COURT OF JUSTICE... WHENEVER *THAT* IS.
S.H.I.
YOU'RE THE LAST TO ARRIVE. THE RUSSIANS AND AMERICANS ARE ALREADY HERE. THE ICJ TEAM IS HERE. THEY'RE ALL IN THE BREAK ROOM WITH HER NOW.
THEY'RE STORING THE BODY IN THE ***BREAK ROOM?***
THE BODY? DAMN, THEY DIDN'T TELL YOU *ANYTHING*, DID THEY?
SHE'S ALIVE, CHARLES. PEGGY CARTER IS ***ALIVE.***

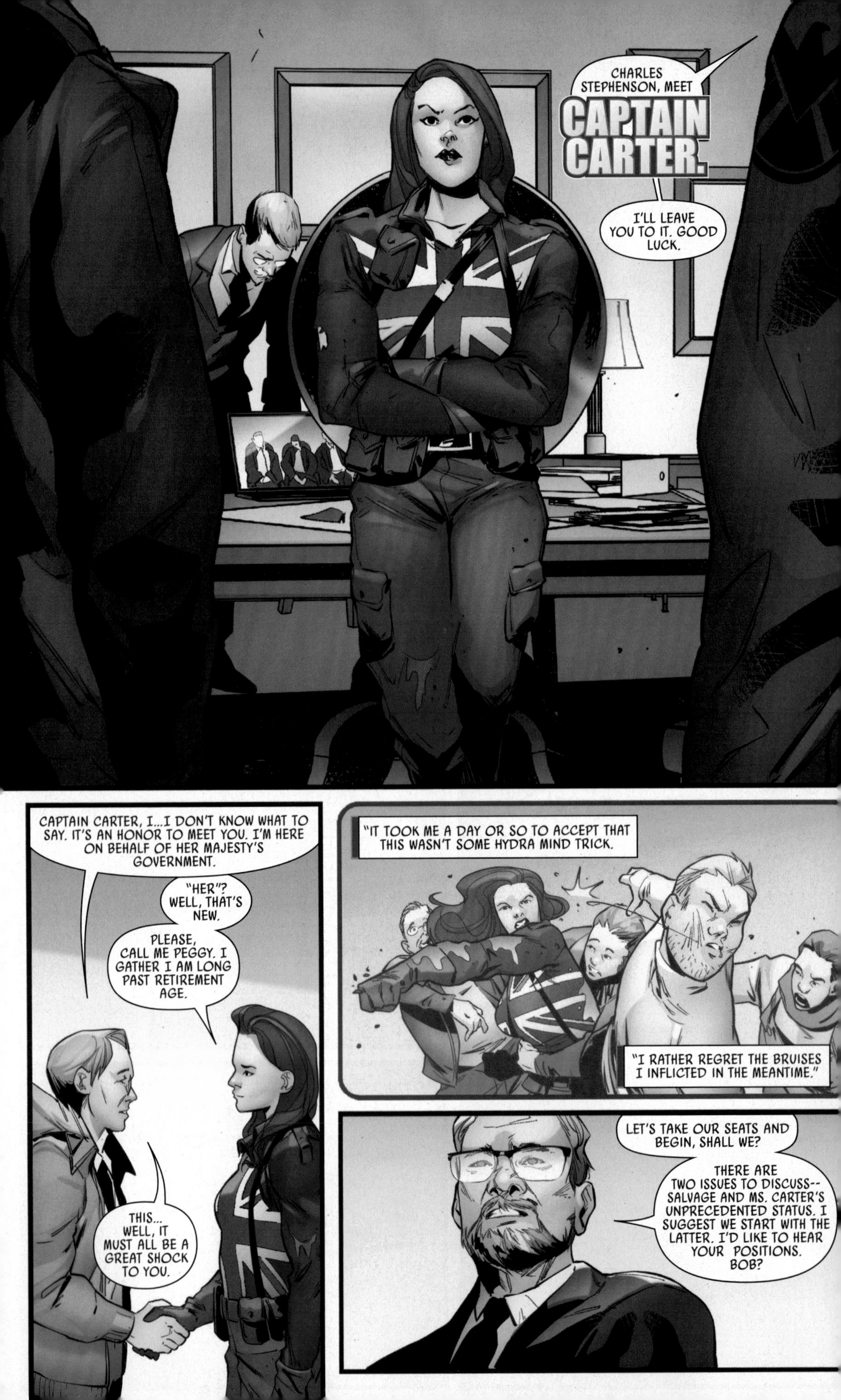

CHARLES STEPHENSON, MEET CAPTAIN CARTER.
I'LL LEAVE YOU TO IT. GOOD LUCK.
CAPTAIN CARTER, I...I DON'T KNOW WHAT TO SAY. IT'S AN HONOR TO MEET YOU. I'M HERE ON BEHALF OF HER MAJESTY'S GOVERNMENT.
"HER"? WELL, THAT'S NEW.
PLEASE, CALL ME PEGGY. I GATHER I AM LONG PAST RETIREMENT AGE.
THIS... WELL, IT MUST ALL BE A GREAT SHOCK TO YOU.
"IT TOOK ME A DAY OR SO TO ACCEPT THAT THIS WASN'T SOME HYDRA MIND TRICK.
"I RATHER REGRET THE BRUISES I INFLICTED IN THE MEANTIME."
LET'S TAKE OUR SEATS AND BEGIN, SHALL WE?
THERE ARE TWO ISSUES TO DISCUSS--SALVAGE AND MS. CARTER'S UNPRECEDENTED STATUS. I SUGGEST WE START WITH THE LATTER. I'D LIKE TO HEAR YOUR POSITIONS. BOB?

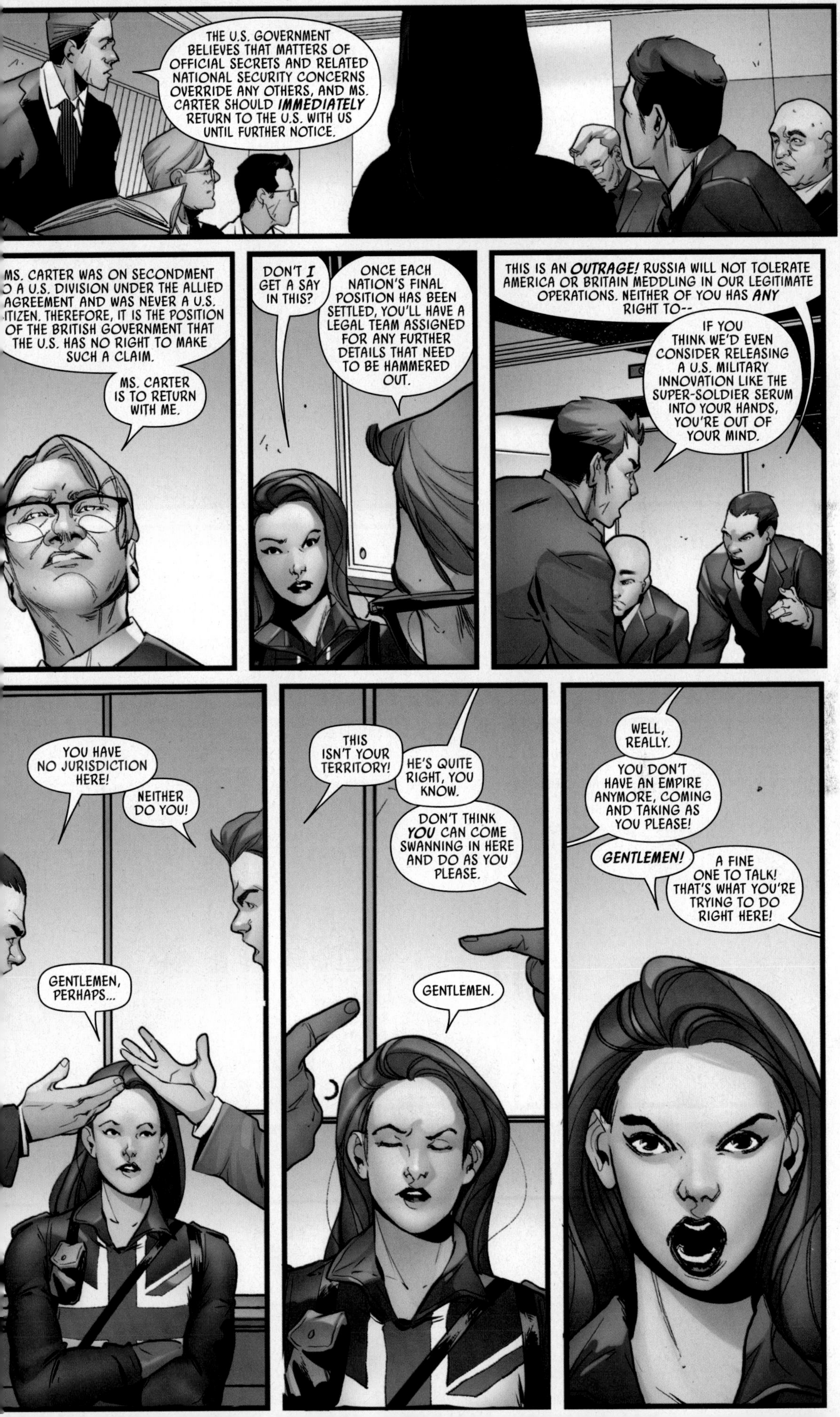

THE U.S. GOVERNMENT BELIEVES THAT MATTERS OF OFFICIAL SECRETS AND RELATED NATIONAL SECURITY CONCERNS OVERRIDE ANY OTHERS, AND MS. CARTER SHOULD *IMMEDIATELY* RETURN TO THE U.S. WITH US UNTIL FURTHER NOTICE.
MS. CARTER WAS ON SECONDMENT TO A U.S. DIVISION UNDER THE ALLIED AGREEMENT AND WAS NEVER A U.S. CITIZEN. THEREFORE, IT IS THE POSITION OF THE BRITISH GOVERNMENT THAT THE U.S. HAS NO RIGHT TO MAKE SUCH A CLAIM.
MS. CARTER IS TO RETURN WITH ME.
DON'T *I* GET A SAY IN THIS?
ONCE EACH NATION'S FINAL POSITION HAS BEEN SETTLED, YOU'LL HAVE A LEGAL TEAM ASSIGNED FOR ANY FURTHER DETAILS THAT NEED TO BE HAMMERED OUT.
THIS IS AN *OUTRAGE!* RUSSIA WILL NOT TOLERATE AMERICA OR BRITAIN MEDDLING IN OUR LEGITIMATE OPERATIONS. NEITHER OF YOU HAS *ANY* RIGHT TO--
IF YOU THINK WE'D EVEN CONSIDER RELEASING A U.S. MILITARY INNOVATION LIKE THE SUPER-SOLDIER SERUM INTO YOUR HANDS, YOU'RE OUT OF YOUR MIND.
YOU HAVE NO JURISDICTION HERE!
NEITHER DO YOU!
GENTLEMEN, PERHAPS...
THIS ISN'T YOUR TERRITORY!
HE'S QUITE RIGHT, YOU KNOW.
DON'T THINK *YOU* CAN COME SWANNING IN HERE AND DO AS YOU PLEASE.
GENTLEMEN.
WELL, REALLY.
YOU DON'T HAVE AN EMPIRE ANYMORE, COMING AND TAKING AS YOU PLEASE!
GENTLEMEN!
A FINE ONE TO TALK! THAT'S WHAT YOU'RE TRYING TO DO RIGHT HERE!

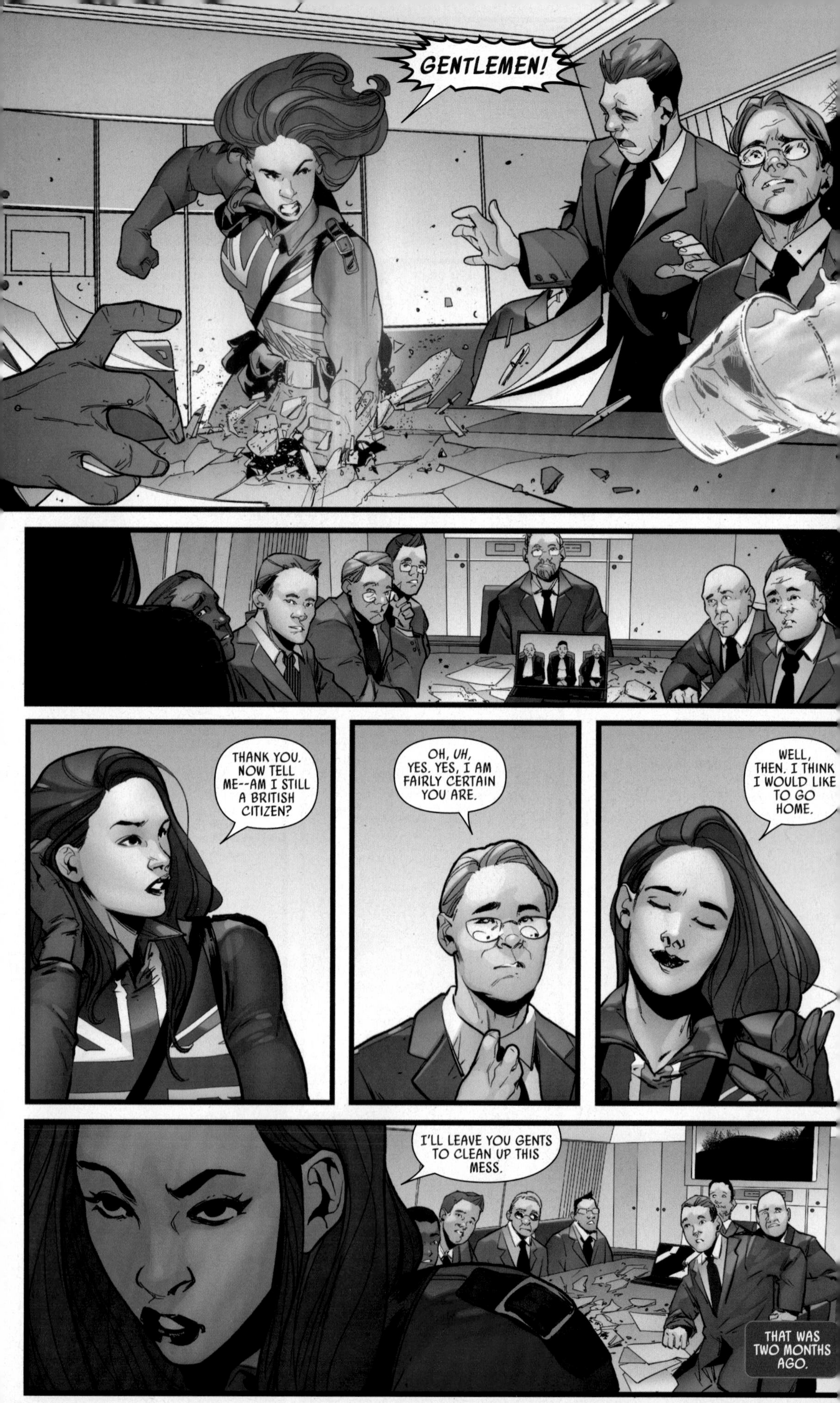
GENTLEMEN!
THANK YOU. NOW TELL ME--AM I STILL A BRITISH CITIZEN?
OH, UH, YES. YES, I AM FAIRLY CERTAIN YOU ARE.
WELL, THEN. I THINK I WOULD LIKE TO GO HOME.
I'LL LEAVE YOU GENTS TO CLEAN UP THIS MESS.
THAT WAS TWO MONTHS AGO.

S BEEN A PERIOD OF...ADJUSTMENT.

I HAD BEEN *M.I.A.* SINCE 1945. NO BRITISH GOVERNMENT SINCE HAS FELT IT POLITICALLY ASTUTE TO DECLARE THE *SUPER-SOLDIER* OFFICIALLY DEAD.

THERE'S BEEN A SALARY--AND THEN A PENSION--AMASSING IN MY BANK ACCOUNT FOR NEARLY *EIGHTY YEARS.* THAT GIVES ME A BIT OF BREATHING SPACE. TIME TO *THINK.*

I TOOK AN APARTMENT IN A FAMILIAR AREA, TO HELP ME RECONNECT WITH LONDON.

SOUGHT OUT OLD HAUNTS. SOME STILL STANDING.

SOME NOT.

I CAN'T HIDE AWAY. I HAVE TO ROLL MY SLEEVES UP AND PUT IN THE WORK TO LIVE IN THIS WORLD. AND THERE *ARE* POSITIVES.

THE FOOD REALLY IS *MUCH* BETTER.

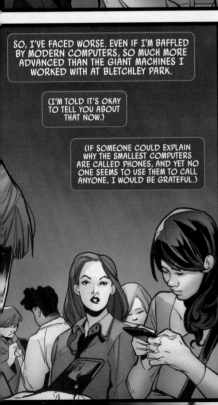

SO, I'VE FACED WORSE. EVEN IF I'M BAFFLED BY MODERN COMPUTERS, SO MUCH MORE ADVANCED THAN THE GIANT MACHINES I WORKED WITH AT BLETCHLEY PARK.

(I'M TOLD IT'S OKAY TO TELL YOU ABOUT THAT NOW.)

(IF SOMEONE COULD EXPLAIN WHY THE SMALLEST COMPUTERS ARE CALLED PHONES, AND YET NO ONE SEEMS TO USE THEM TO CALL ANYONE, I WOULD BE GRATEFUL.)

THE TELEVISION DRAMAS MOVE SO FAST, I FEEL LIKE I MIGHT GET NAUSEA.

(AND THEY SHOW A *LOT* MORE SKIN THAN I'M ACCUSTOMED TO.)

GOOD LORD.

DOOF DOOF DOOF DOOF

AND I DON'T REALLY UNDERSTAND THE MUSIC.

OR QUITE *WHY* YOUNG PEOPLE FEEL THE NEED TO PLAY IT SO LOUD.

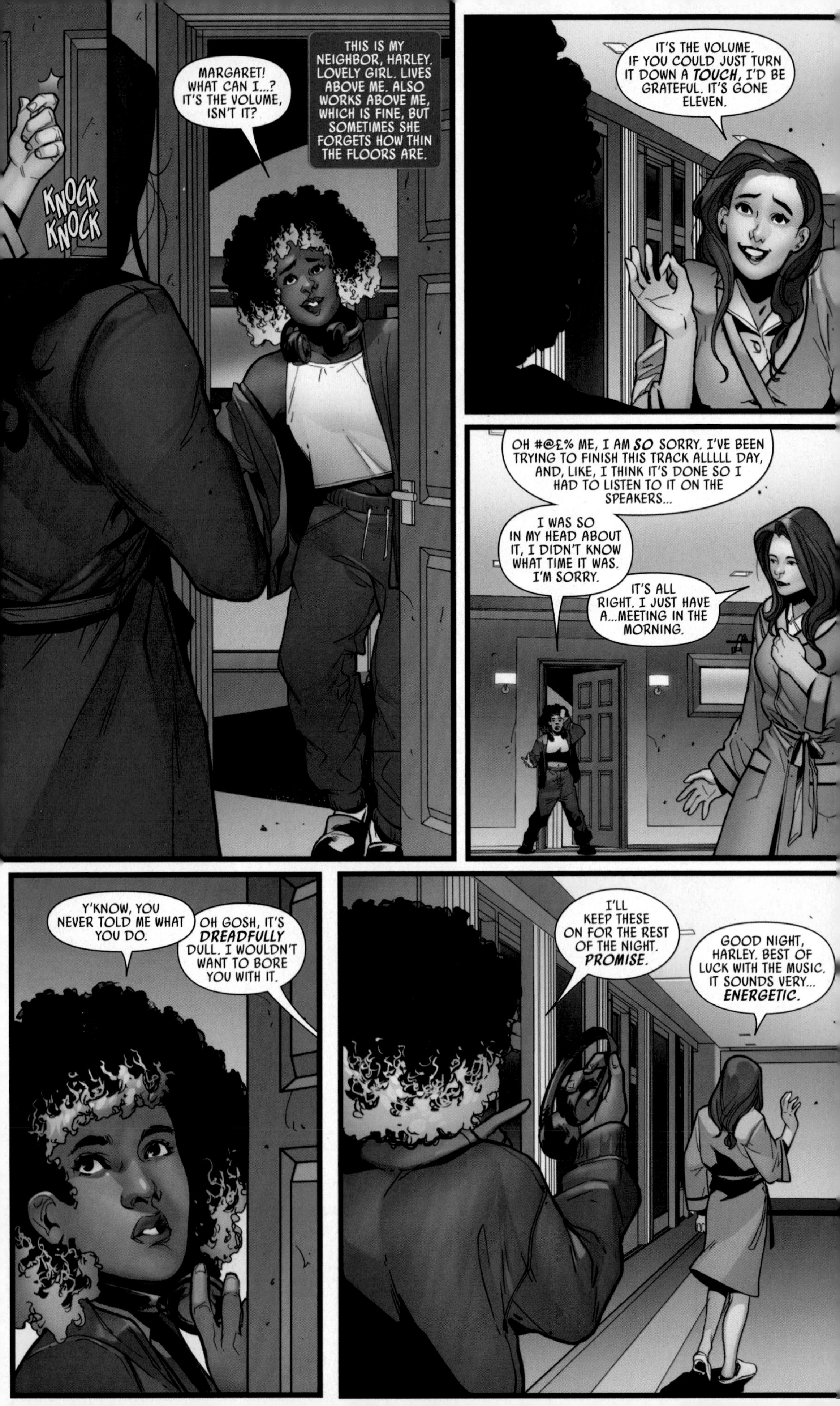
MARGARET! WHAT CAN I...? IT'S THE VOLUME, ISN'T IT?
THIS IS MY NEIGHBOR, HARLEY. LOVELY GIRL. LIVES ABOVE ME. ALSO WORKS ABOVE ME, WHICH IS FINE, BUT SOMETIMES SHE FORGETS HOW THIN THE FLOORS ARE.
KNOCK KNOCK
IT'S THE VOLUME. IF YOU COULD JUST TURN IT DOWN A TOUCH, I'D BE GRATEFUL. IT'S GONE ELEVEN.
OH #@£% ME, I AM SO SORRY. I'VE BEEN TRYING TO FINISH THIS TRACK ALLLLL DAY, AND, LIKE, I THINK IT'S DONE SO I HAD TO LISTEN TO IT ON THE SPEAKERS...
I WAS SO IN MY HEAD ABOUT IT, I DIDN'T KNOW WHAT TIME IT WAS. I'M SORRY.
IT'S ALL RIGHT. I JUST HAVE A...MEETING IN THE MORNING.
Y'KNOW, YOU NEVER TOLD ME WHAT YOU DO.
OH GOSH, IT'S DREADFULLY DULL. I WOULDN'T WANT TO BORE YOU WITH IT.
I'LL KEEP THESE ON FOR THE REST OF THE NIGHT. PROMISE.
GOOD NIGHT, HARLEY. BEST OF LUCK WITH THE MUSIC. IT SOUNDS VERY... ENERGETIC.

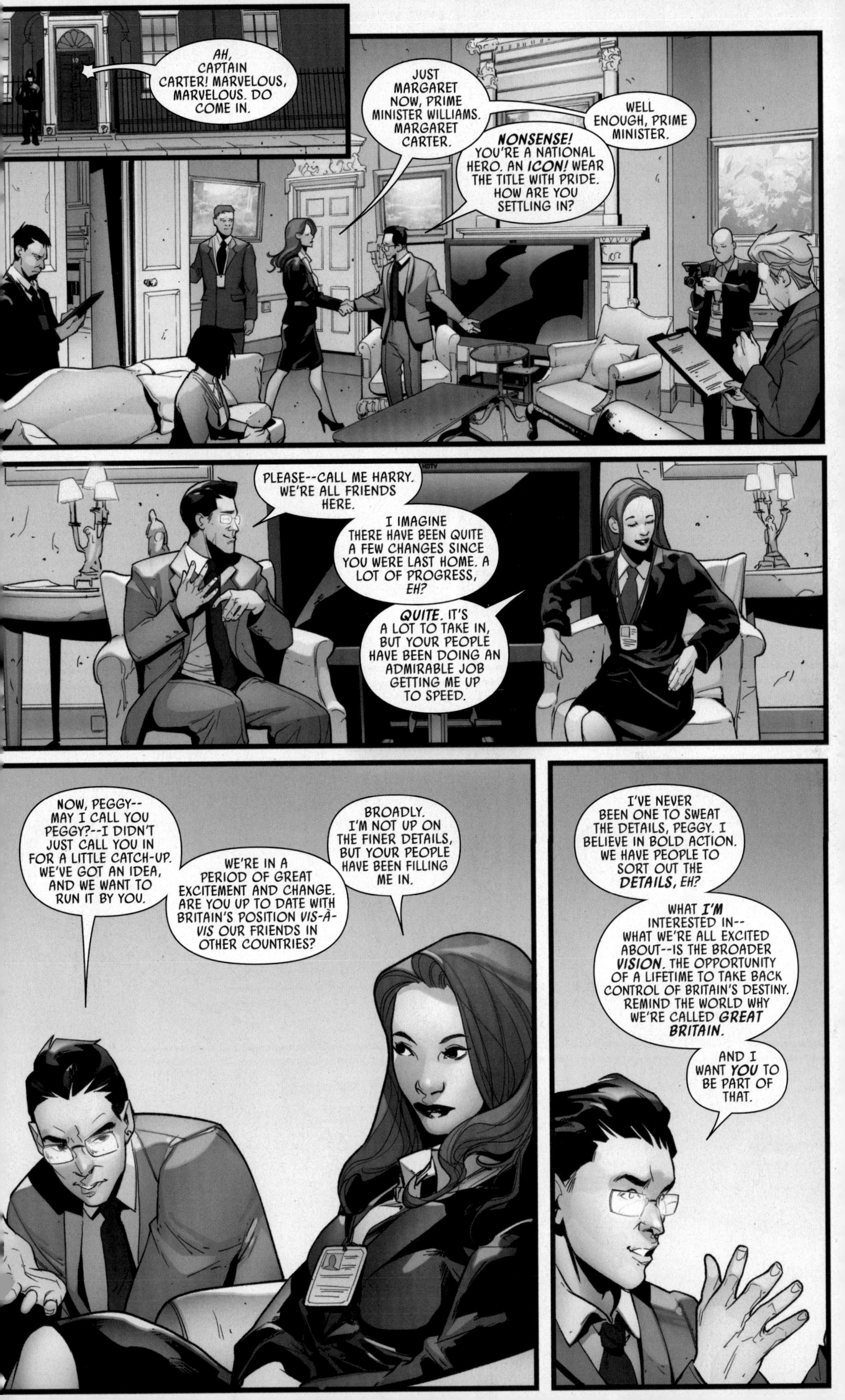
AH, CAPTAIN CARTER! MARVELOUS, MARVELOUS. DO COME IN.
JUST MARGARET NOW, PRIME MINISTER WILLIAMS. MARGARET CARTER.
NONSENSE! YOU'RE A NATIONAL HERO. AN ICON! WEAR THE TITLE WITH PRIDE. HOW ARE YOU SETTLING IN?
WELL ENOUGH, PRIME MINISTER.
PLEASE--CALL ME HARRY. WE'RE ALL FRIENDS HERE.
I IMAGINE THERE HAVE BEEN QUITE A FEW CHANGES SINCE YOU WERE LAST HOME. A LOT OF PROGRESS, EH?
QUITE. IT'S A LOT TO TAKE IN, BUT YOUR PEOPLE HAVE BEEN DOING AN ADMIRABLE JOB GETTING ME UP TO SPEED.
NOW, PEGGY--MAY I CALL YOU PEGGY?--I DIDN'T JUST CALL YOU IN FOR A LITTLE CATCH-UP. WE'VE GOT AN IDEA, AND WE WANT TO RUN IT BY YOU.
WE'RE IN A PERIOD OF GREAT EXCITEMENT AND CHANGE. ARE YOU UP TO DATE WITH BRITAIN'S POSITION VIS-À-VIS OUR FRIENDS IN OTHER COUNTRIES?
BROADLY. I'M NOT UP ON THE FINER DETAILS, BUT YOUR PEOPLE HAVE BEEN FILLING ME IN.
I'VE NEVER BEEN ONE TO SWEAT THE DETAILS, PEGGY. I BELIEVE IN BOLD ACTION. WE HAVE PEOPLE TO SORT OUT THE DETAILS, EH?
WHAT I'M INTERESTED IN--WHAT WE'RE ALL EXCITED ABOUT--IS THE BROADER VISION. THE OPPORTUNITY OF A LIFETIME TO TAKE BACK CONTROL OF BRITAIN'S DESTINY. REMIND THE WORLD WHY WE'RE CALLED GREAT BRITAIN.
AND I WANT YOU TO BE PART OF THAT.

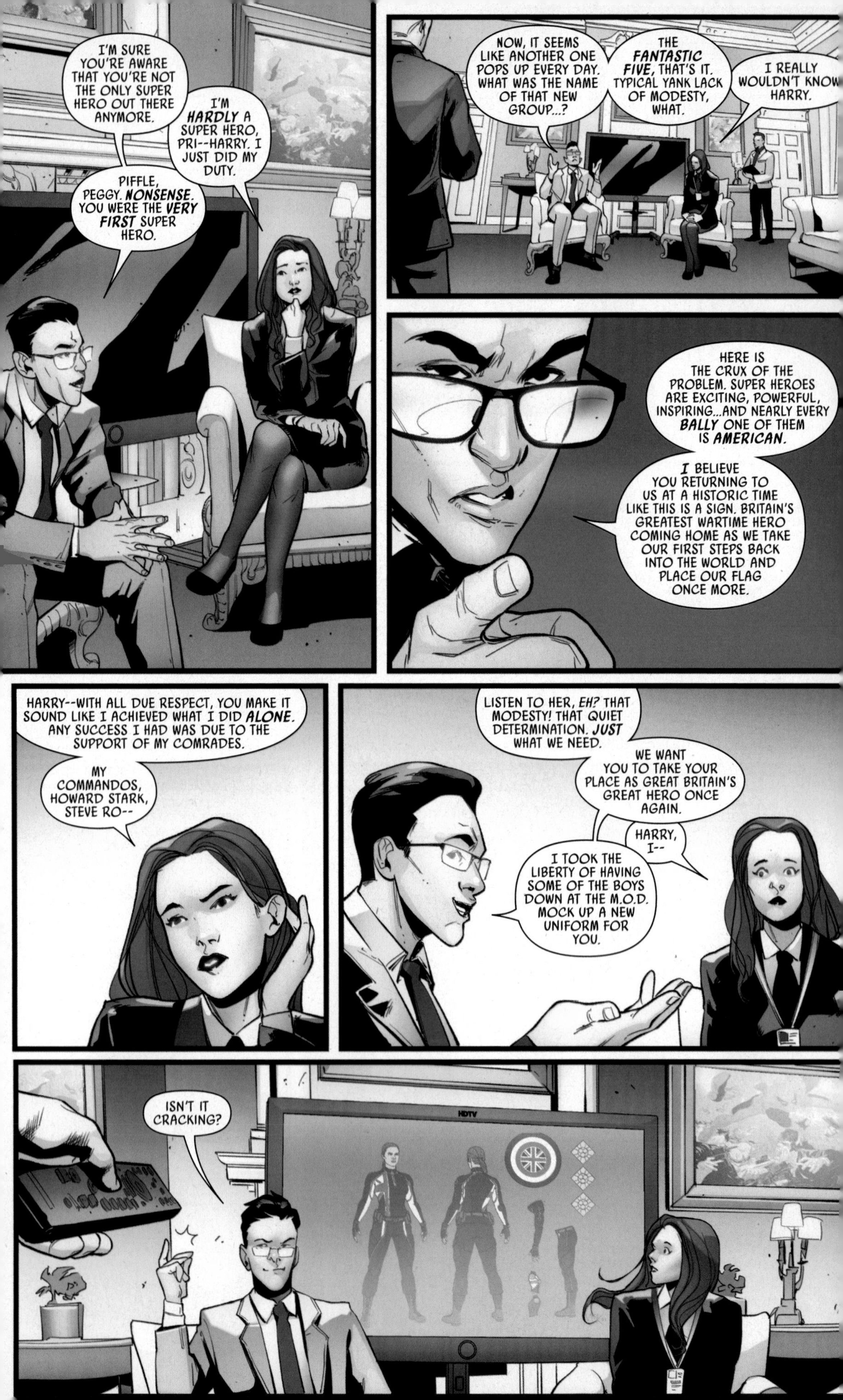
I'M SURE YOU'RE AWARE THAT YOU'RE NOT THE ONLY SUPER HERO OUT THERE ANYMORE.
I'M *HARDLY* A SUPER HERO, PRI--HARRY. I JUST DID MY DUTY.
PIFFLE, PEGGY. **NONSENSE.** YOU WERE THE ***VERY FIRST*** SUPER HERO.
NOW, IT SEEMS LIKE ANOTHER ONE POPS UP EVERY DAY. WHAT WAS THE NAME OF THAT NEW GROUP...?
THE ***FANTASTIC FIVE,*** THAT'S IT. TYPICAL YANK LACK OF MODESTY, WHAT.
I REALLY WOULDN'T KNOW, HARRY.
HERE IS THE CRUX OF THE PROBLEM. SUPER HEROES ARE EXCITING, POWERFUL, INSPIRING...AND NEARLY EVERY ***BALLY*** ONE OF THEM IS ***AMERICAN.***
I BELIEVE YOU RETURNING TO US AT A HISTORIC TIME LIKE THIS IS A SIGN. BRITAIN'S GREATEST WARTIME HERO COMING HOME AS WE TAKE OUR FIRST STEPS BACK INTO THE WORLD AND PLACE OUR FLAG ONCE MORE.
HARRY--WITH ALL DUE RESPECT, YOU MAKE IT SOUND LIKE I ACHIEVED WHAT I DID *ALONE.* ANY SUCCESS I HAD WAS DUE TO THE SUPPORT OF MY COMRADES.
MY COMMANDOS, HOWARD STARK, STEVE RO--
LISTEN TO HER, *EH?* THAT MODESTY! THAT QUIET DETERMINATION. ***JUST*** WHAT WE NEED.
WE WANT YOU TO TAKE YOUR PLACE AS GREAT BRITAIN'S GREAT HERO ONCE AGAIN.
HARRY, I--
I TOOK THE LIBERTY OF HAVING SOME OF THE BOYS DOWN AT THE M.O.D. MOCK UP A NEW UNIFORM FOR YOU.
ISN'T IT CRACKING?
HDTV

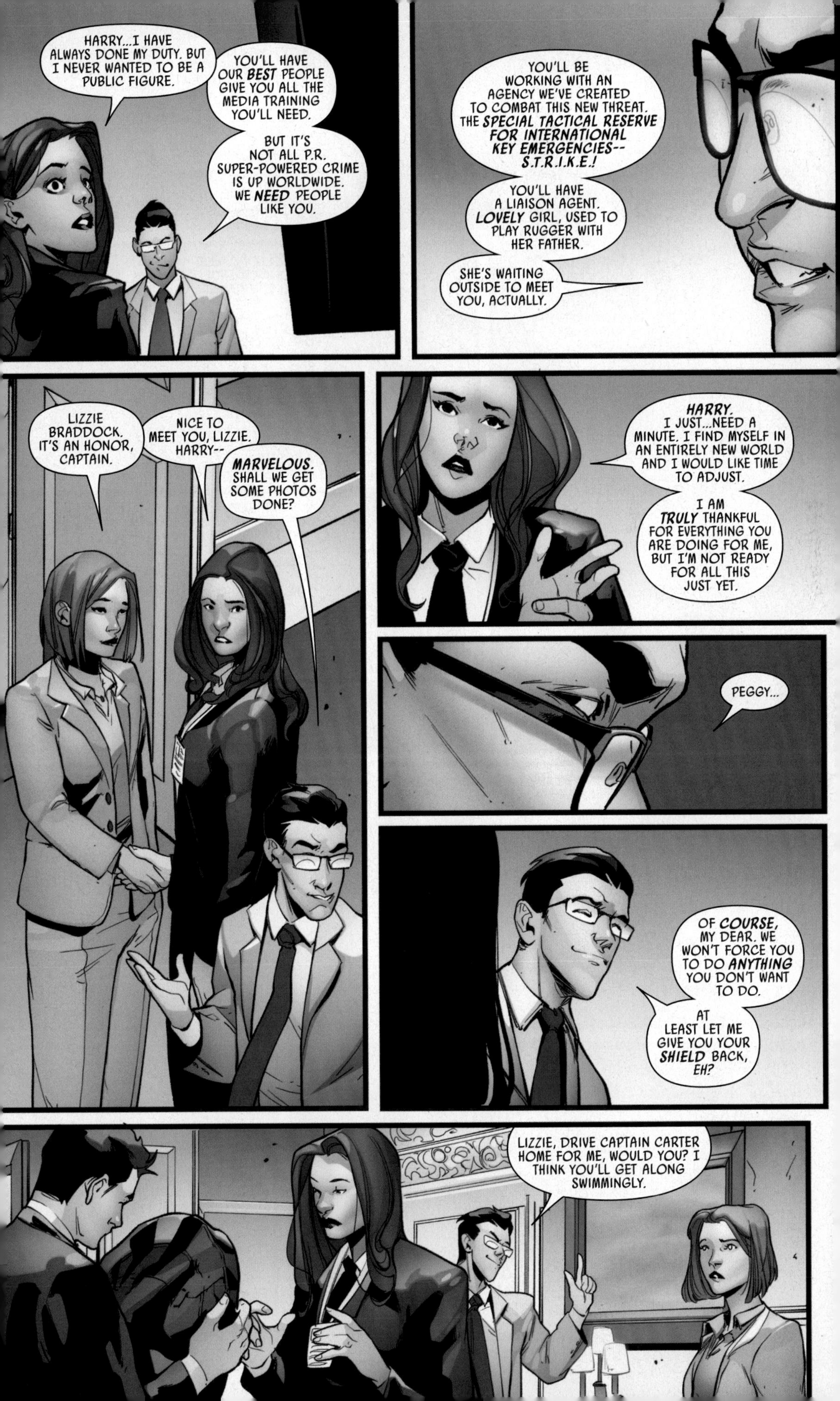
HARRY...I HAVE ALWAYS DONE MY DUTY. BUT I NEVER WANTED TO BE A PUBLIC FIGURE.
YOU'LL HAVE OUR BEST PEOPLE GIVE YOU ALL THE MEDIA TRAINING YOU'LL NEED.
BUT IT'S NOT ALL P.R. SUPER-POWERED CRIME IS UP WORLDWIDE. WE NEED PEOPLE LIKE YOU.
YOU'LL BE WORKING WITH AN AGENCY WE'VE CREATED TO COMBAT THIS NEW THREAT. THE SPECIAL TACTICAL RESERVE FOR INTERNATIONAL KEY EMERGENCIES-- S.T.R.I.K.E.!
YOU'LL HAVE A LIAISON AGENT. LOVELY GIRL, USED TO PLAY RUGGER WITH HER FATHER.
SHE'S WAITING OUTSIDE TO MEET YOU, ACTUALLY.
LIZZIE BRADDOCK. IT'S AN HONOR, CAPTAIN.
NICE TO MEET YOU, LIZZIE. HARRY--
MARVELOUS. SHALL WE GET SOME PHOTOS DONE?
HARRY. I JUST...NEED A MINUTE. I FIND MYSELF IN AN ENTIRELY NEW WORLD AND I WOULD LIKE TIME TO ADJUST.
I AM TRULY THANKFUL FOR EVERYTHING YOU ARE DOING FOR ME, BUT I'M NOT READY FOR ALL THIS JUST YET.
PEGGY...
OF COURSE, MY DEAR. WE WON'T FORCE YOU TO DO ANYTHING YOU DON'T WANT TO DO.
AT LEAST LET ME GIVE YOU YOUR SHIELD BACK, EH?
LIZZIE, DRIVE CAPTAIN CARTER HOME FOR ME, WOULD YOU? I THINK YOU'LL GET ALONG SWIMMINGLY.

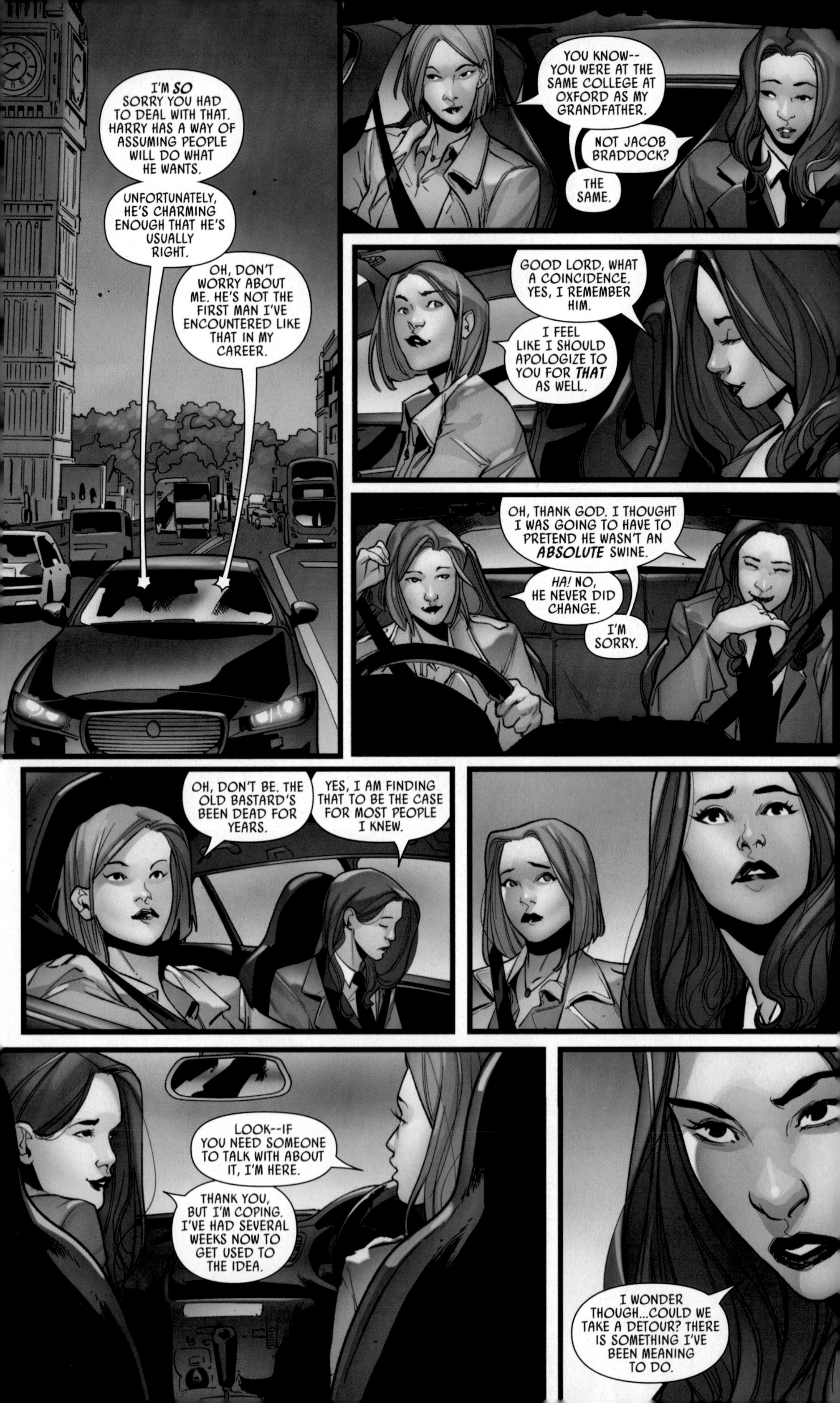
I'M SO SORRY YOU HAD TO DEAL WITH THAT. HARRY HAS A WAY OF ASSUMING PEOPLE WILL DO WHAT HE WANTS.
UNFORTUNATELY, HE'S CHARMING ENOUGH THAT HE'S USUALLY RIGHT.
OH, DON'T WORRY ABOUT ME. HE'S NOT THE FIRST MAN I'VE ENCOUNTERED LIKE THAT IN MY CAREER.
YOU KNOW-- YOU WERE AT THE SAME COLLEGE AT OXFORD AS MY GRANDFATHER.
NOT JACOB BRADDOCK?
THE SAME.
GOOD LORD, WHAT A COINCIDENCE. YES, I REMEMBER HIM.
I FEEL LIKE I SHOULD APOLOGIZE TO YOU FOR THAT AS WELL.
OH, THANK GOD. I THOUGHT I WAS GOING TO HAVE TO PRETEND HE WASN'T AN ABSOLUTE SWINE.
HA! NO, HE NEVER DID CHANGE.
I'M SORRY.
OH, DON'T BE. THE OLD BASTARD'S BEEN DEAD FOR YEARS.
YES, I AM FINDING THAT TO BE THE CASE FOR MOST PEOPLE I KNEW.
LOOK--IF YOU NEED SOMEONE TO TALK WITH ABOUT IT, I'M HERE.
THANK YOU, BUT I'M COPING. I'VE HAD SEVERAL WEEKS NOW TO GET USED TO THE IDEA.
I WONDER THOUGH...COULD WE TAKE A DETOUR? THERE IS SOMETHING I'VE BEEN MEANING TO DO.

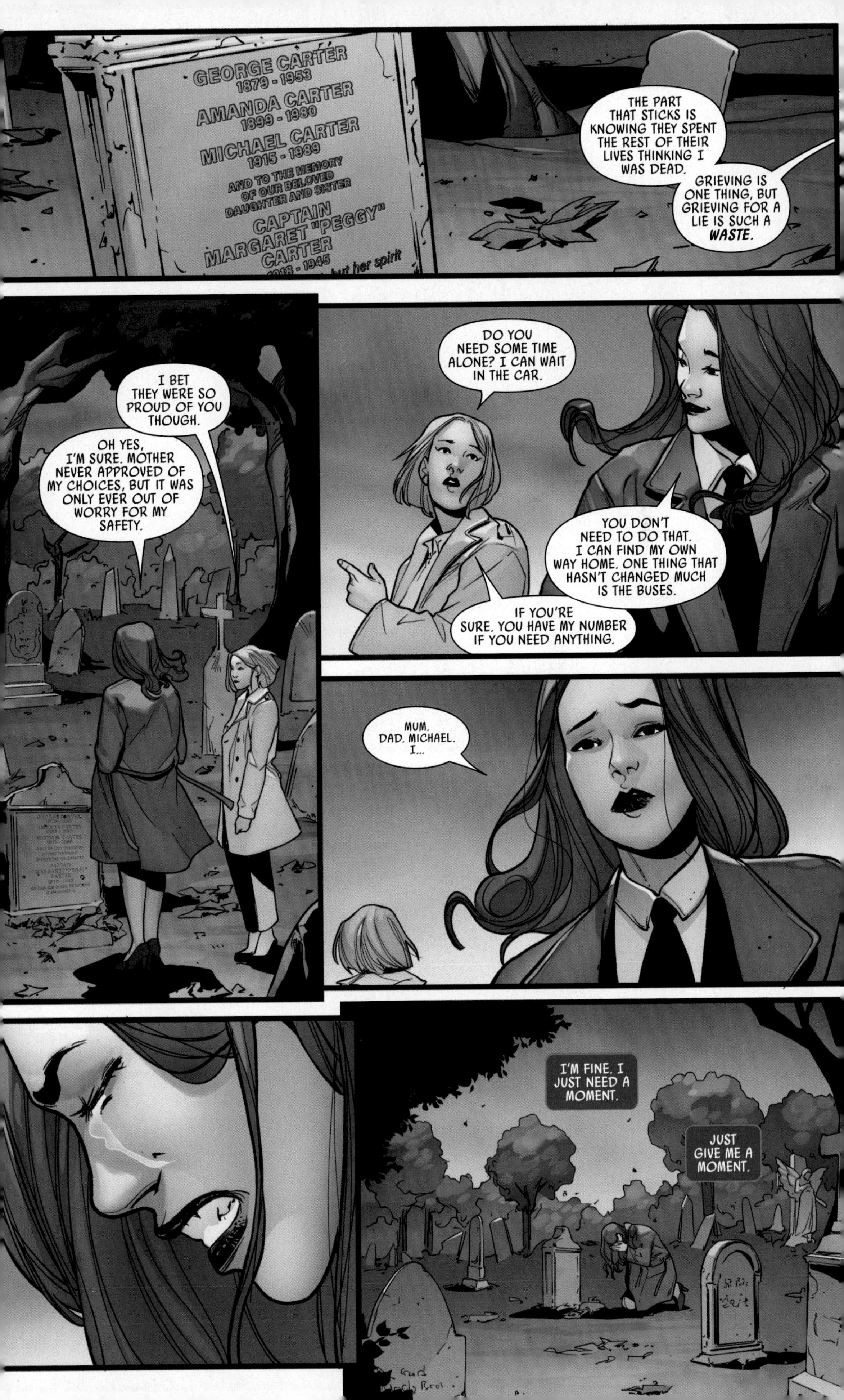

GEORGE CARTER
1879 - 1953
AMANDA CARTER
1899 - 1980
MICHAEL CARTER
1915 - 1989
AND TO THE MEMORY
OF OUR BELOVED
DAUGHTER AND SISTER
CAPTAIN
MARGARET "PEGGY"
CARTER
but her spirit
THE PART THAT STICKS IS KNOWING THEY SPENT THE REST OF THEIR LIVES THINKING I WAS DEAD.
GRIEVING IS ONE THING, BUT GRIEVING FOR A LIE IS SUCH A WASTE.
I BET THEY WERE SO PROUD OF YOU THOUGH.
OH YES, I'M SURE. MOTHER NEVER APPROVED OF MY CHOICES, BUT IT WAS ONLY EVER OUT OF WORRY FOR MY SAFETY.
DO YOU NEED SOME TIME ALONE? I CAN WAIT IN THE CAR.
YOU DON'T NEED TO DO THAT. I CAN FIND MY OWN WAY HOME. ONE THING THAT HASN'T CHANGED MUCH IS THE BUSES.
IF YOU'RE SURE. YOU HAVE MY NUMBER IF YOU NEED ANYTHING.
MUM. DAD. MICHAEL. I...
I'M FINE. I JUST NEED A MOMENT.
JUST GIVE ME A MOMENT.

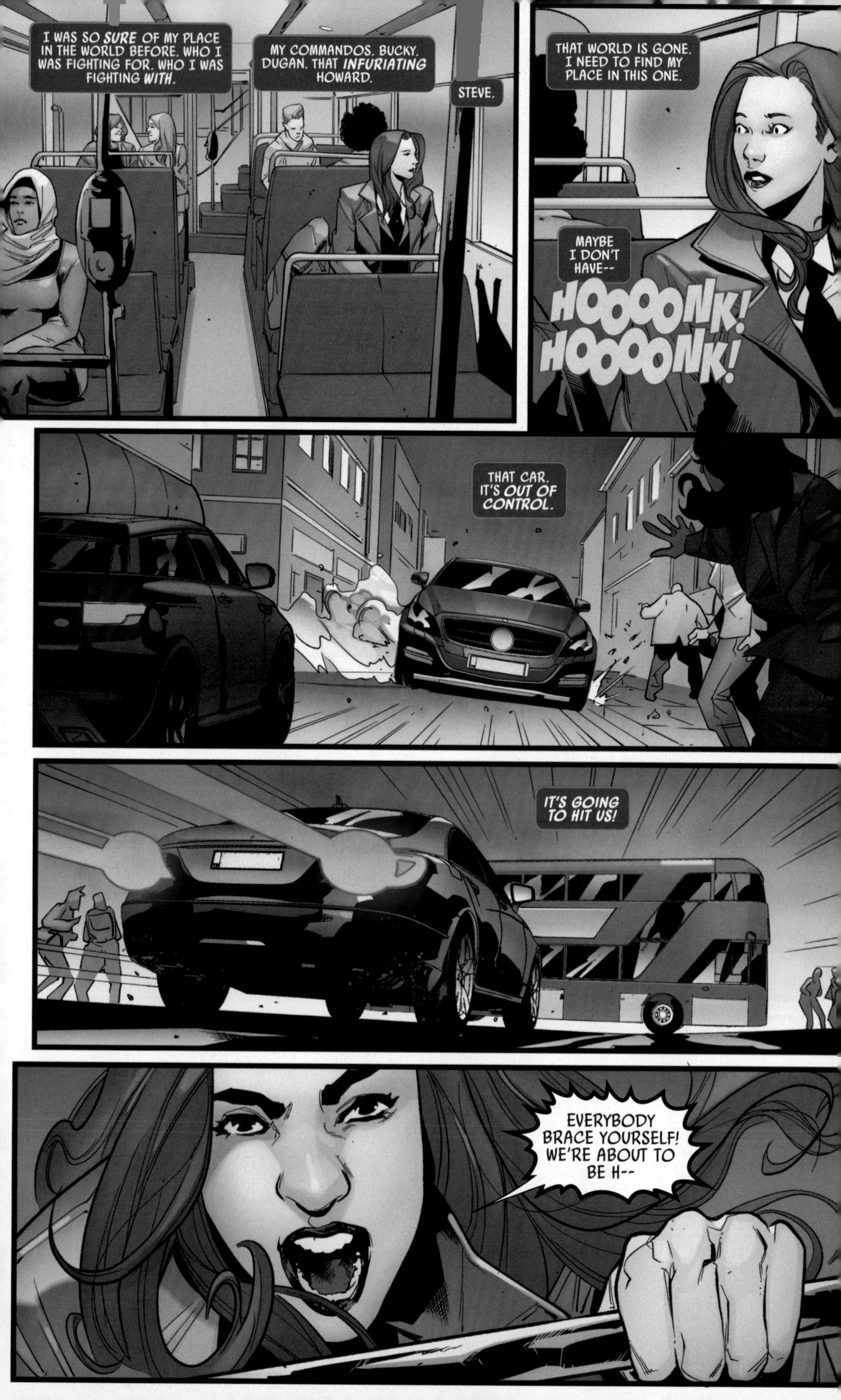

I WAS SO SURE OF MY PLACE IN THE WORLD BEFORE. WHO I WAS FIGHTING FOR. WHO I WAS FIGHTING WITH.
MY COMMANDOS. BUCKY. DUGAN. THAT INFURIATING HOWARD.
STEVE.
THAT WORLD IS GONE. I NEED TO FIND MY PLACE IN THIS ONE.
MAYBE I DON'T HAVE--
HOOOOONK! HOOOOONK!
THAT CAR. IT'S OUT OF CONTROL.
IT'S GOING TO HIT US!
EVERYBODY BRACE YOURSELF! WE'RE ABOUT TO BE H--

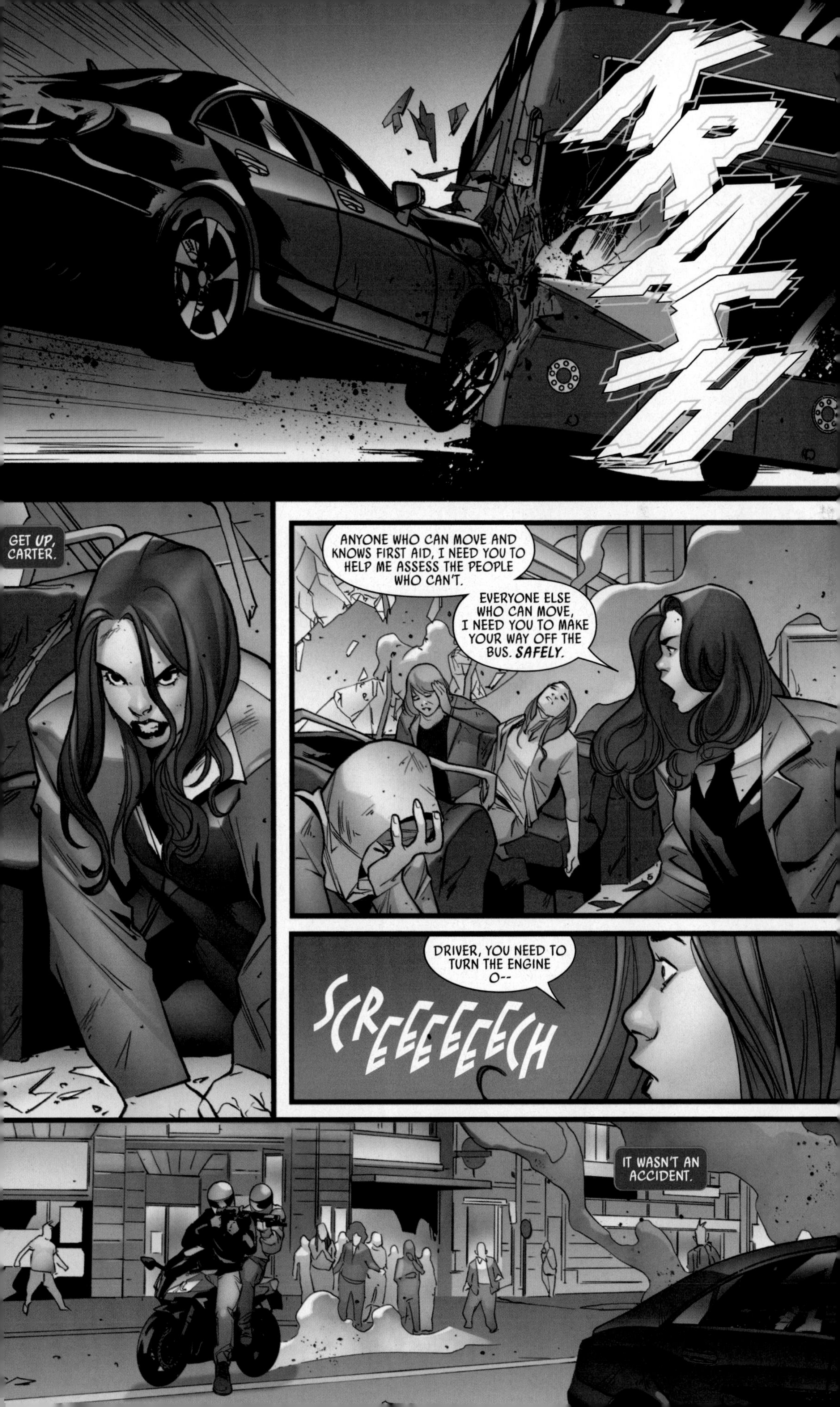
KRASH
GET UP, CARTER.
ANYONE WHO CAN MOVE AND KNOWS FIRST AID, I NEED YOU TO HELP ME ASSESS THE PEOPLE WHO CAN'T.
EVERYONE ELSE WHO CAN MOVE, I NEED YOU TO MAKE YOUR WAY OFF THE BUS. *SAFELY.*
DRIVER, YOU NEED TO TURN THE ENGINE O--
SCREEEEEEECH
IT WASN'T AN ACCIDENT.

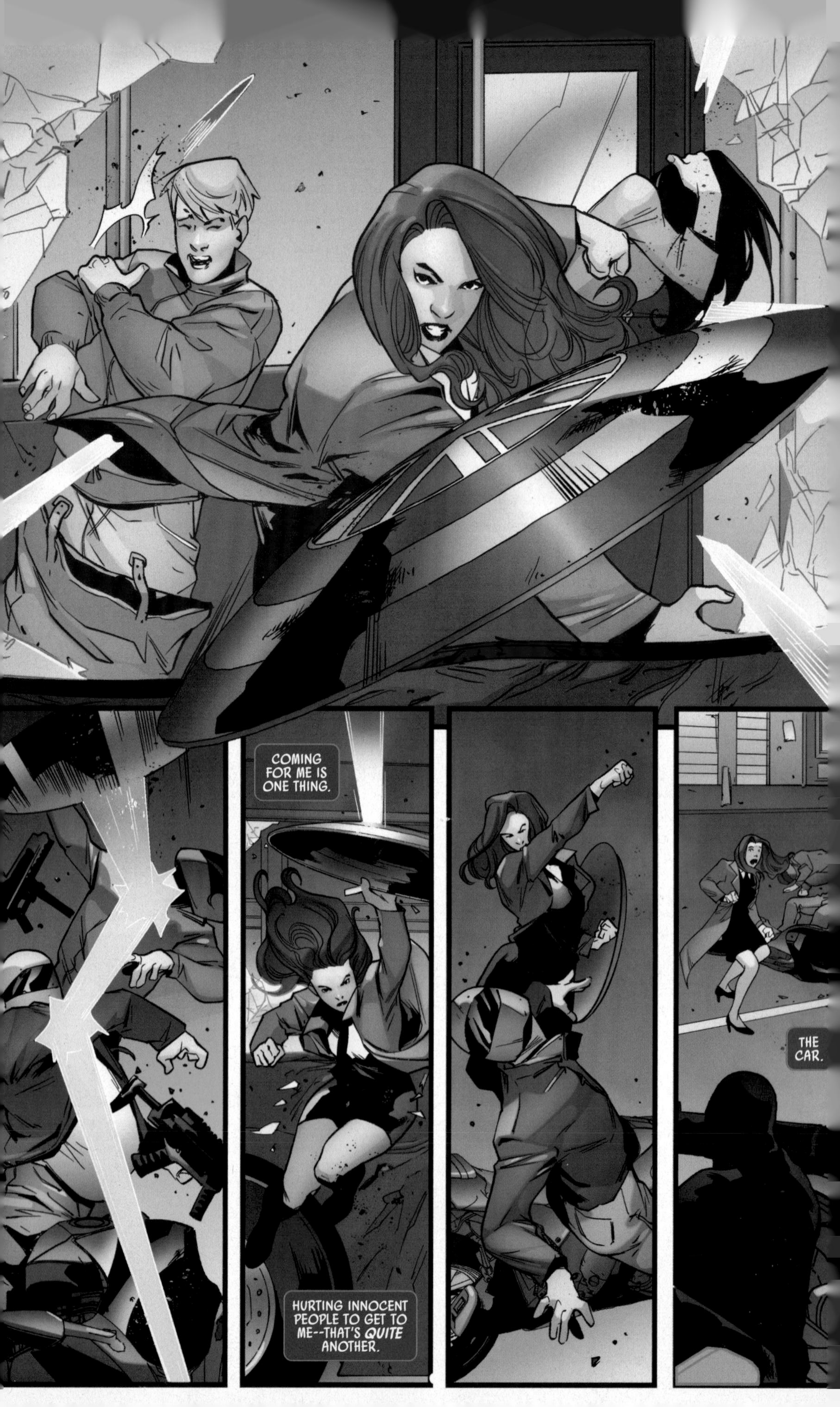
COMING FOR ME IS ONE THING.
HURTING INNOCENT PEOPLE TO GET TO ME--THAT'S *QUITE* ANOTHER.
THE CAR.

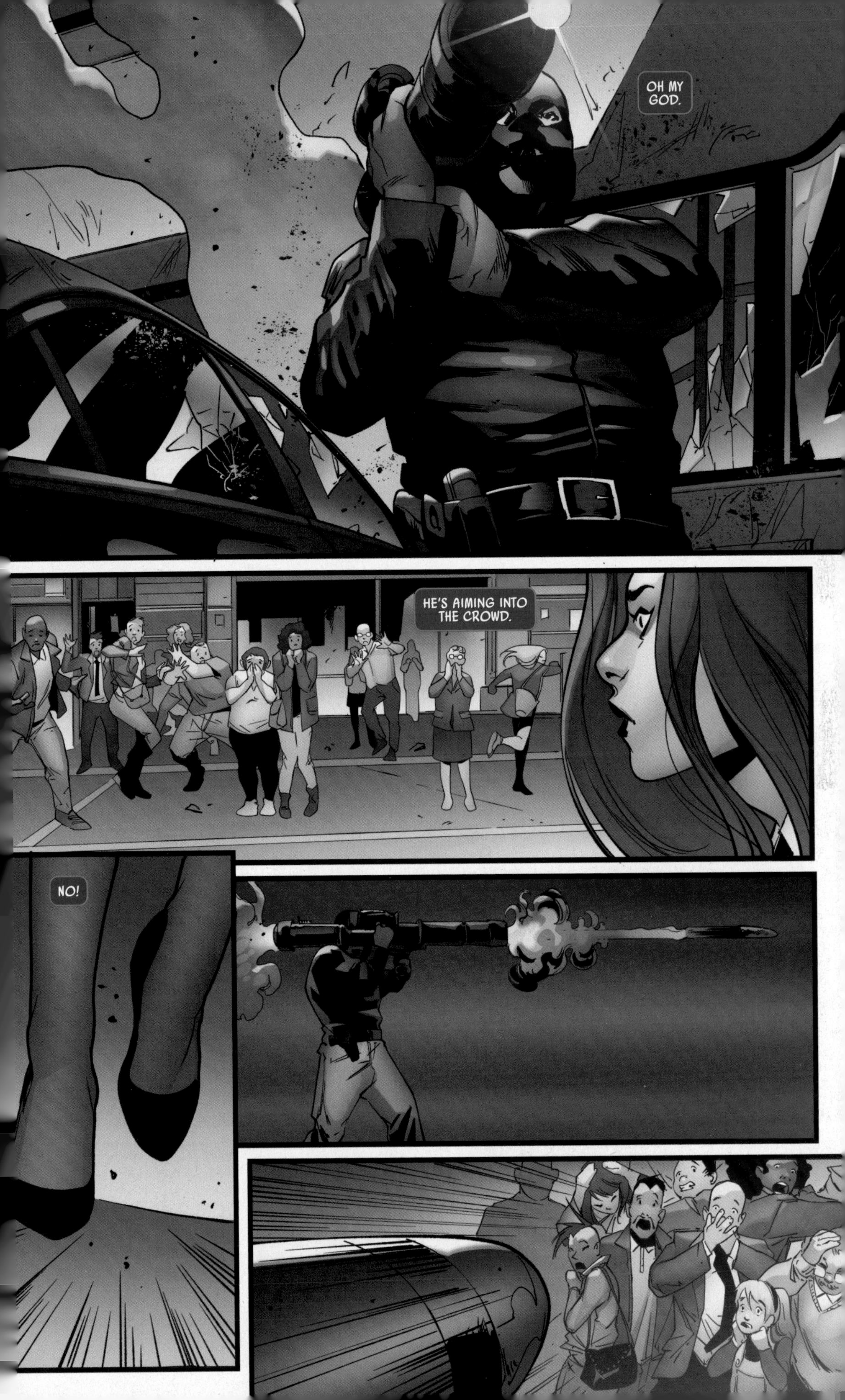
OH MY GOD.
HE'S AIMING INTO THE CROWD.
NO!

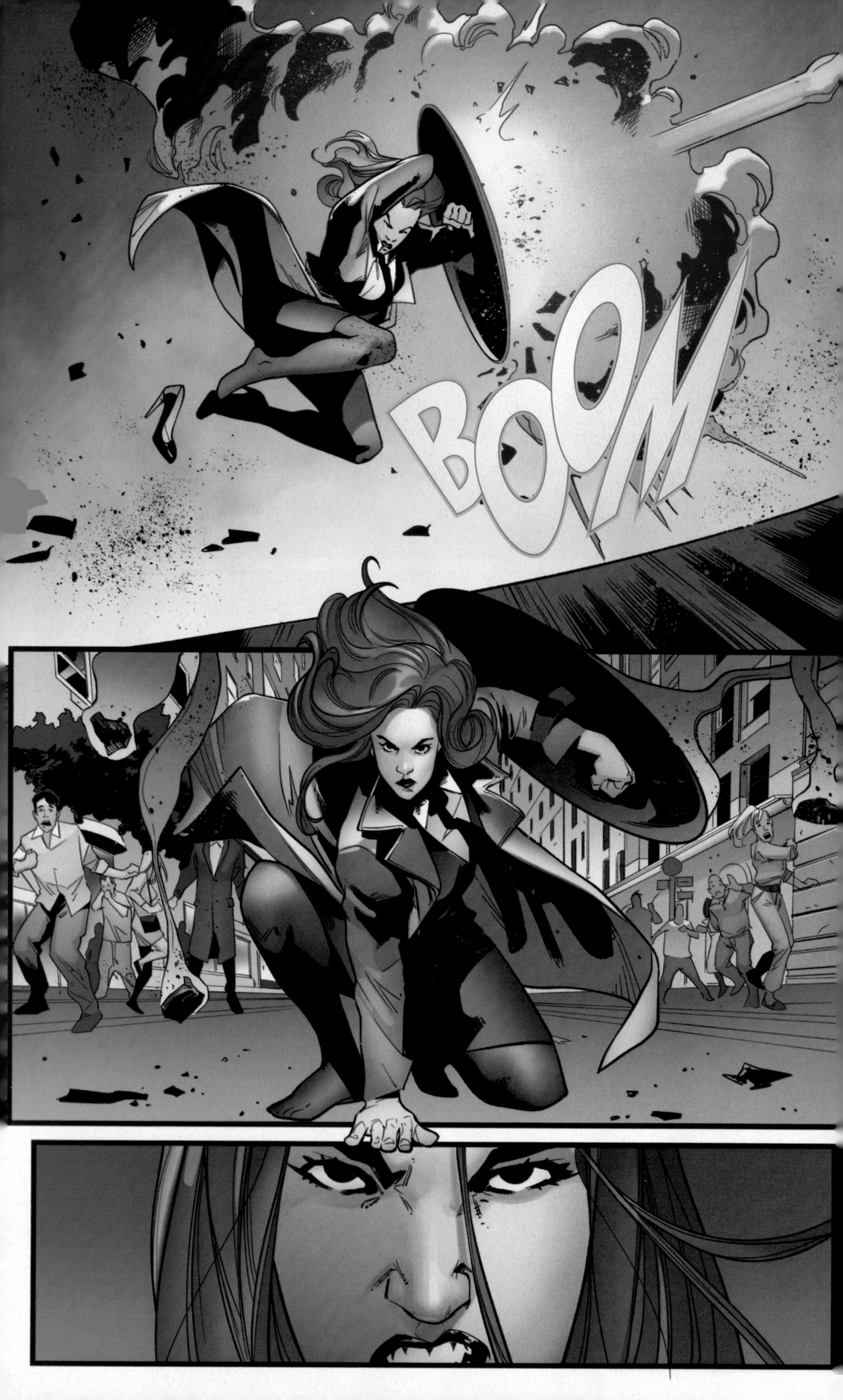
BOOM

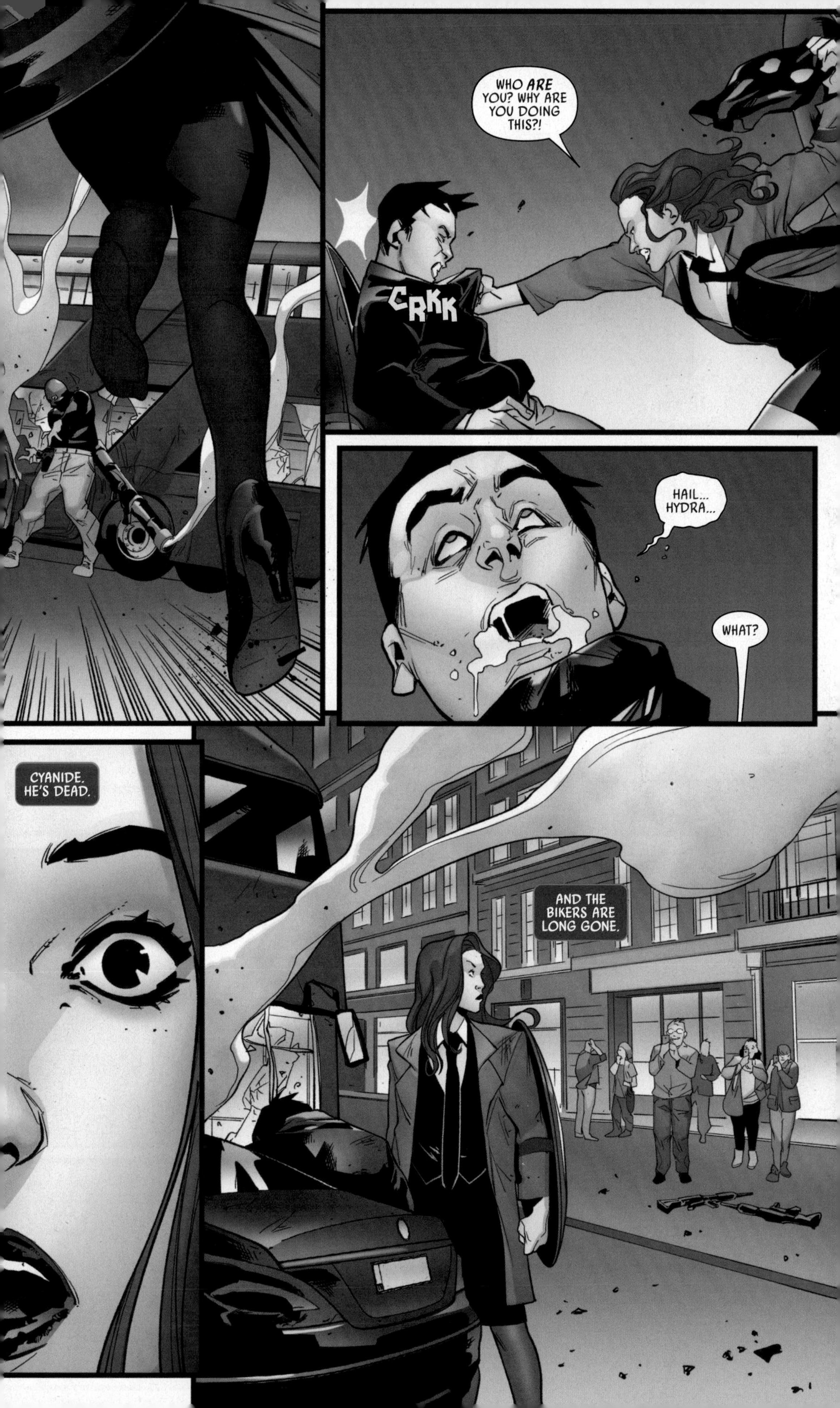

WHO ARE YOU? WHY ARE YOU DOING THIS?!
CRKK
HAIL... HYDRA...
WHAT?
CYANIDE. HE'S DEAD.
AND THE BIKERS ARE LONG GONE.

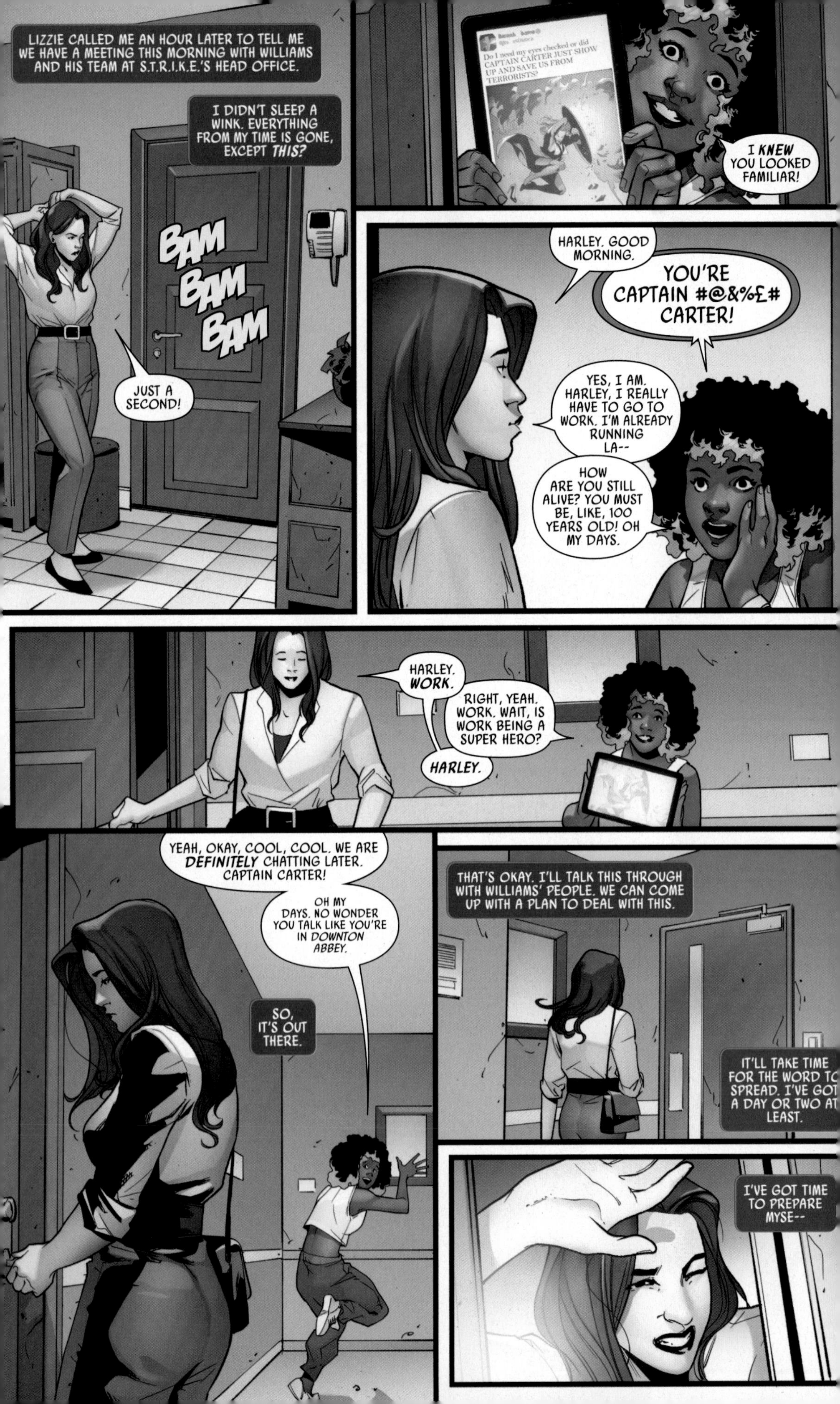
LIZZIE CALLED ME AN HOUR LATER TO TELL ME WE HAVE A MEETING THIS MORNING WITH WILLIAMS AND HIS TEAM AT S.T.R.I.K.E.'S HEAD OFFICE.
I DIDN'T SLEEP A WINK. EVERYTHING FROM MY TIME IS GONE, EXCEPT THIS?
BAM BAM BAM
JUST A SECOND!
Do I need my eyes checked or did CAPTAIN CARTER JUST SHOW UP AND SAVE US FROM TERRORISTS?
I KNEW YOU LOOKED FAMILIAR!
HARLEY. GOOD MORNING.
YOU'RE CAPTAIN #@&%£# CARTER!
YES, I AM. HARLEY, I REALLY HAVE TO GO TO WORK. I'M ALREADY RUNNING LA--
HOW ARE YOU STILL ALIVE? YOU MUST BE, LIKE, 100 YEARS OLD! OH MY DAYS.
HARLEY. WORK.
RIGHT, YEAH. WORK. WAIT, IS WORK BEING A SUPER HERO?
HARLEY.
YEAH, OKAY, COOL, COOL. WE ARE DEFINITELY CHATTING LATER. CAPTAIN CARTER!
OH MY DAYS. NO WONDER YOU TALK LIKE YOU'RE IN DOWNTON ABBEY.
SO, IT'S OUT THERE.
THAT'S OKAY. I'LL TALK THIS THROUGH WITH WILLIAMS' PEOPLE. WE CAN COME UP WITH A PLAN TO DEAL WITH THIS.
IT'LL TAKE TIME FOR THE WORD TO SPREAD. I'VE GOT A DAY OR TWO AT LEAST.
I'VE GOT TIME TO PREPARE MYSE--

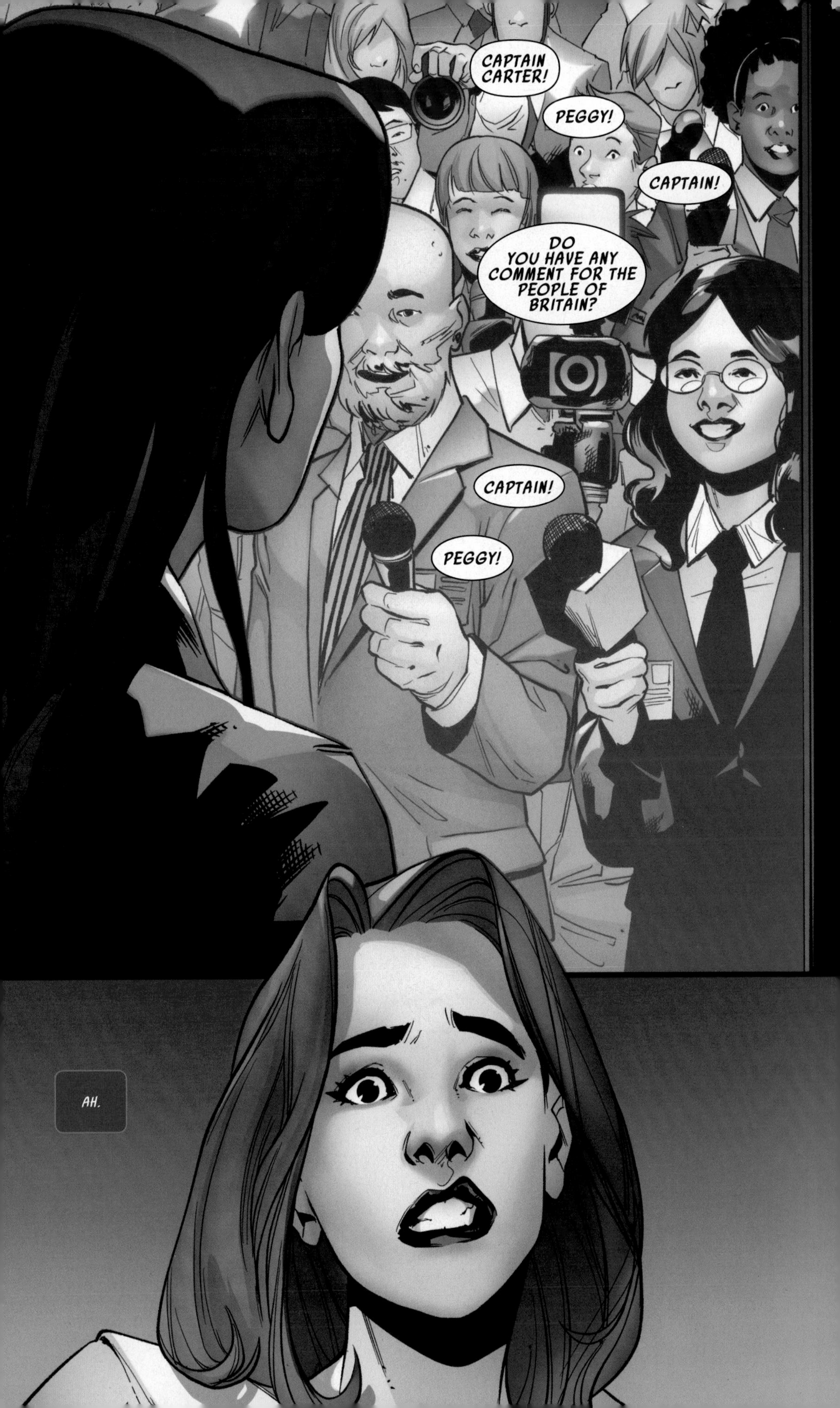
CAPTAIN CARTER!
PEGGY!
CAPTAIN!
DO YOU HAVE ANY COMMENT FOR THE PEOPLE OF BRITAIN?
CAPTAIN!
PEGGY!
AH.

#2

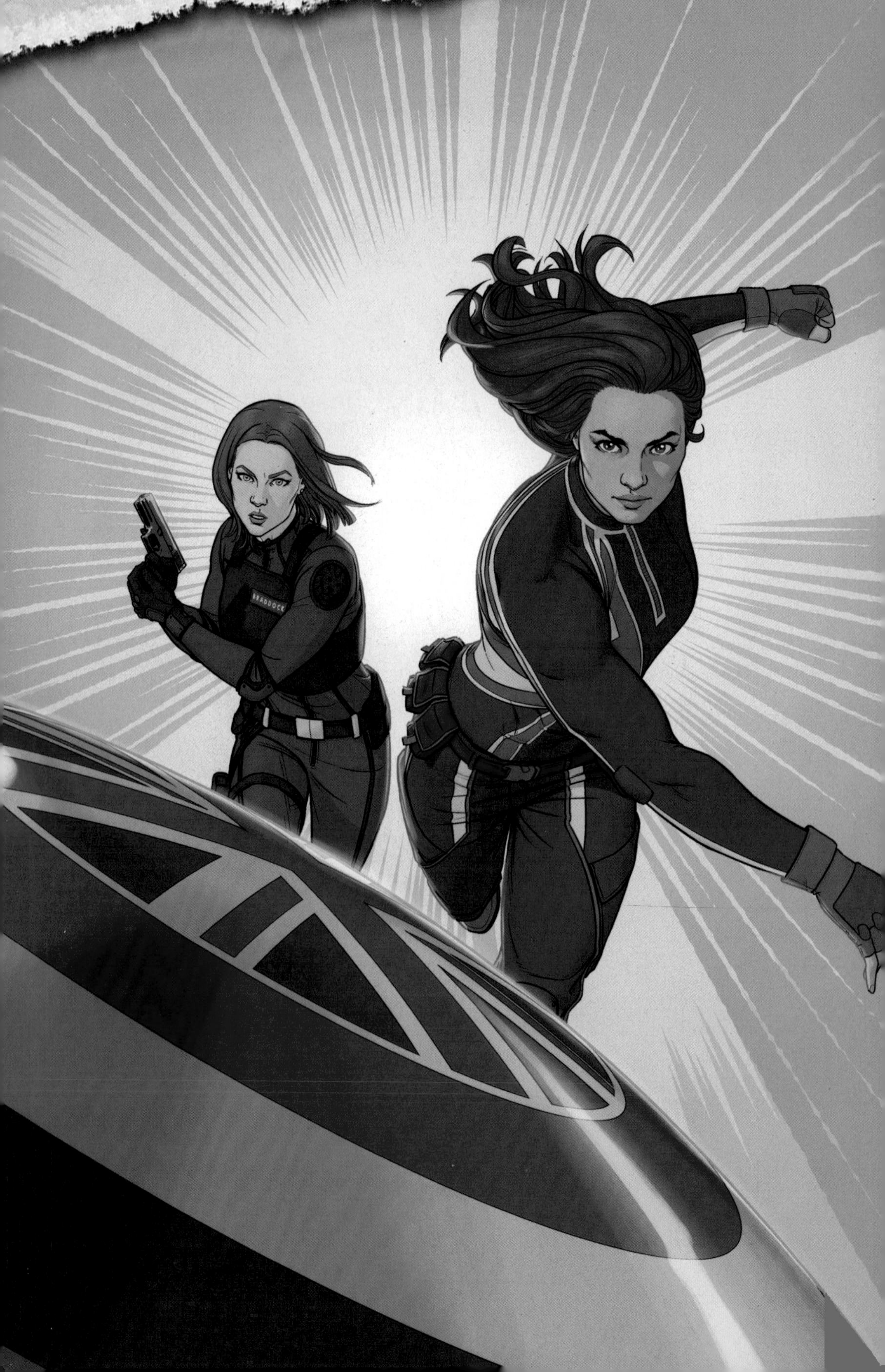
BRADDOCK

THE DAILY NEWS

Thursday April 14 2022 · No 73718

Captain Carter alive and well

Carter foils another Hydra plot

● Terrorists planned to attack Parliament ● S.T.R.I.K.

...n science
...covered
...g WWII
...with British
...rozen inside
...this year
...ain Carter
...ed to active
...ollowing the
...earance of the
...a organisation

BUSINESS TIM

...April 2022

contrast

...Tony Stark on business and
...change of heart — PAGE 7

High street woes
We crunch the data on the hardest hit areas of
the UK - and those that are getting by — PAGE 21

Su
Sup
it n

£

...ntroversial "Anti-Hydra" Bill to
debated in Commons this wee

...me Secretary dismisses overreach concerns ● Opposition ...ps divided over

Some Opposition MPs
...accelerated passage of the
...allow enough time for
The Shadow Education
Katherine Molcher, saf
recognise the need for
...ckle threats of this
... careful to balance it
...commitment to a fre
...we pass this ill
...ndment, we re
...surveillance
...everyone re
...is expos
... whip will
...th the
...majori
...with
...wit
...fr

...nment is fast-tracking the
...the new Anti-Terrorism Bill,
...cond reading in the House of
...will take place on Thursday.
...ove comes in response
...n in terrorism

By MATT THOMAS

The Daily

Wednesday, April 27, 2022

GOVERNMENT
boffins think the number
of mutant babies being
born is growing faster
than ever. Should you be
worried? Today we tell
you the signs to watch
out for.

Full story--Page Five

● 'SUPER VILLAIN'
● OUR PEGGY STOPS

CARTE
VEXES
VIXEN

UK exports drop by more than 10%
Services hit by 4.6% export fall Page 6

Mystery e...
Dr Siobhan

The Morning Sen
Monday May 2 2022

**Civil rights groups warn
bill "risks curb on rights"**

...ll before
...ks Bill
...s from

70p

...AIN'S BEST NEWSPAPER - EARNING YOUR TRUST EVERY DAY

"I'm just doing my job"

EXCLUSIVE: CAPTAIN CARTER INTERVIEW

LONDONER
FREE

THE CAPITAL'S PREMIER FREE NEWSPAPER

...RA LAUNCHES NEW ATTACK, BUT...

SAVES

...ARTER
...APITAL

DAILY Herald
Wednesday, May 14, 2022
95p

Telling it like it is

HYDRA - what we know
● Who are they?
● What do they want?
● How can they be stopped?

EXPERT ANSWERS - P9

● MINISTERS SAY CRACK TEAM IS NOT DOING ENOUGH TO STOP HYDRA ● PM PROMISES NEW POWERS WILL HELP ● IS THAT THE ANSWER?

S.T.R.I.K.E. UNDER

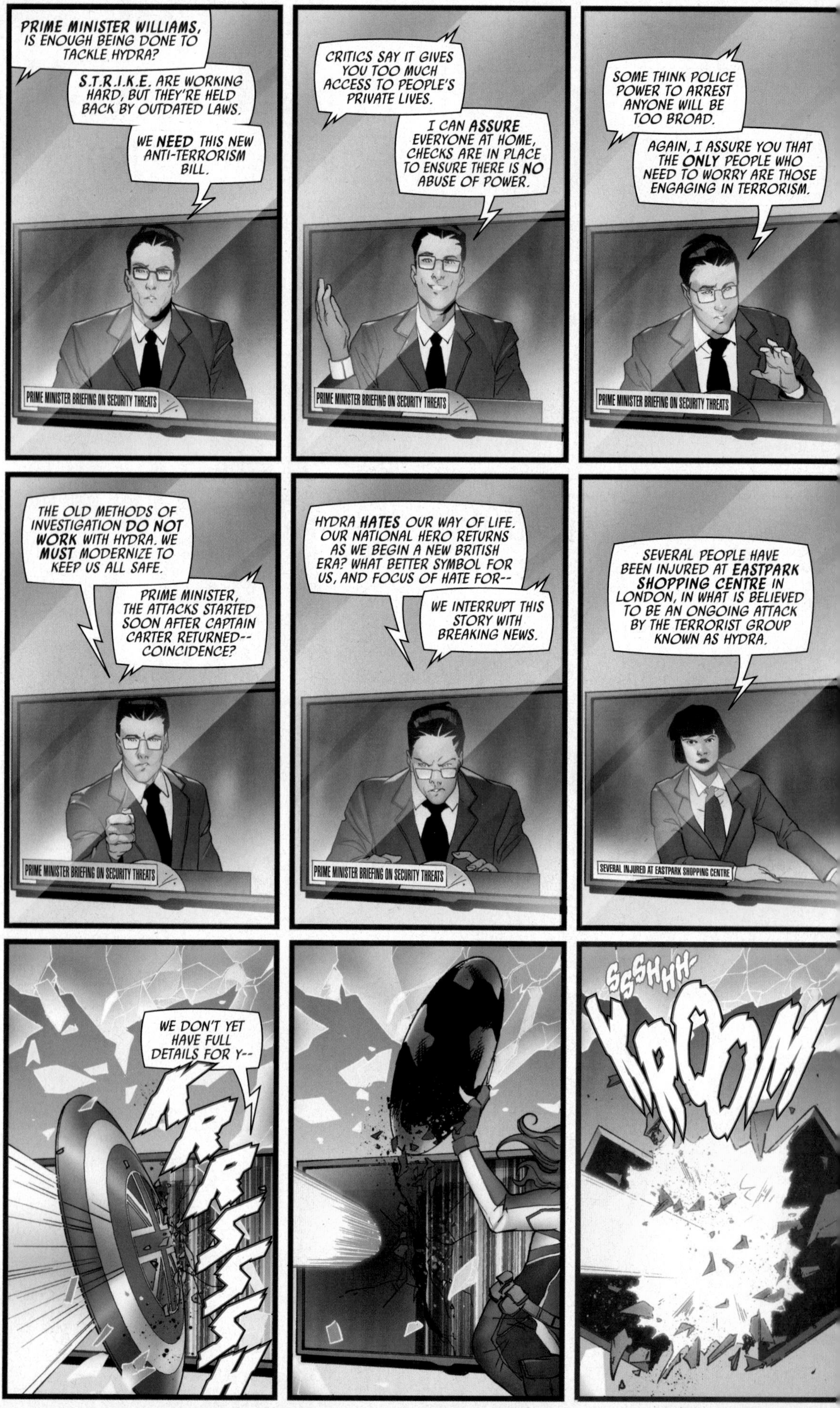

PRIME MINISTER WILLIAMS, IS ENOUGH BEING DONE TO TACKLE HYDRA?
S.T.R.I.K.E. ARE WORKING HARD, BUT THEY'RE HELD BACK BY OUTDATED LAWS.
WE NEED THIS NEW ANTI-TERRORISM BILL.
PRIME MINISTER BRIEFING ON SECURITY THREATS
CRITICS SAY IT GIVES YOU TOO MUCH ACCESS TO PEOPLE'S PRIVATE LIVES.
I CAN ASSURE EVERYONE AT HOME, CHECKS ARE IN PLACE TO ENSURE THERE IS NO ABUSE OF POWER.
PRIME MINISTER BRIEFING ON SECURITY THREATS
SOME THINK POLICE POWER TO ARREST ANYONE WILL BE TOO BROAD.
AGAIN, I ASSURE YOU THAT THE ONLY PEOPLE WHO NEED TO WORRY ARE THOSE ENGAGING IN TERRORISM.
PRIME MINISTER BRIEFING ON SECURITY THREATS
THE OLD METHODS OF INVESTIGATION DO NOT WORK WITH HYDRA. WE MUST MODERNIZE TO KEEP US ALL SAFE.
PRIME MINISTER, THE ATTACKS STARTED SOON AFTER CAPTAIN CARTER RETURNED-- COINCIDENCE?
PRIME MINISTER BRIEFING ON SECURITY THREATS
HYDRA HATES OUR WAY OF LIFE. OUR NATIONAL HERO RETURNS AS WE BEGIN A NEW BRITISH ERA? WHAT BETTER SYMBOL FOR US, AND FOCUS OF HATE FOR--
WE INTERRUPT THIS STORY WITH BREAKING NEWS.
PRIME MINISTER BRIEFING ON SECURITY THREATS
SEVERAL PEOPLE HAVE BEEN INJURED AT EASTPARK SHOPPING CENTRE IN LONDON, IN WHAT IS BELIEVED TO BE AN ONGOING ATTACK BY THE TERRORIST GROUP KNOWN AS HYDRA.
SEVERAL INJURED AT EASTPARK SHOPPING CENTRE
WE DON'T YET HAVE FULL DETAILS FOR Y--
KRRISSSH
SSSHHH-
KROOM

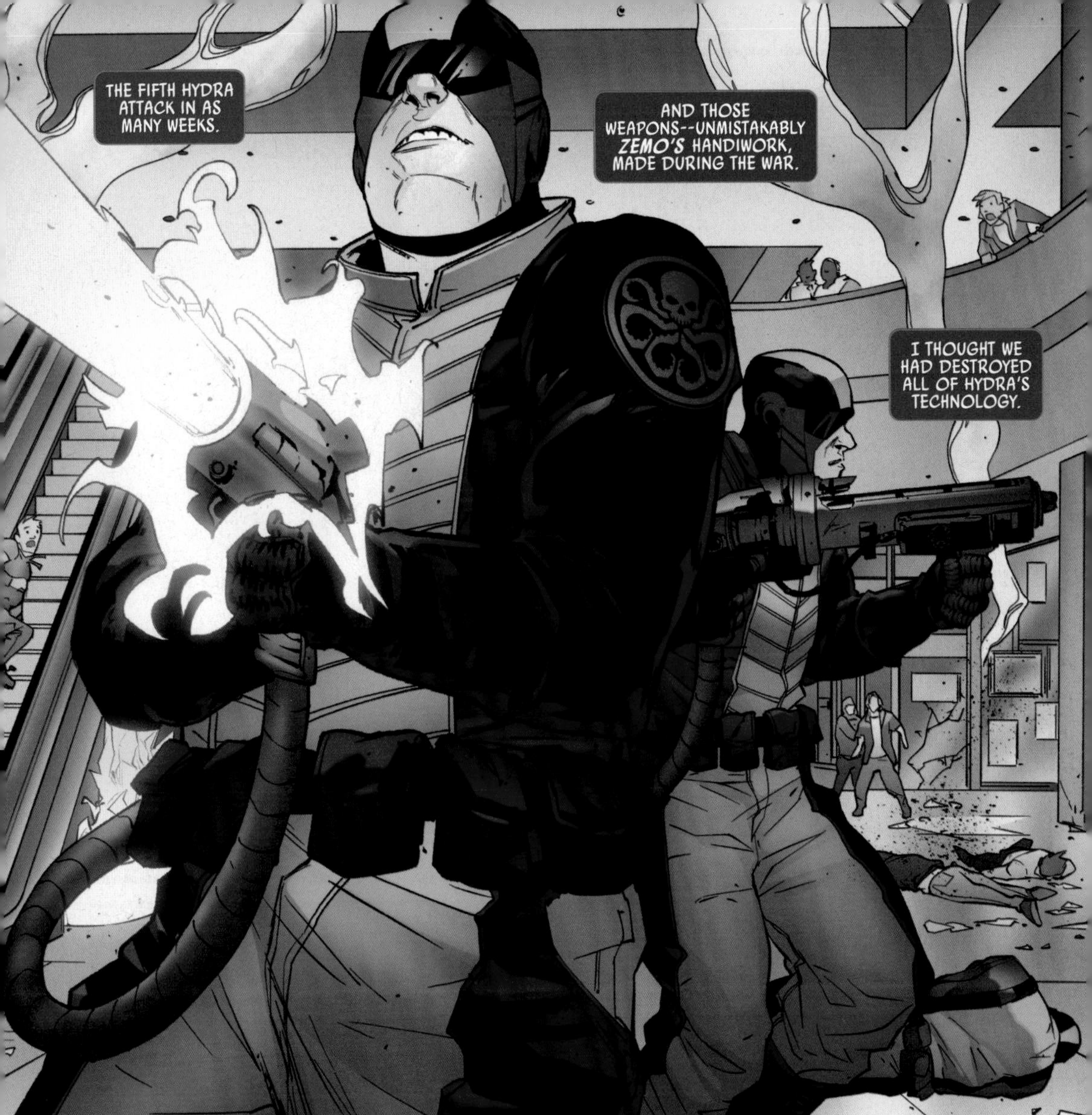
THE FIFTH HYDRA ATTACK IN AS MANY WEEKS.
AND THOSE WEAPONS--UNMISTAKABLY ZEMO'S HANDIWORK, MADE DURING THE WAR.
I THOUGHT WE HAD DESTROYED ALL OF HYDRA'S TECHNOLOGY.

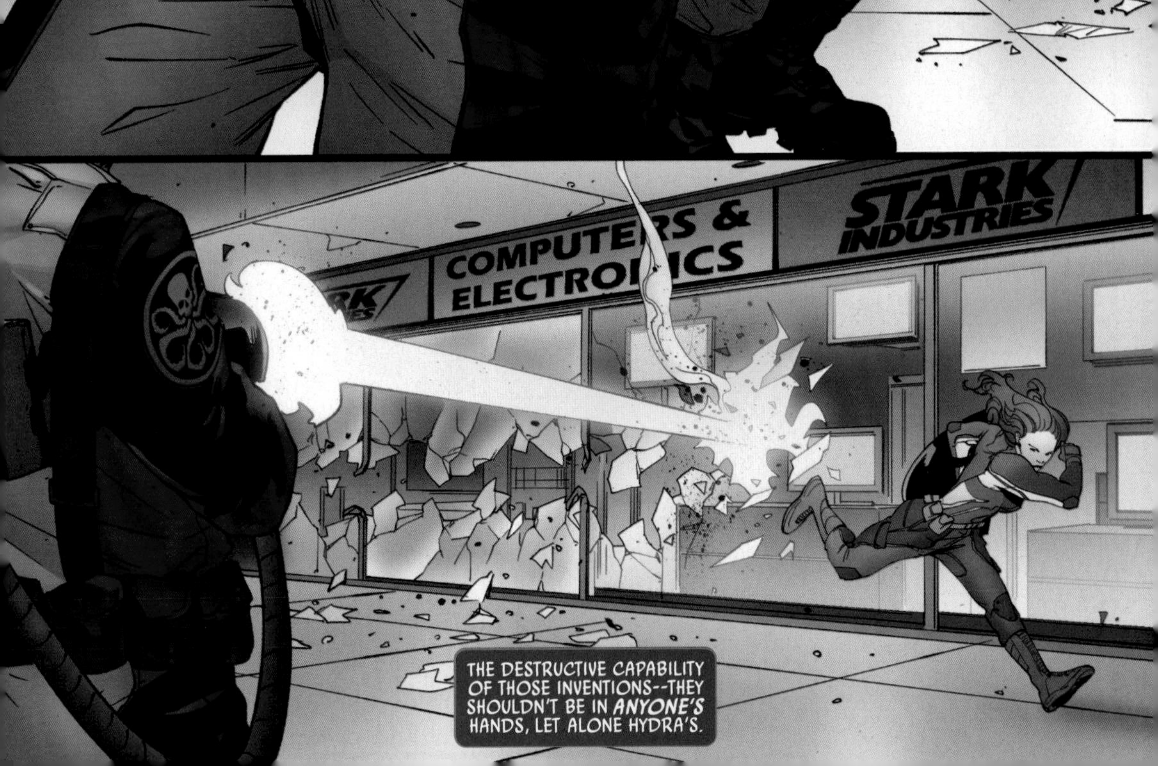
COMPUTERS & ELECTRONICS
STARK INDUSTRIES
THE DESTRUCTIVE CAPABILITY OF THOSE INVENTIONS--THEY SHOULDN'T BE IN ANYONE'S HANDS, LET ALONE HYDRA'S.

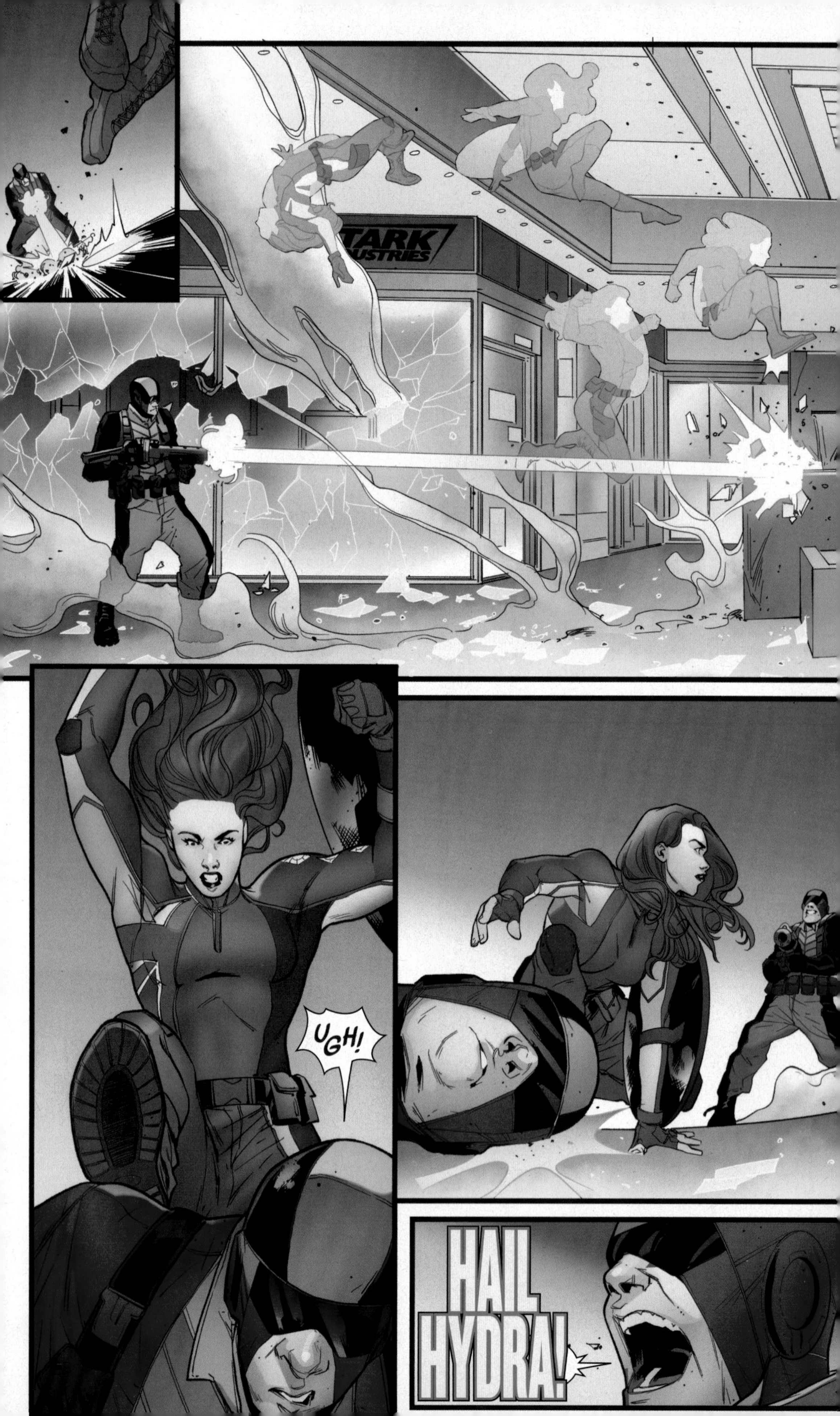

STARK INDUSTRIES
UGH!
HAIL HYDRA!

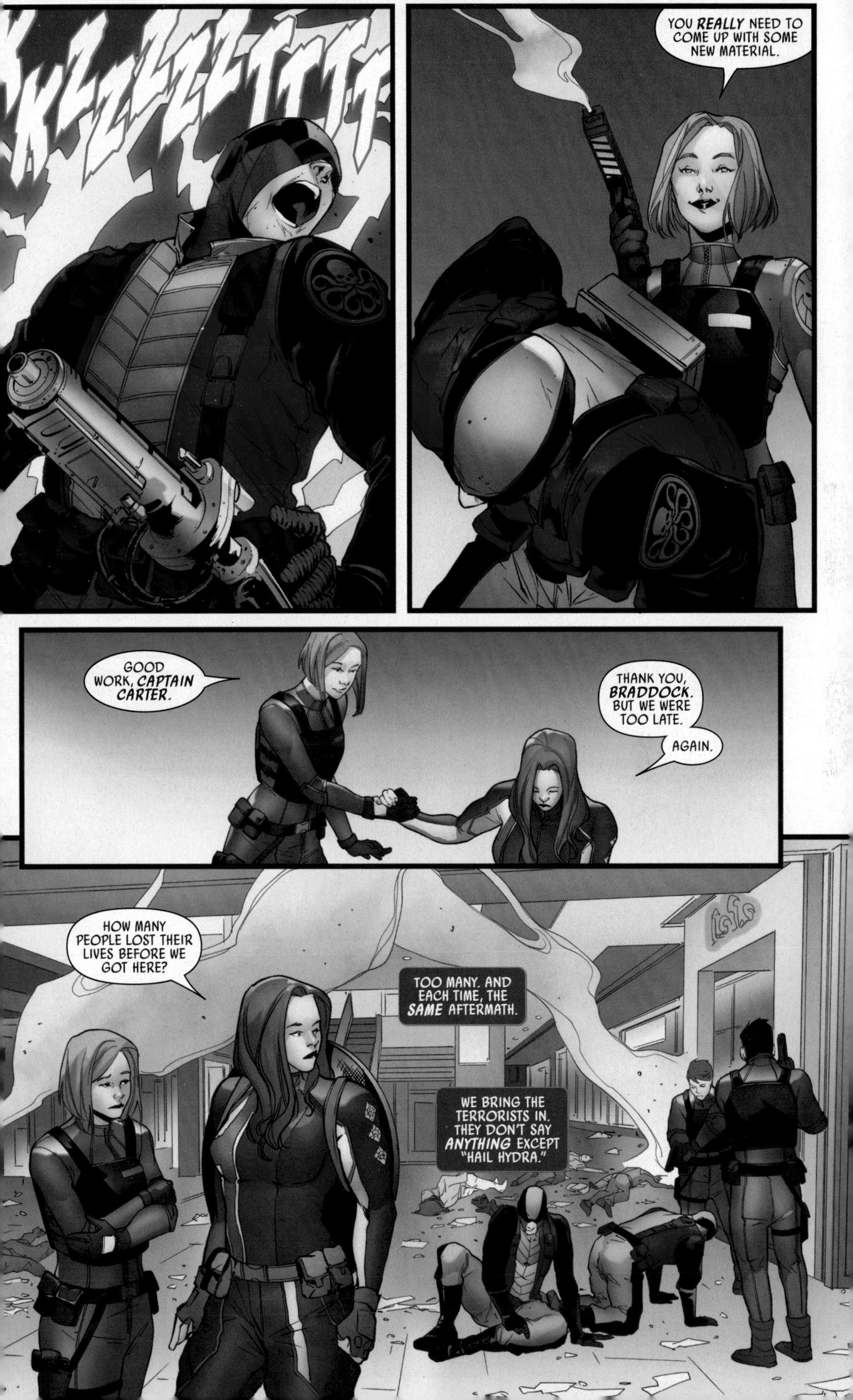
KZZZZZZTTTT
YOU REALLY NEED TO COME UP WITH SOME NEW MATERIAL.
GOOD WORK, CAPTAIN CARTER.
THANK YOU, BRADDOCK. BUT WE WERE TOO LATE.
AGAIN.
HOW MANY PEOPLE LOST THEIR LIVES BEFORE WE GOT HERE?
TOO MANY. AND EACH TIME, THE SAME AFTERMATH.
WE BRING THE TERRORISTS IN. THEY DON'T SAY ANYTHING EXCEPT "HAIL HYDRA."

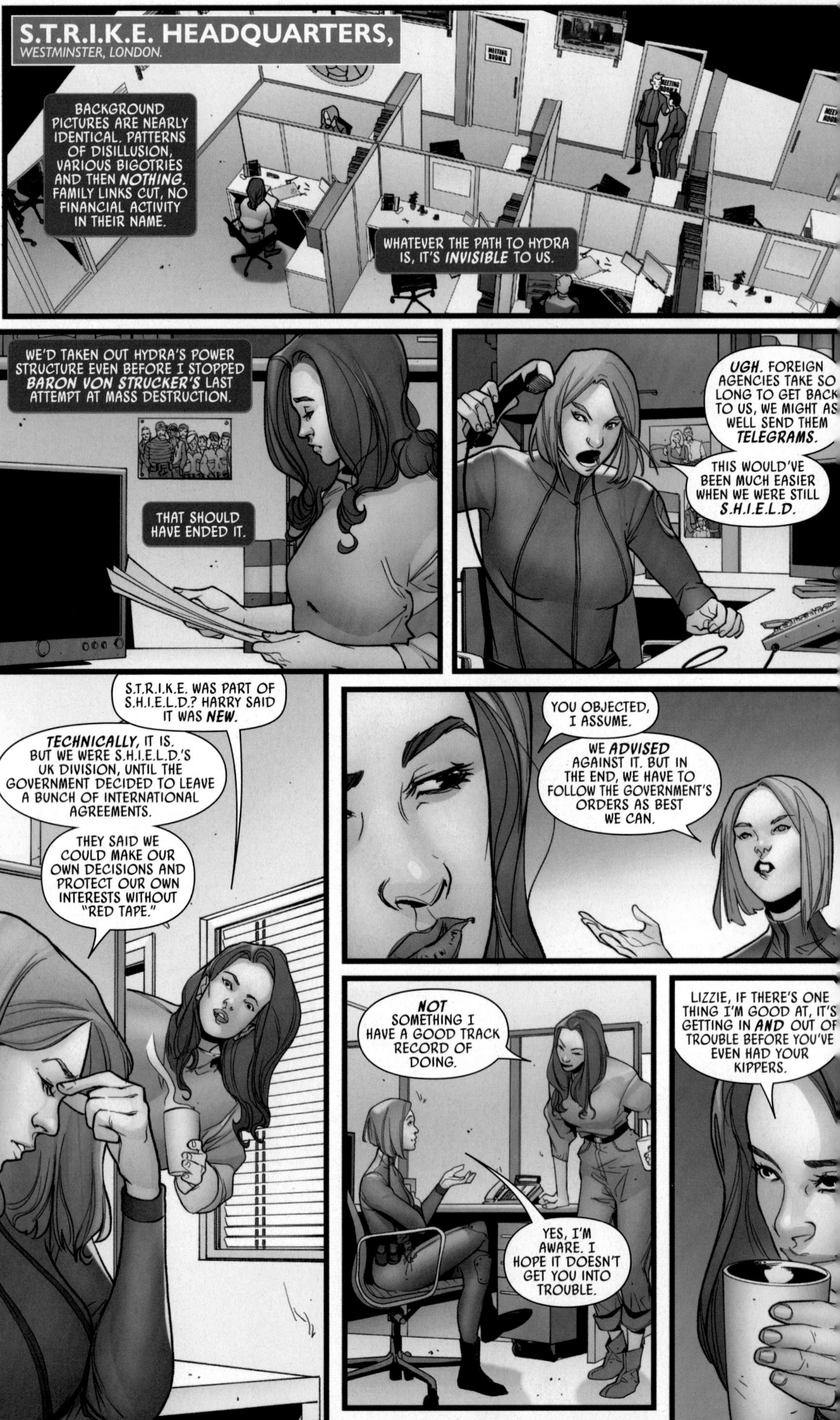
S.T.R.I.K.E. HEADQUARTERS,
WESTMINSTER, LONDON.
BACKGROUND PICTURES ARE NEARLY IDENTICAL. PATTERNS OF DISILLUSION, VARIOUS BIGOTRIES AND THEN NOTHING. FAMILY LINKS CUT, NO FINANCIAL ACTIVITY IN THEIR NAME.
WHATEVER THE PATH TO HYDRA IS, IT'S INVISIBLE TO US.
MEETING ROOM A
WE'D TAKEN OUT HYDRA'S POWER STRUCTURE EVEN BEFORE I STOPPED BARON VON STRUCKER'S LAST ATTEMPT AT MASS DESTRUCTION.
THAT SHOULD HAVE ENDED IT.
UGH. FOREIGN AGENCIES TAKE SO LONG TO GET BACK TO US, WE MIGHT AS WELL SEND THEM TELEGRAMS.
THIS WOULD'VE BEEN MUCH EASIER WHEN WE WERE STILL S.H.I.E.L.D.
S.T.R.I.K.E. WAS PART OF S.H.I.E.L.D.? HARRY SAID IT WAS NEW.
TECHNICALLY, IT IS. BUT WE WERE S.H.I.E.L.D.'S UK DIVISION, UNTIL THE GOVERNMENT DECIDED TO LEAVE A BUNCH OF INTERNATIONAL AGREEMENTS.
THEY SAID WE COULD MAKE OUR OWN DECISIONS AND PROTECT OUR OWN INTERESTS WITHOUT "RED TAPE."
YOU OBJECTED, I ASSUME.
WE ADVISED AGAINST IT. BUT IN THE END, WE HAVE TO FOLLOW THE GOVERNMENT'S ORDERS AS BEST WE CAN.
NOT SOMETHING I HAVE A GOOD TRACK RECORD OF DOING.
YES, I'M AWARE. I HOPE IT DOESN'T GET YOU INTO TROUBLE.
LIZZIE, IF THERE'S ONE THING I'M GOOD AT, IT'S GETTING IN AND OUT OF TROUBLE BEFORE YOU'VE EVEN HAD YOUR KIPPERS.

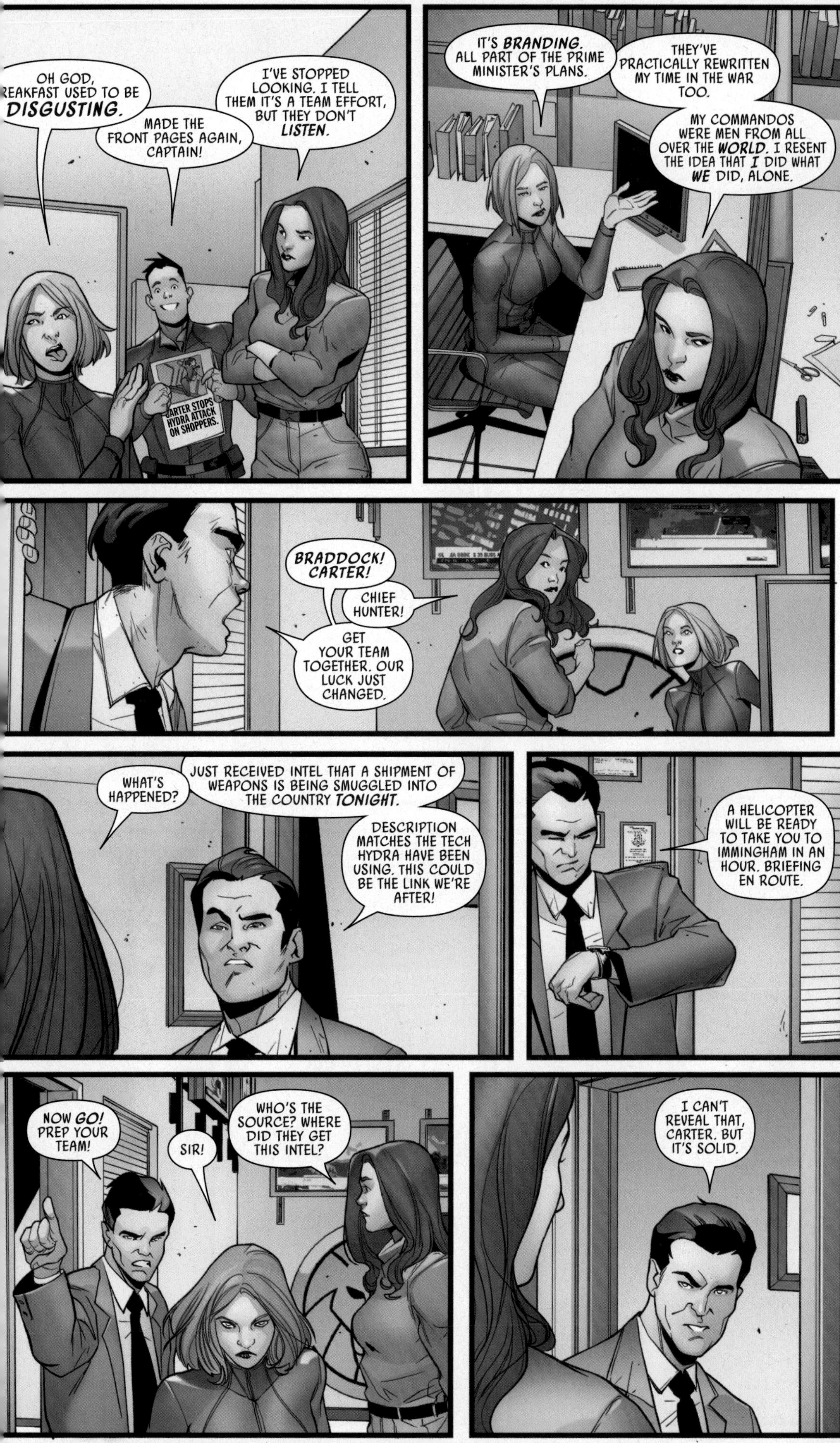
OH GOD, REAKFAST USED TO BE DISGUSTING.
MADE THE FRONT PAGES AGAIN, CAPTAIN!
I'VE STOPPED LOOKING. I TELL THEM IT'S A TEAM EFFORT, BUT THEY DON'T LISTEN.
CARTER STOPS HYDRA ATTACK ON SHOPPERS.
IT'S BRANDING. ALL PART OF THE PRIME MINISTER'S PLANS.
THEY'VE PRACTICALLY REWRITTEN MY TIME IN THE WAR TOO.
MY COMMANDOS WERE MEN FROM ALL OVER THE WORLD. I RESENT THE IDEA THAT I DID WHAT WE DID, ALONE.
BRADDOCK! CARTER!
CHIEF HUNTER!
GET YOUR TEAM TOGETHER. OUR LUCK JUST CHANGED.
WHAT'S HAPPENED?
JUST RECEIVED INTEL THAT A SHIPMENT OF WEAPONS IS BEING SMUGGLED INTO THE COUNTRY TONIGHT.
DESCRIPTION MATCHES THE TECH HYDRA HAVE BEEN USING. THIS COULD BE THE LINK WE'RE AFTER!
A HELICOPTER WILL BE READY TO TAKE YOU TO IMMINGHAM IN AN HOUR. BRIEFING EN ROUTE.
NOW GO! PREP YOUR TEAM!
SIR!
WHO'S THE SOURCE? WHERE DID THEY GET THIS INTEL?
I CAN'T REVEAL THAT, CARTER. BUT IT'S SOLID.

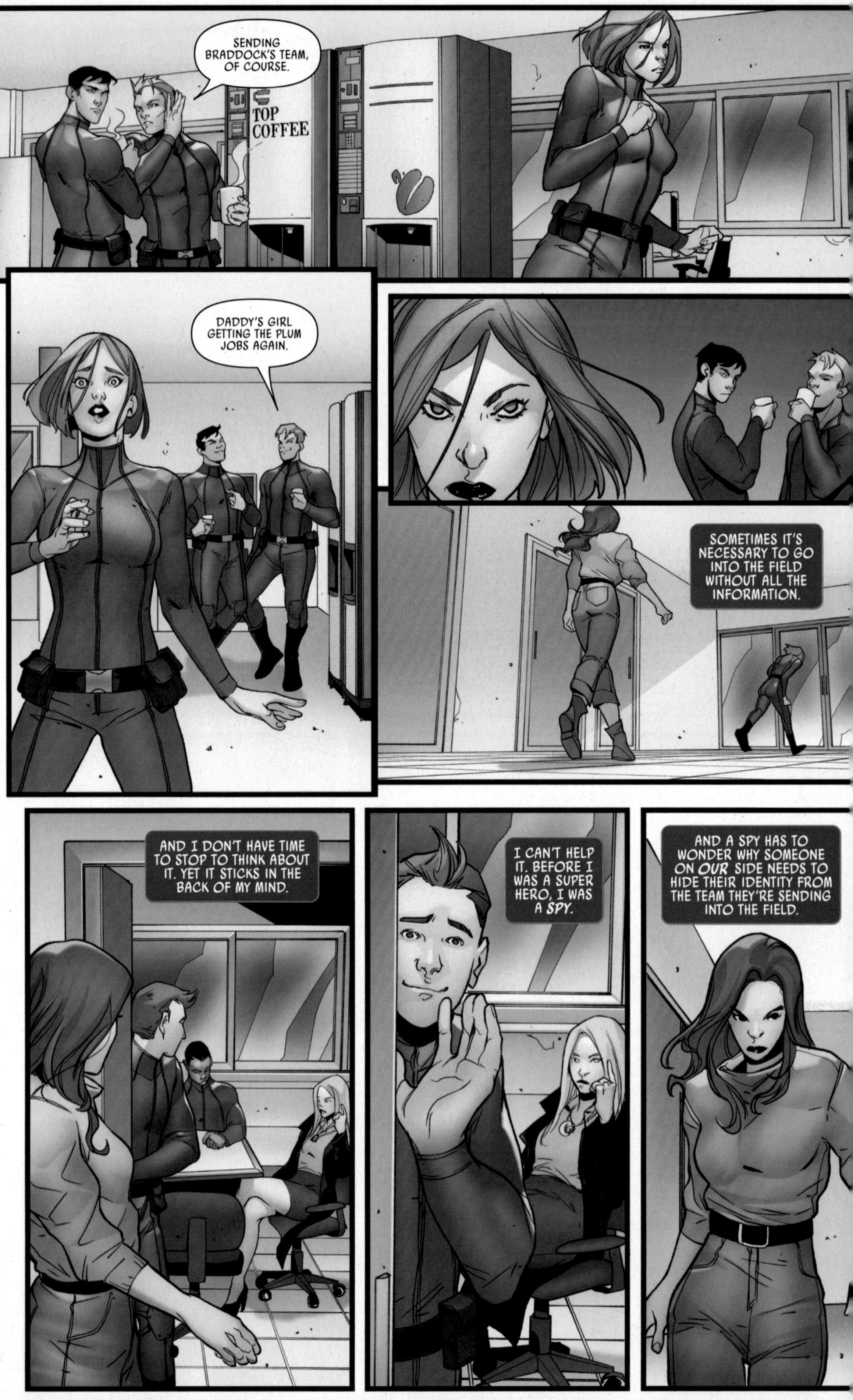
SENDING BRADDOCK'S TEAM, OF COURSE.
TOP COFFEE
DADDY'S GIRL GETTING THE PLUM JOBS AGAIN.
SOMETIMES IT'S NECESSARY TO GO INTO THE FIELD WITHOUT ALL THE INFORMATION.
AND I DON'T HAVE TIME TO STOP TO THINK ABOUT IT. YET IT STICKS IN THE BACK OF MY MIND.
I CAN'T HELP IT. BEFORE I WAS A SUPER HERO, I WAS A SPY.
AND A SPY HAS TO WONDER WHY SOMEONE ON OUR SIDE NEEDS TO HIDE THEIR IDENTITY FROM THE TEAM THEY'RE SENDING INTO THE FIELD.

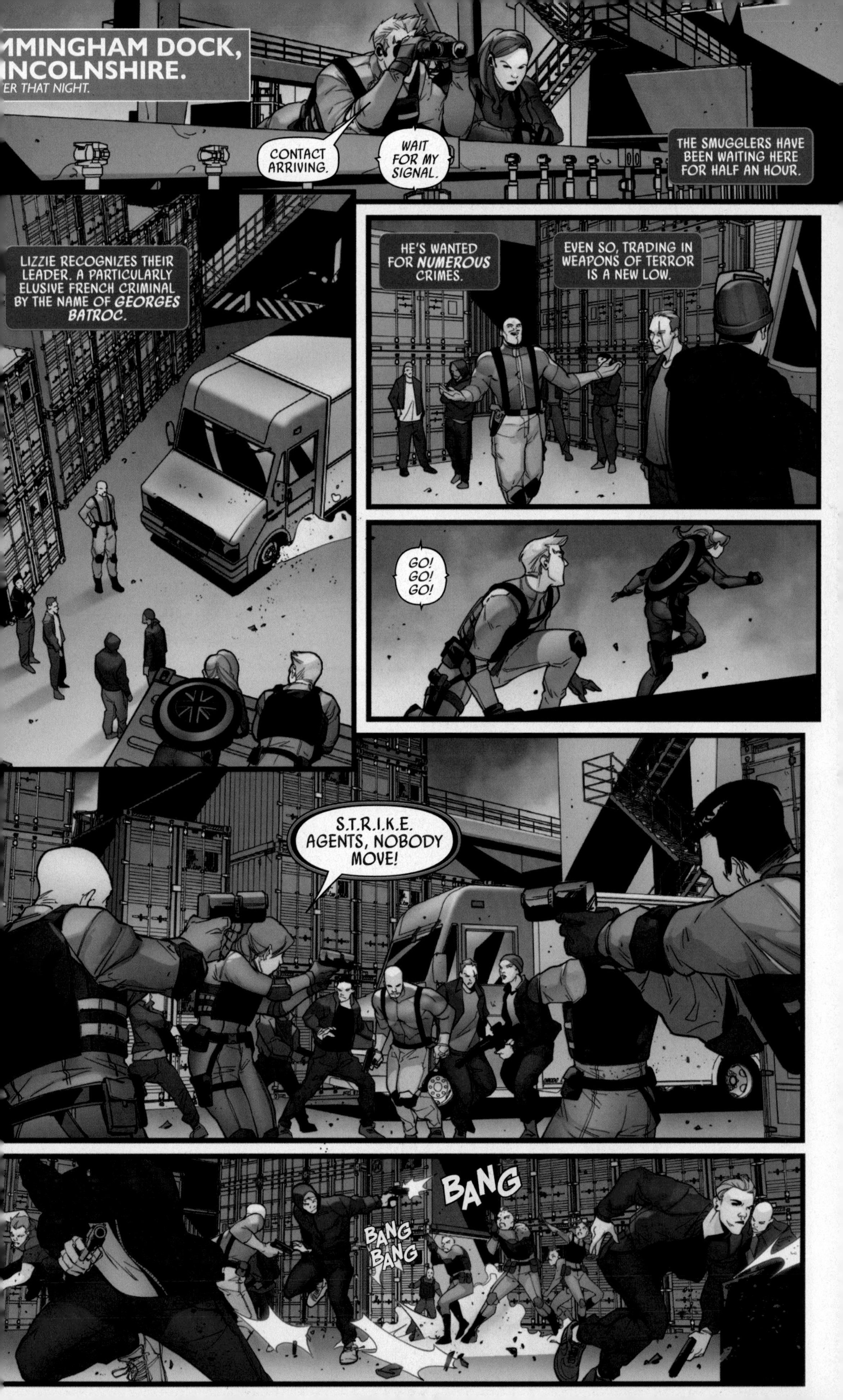

MMINGHAM DOCK,
NCOLNSHIRE.
ER THAT NIGHT.
CONTACT ARRIVING.
WAIT FOR MY SIGNAL.
THE SMUGGLERS HAVE BEEN WAITING HERE FOR HALF AN HOUR.
LIZZIE RECOGNIZES THEIR LEADER. A PARTICULARLY ELUSIVE FRENCH CRIMINAL BY THE NAME OF GEORGES BATROC.
HE'S WANTED FOR NUMEROUS CRIMES.
EVEN SO, TRADING IN WEAPONS OF TERROR IS A NEW LOW.
GO! GO! GO!
S.T.R.I.K.E. AGENTS, NOBODY MOVE!
BANG
BANG
BANG

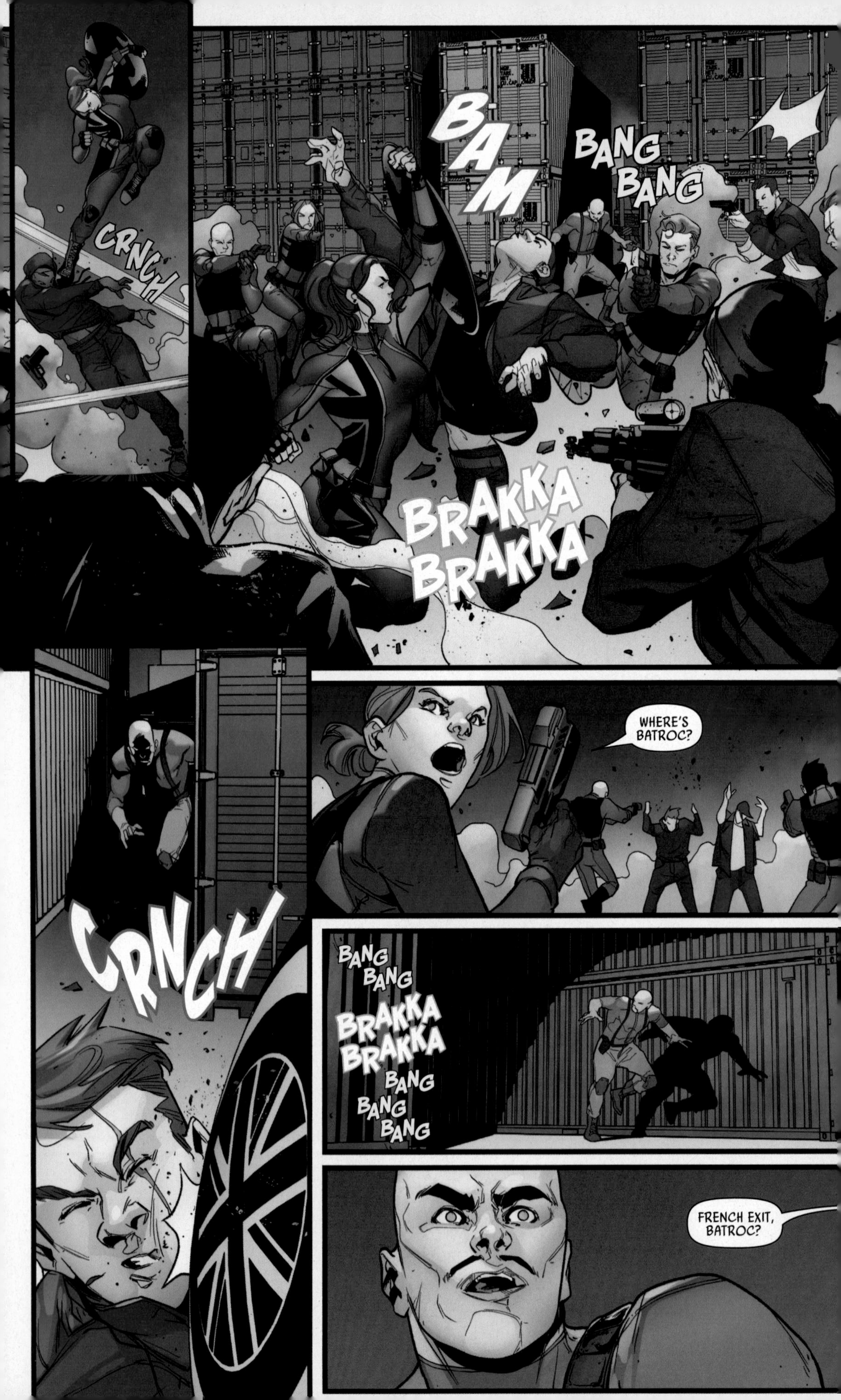
CRNCH
BAM
BANG
BANG
BRAKKA
BRAKKA
CRNCH
WHERE'S BATROC?
BANG
BANG
BRAKKA
BRAKKA
BANG
BANG
BANG
FRENCH EXIT, BATROC?

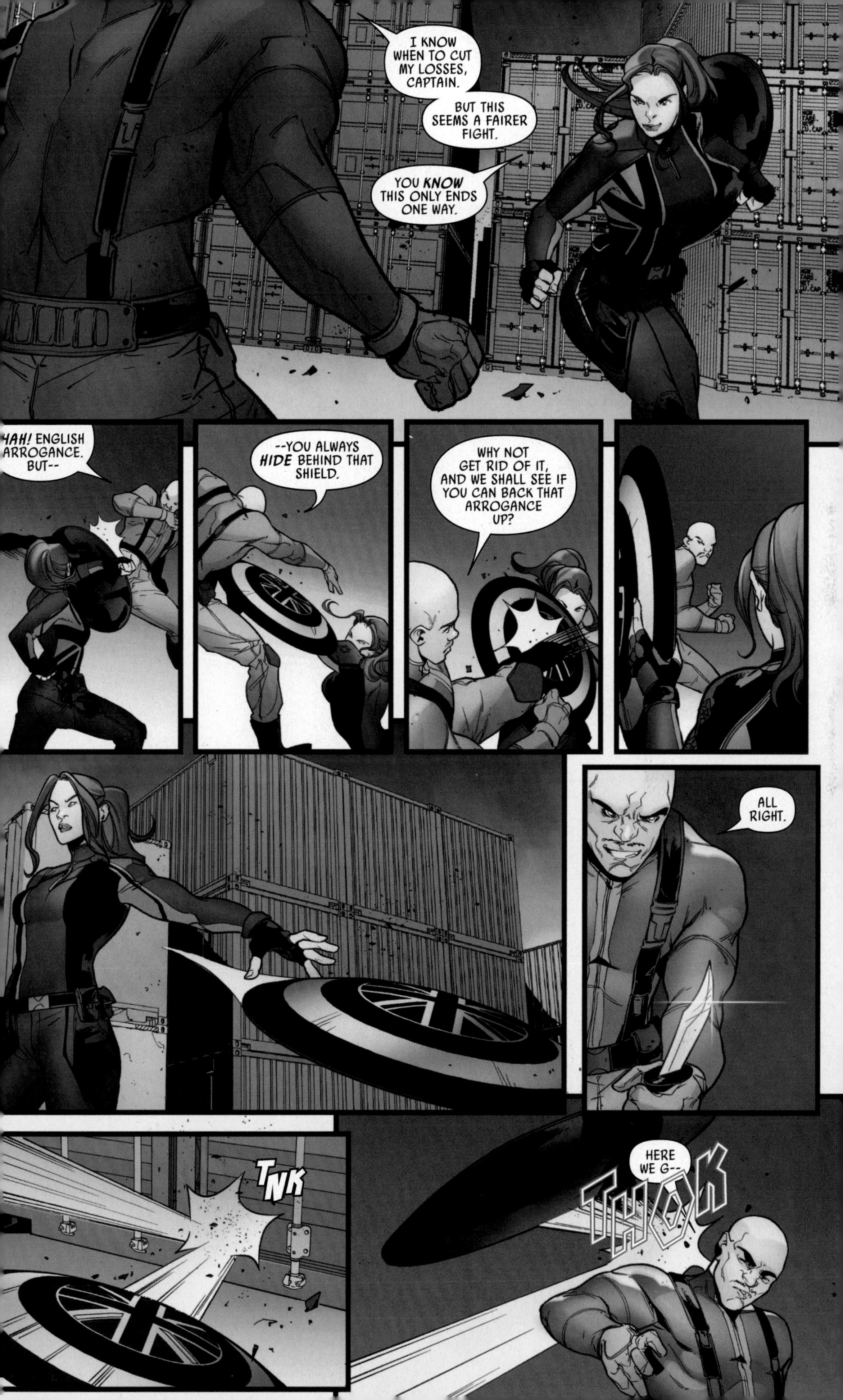
I KNOW WHEN TO CUT MY LOSSES, CAPTAIN.
BUT THIS SEEMS A FAIRER FIGHT.
YOU KNOW THIS ONLY ENDS ONE WAY.
HAH! ENGLISH ARROGANCE. BUT--
--YOU ALWAYS HIDE BEHIND THAT SHIELD.
WHY NOT GET RID OF IT, AND WE SHALL SEE IF YOU CAN BACK THAT ARROGANCE UP?
ALL RIGHT.
TNK
HERE WE G--
THOK

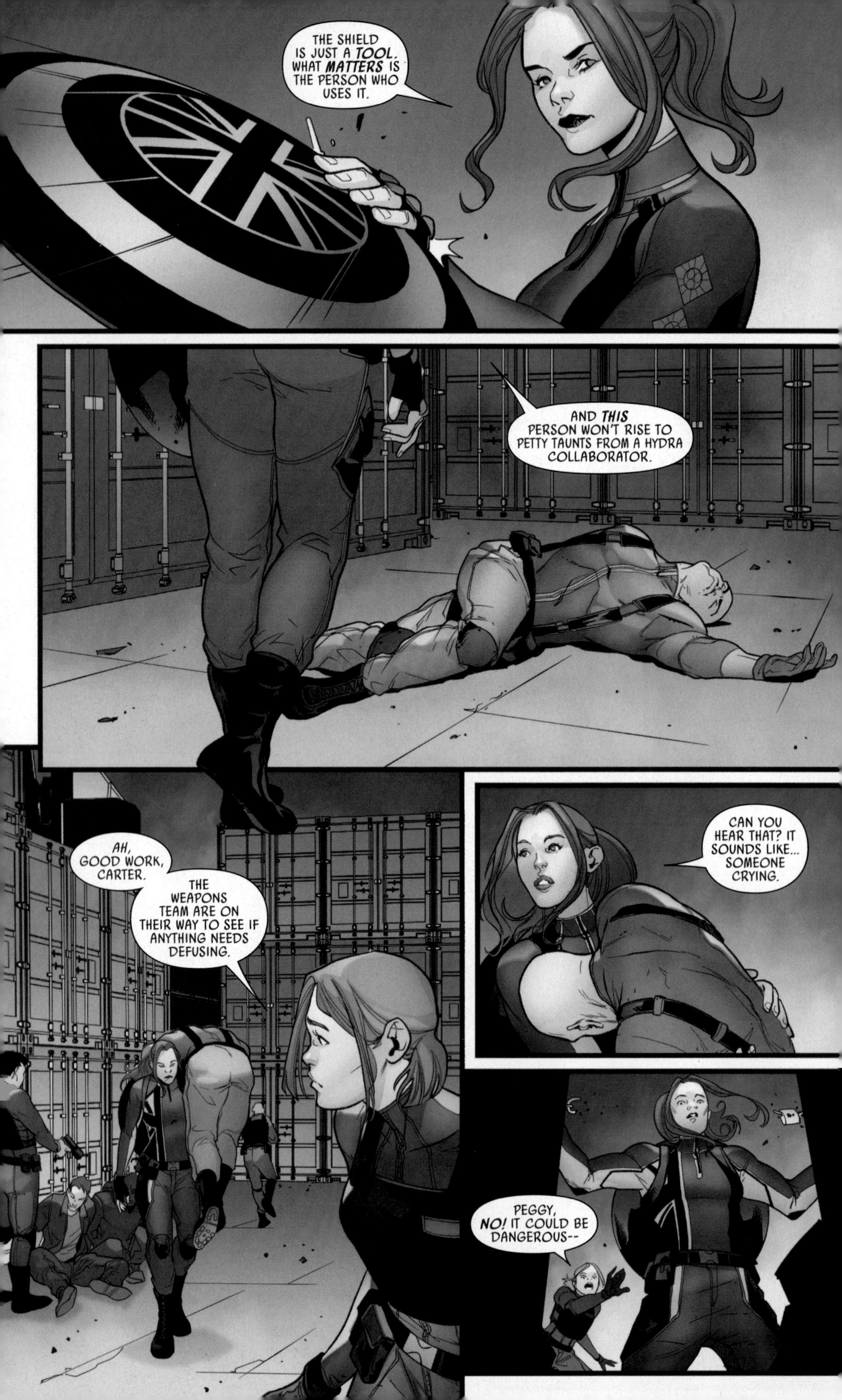
THE SHIELD IS JUST A *TOOL*. WHAT *MATTERS* IS THE PERSON WHO USES IT.
AND *THIS* PERSON WON'T RISE TO PETTY TAUNTS FROM A HYDRA COLLABORATOR.
AH, GOOD WORK, CARTER.
THE WEAPONS TEAM ARE ON THEIR WAY TO SEE IF ANYTHING NEEDS DEFUSING.
CAN YOU HEAR THAT? IT SOUNDS LIKE... SOMEONE CRYING.
PEGGY, *NO!* IT COULD BE DANGEROUS--

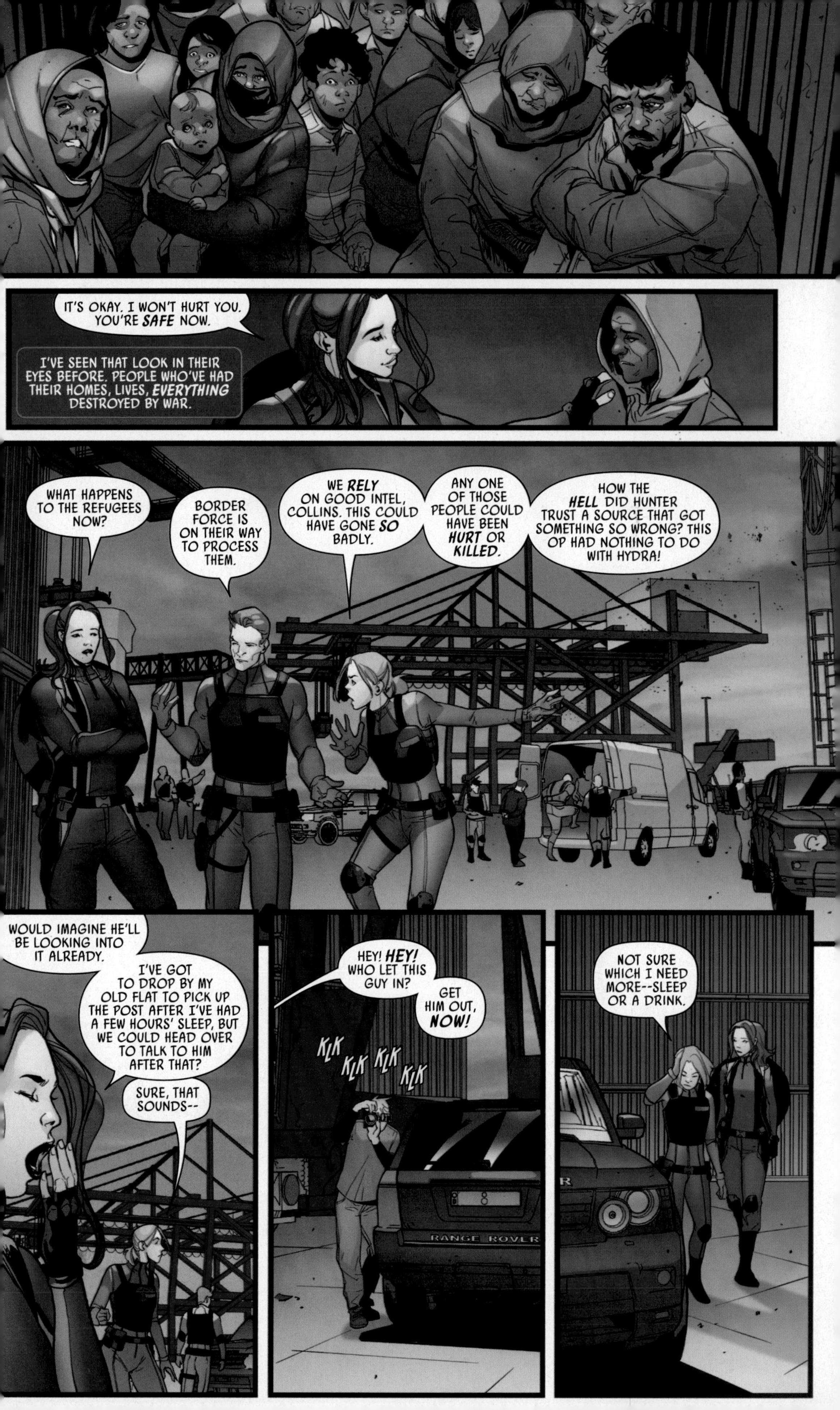

IT'S OKAY. I WON'T HURT YOU. YOU'RE *SAFE* NOW.
I'VE SEEN THAT LOOK IN THEIR EYES BEFORE. PEOPLE WHO'VE HAD THEIR HOMES, LIVES, *EVERYTHING* DESTROYED BY WAR.
WHAT HAPPENS TO THE REFUGEES NOW?
BORDER FORCE IS ON THEIR WAY TO PROCESS THEM.
WE *RELY* ON GOOD INTEL, COLLINS. THIS COULD HAVE GONE *SO* BADLY.
ANY ONE OF THOSE PEOPLE COULD HAVE BEEN *HURT* OR *KILLED.*
HOW THE *HELL* DID HUNTER TRUST A SOURCE THAT GOT SOMETHING SO WRONG? THIS OP HAD NOTHING TO DO WITH HYDRA!
WOULD IMAGINE HE'LL BE LOOKING INTO IT ALREADY.
I'VE GOT TO DROP BY MY OLD FLAT TO PICK UP THE POST AFTER I'VE HAD A FEW HOURS' SLEEP, BUT WE COULD HEAD OVER TO TALK TO HIM AFTER THAT?
SURE, THAT SOUNDS--
HEY! *HEY!* WHO LET THIS GUY IN?
GET HIM OUT, *NOW!*
KLK KLK KLK KLK
RANGE ROVER
NOT SURE WHICH I NEED MORE--SLEEP OR A DRINK.

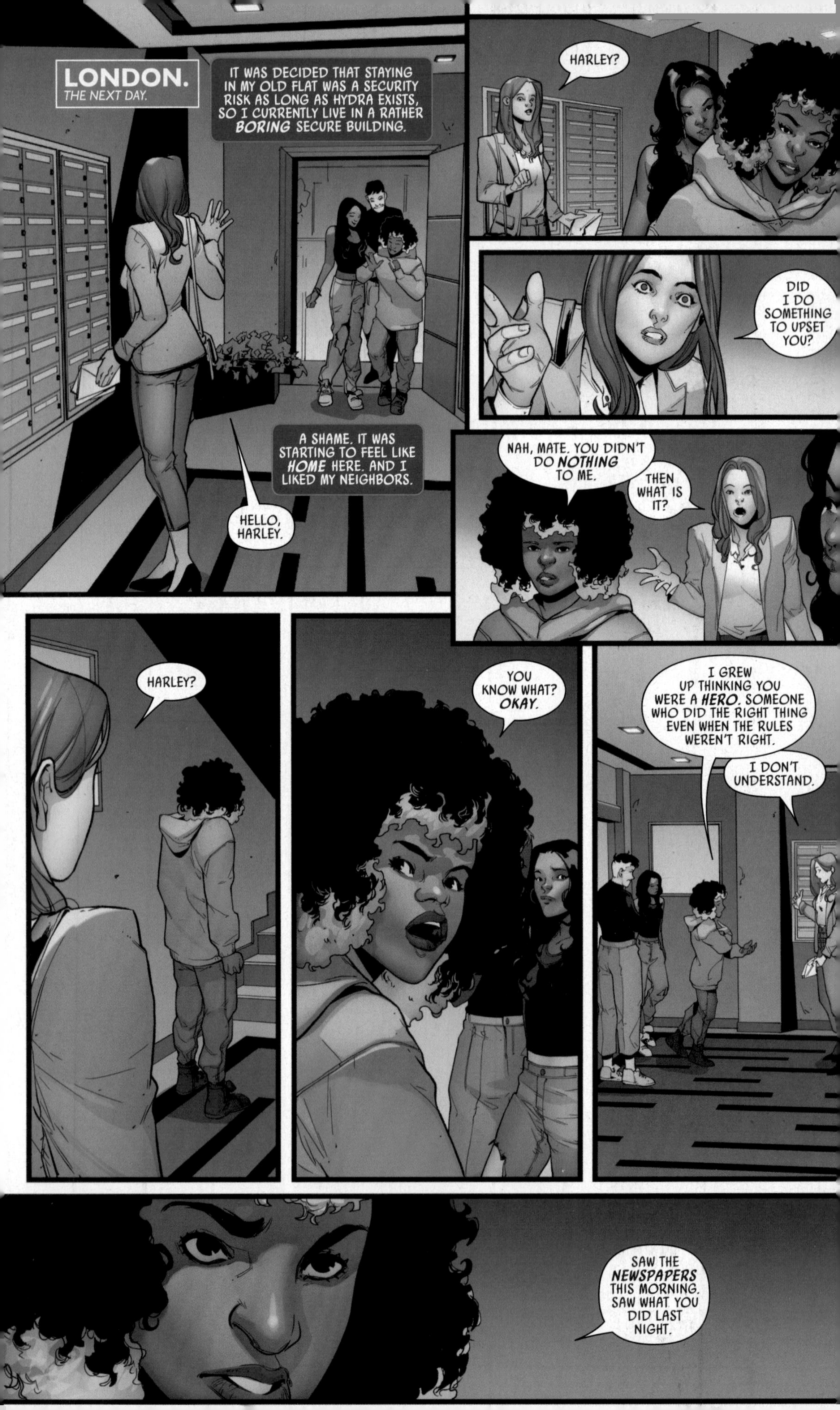
LONDON.
THE NEXT DAY.
IT WAS DECIDED THAT STAYING IN MY OLD FLAT WAS A SECURITY RISK AS LONG AS HYDRA EXISTS, SO I CURRENTLY LIVE IN A RATHER BORING SECURE BUILDING.
A SHAME. IT WAS STARTING TO FEEL LIKE HOME HERE. AND I LIKED MY NEIGHBORS.
HELLO, HARLEY.
HARLEY?
DID I DO SOMETHING TO UPSET YOU?
NAH, MATE. YOU DIDN'T DO NOTHING TO ME.
THEN WHAT IS IT?
HARLEY?
YOU KNOW WHAT? OKAY.
I GREW UP THINKING YOU WERE A HERO. SOMEONE WHO DID THE RIGHT THING EVEN WHEN THE RULES WEREN'T RIGHT.
I DON'T UNDERSTAND.
SAW THE NEWSPAPERS THIS MORNING. SAW WHAT YOU DID LAST NIGHT.

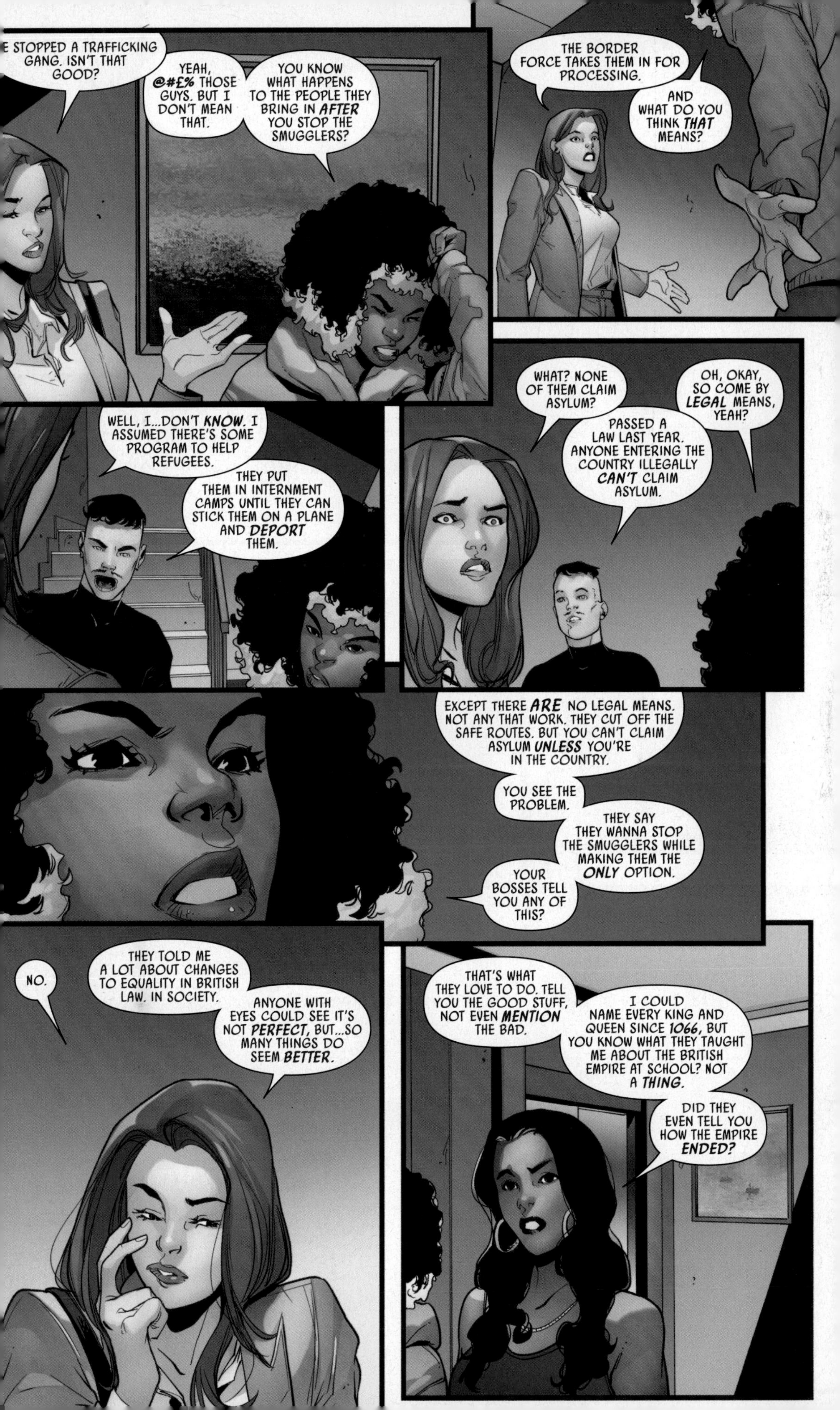
E STOPPED A TRAFFICKING GANG. ISN'T THAT GOOD?
YEAH, @#£% THOSE GUYS. BUT I DON'T MEAN THAT.
YOU KNOW WHAT HAPPENS TO THE PEOPLE THEY BRING IN AFTER YOU STOP THE SMUGGLERS?
THE BORDER FORCE TAKES THEM IN FOR PROCESSING.
AND WHAT DO YOU THINK THAT MEANS?
WELL, I...DON'T KNOW. I ASSUMED THERE'S SOME PROGRAM TO HELP REFUGEES.
THEY PUT THEM IN INTERNMENT CAMPS UNTIL THEY CAN STICK THEM ON A PLANE AND DEPORT THEM.
WHAT? NONE OF THEM CLAIM ASYLUM?
PASSED A LAW LAST YEAR. ANYONE ENTERING THE COUNTRY ILLEGALLY CAN'T CLAIM ASYLUM.
OH, OKAY, SO COME BY LEGAL MEANS, YEAH?
EXCEPT THERE ARE NO LEGAL MEANS. NOT ANY THAT WORK. THEY CUT OFF THE SAFE ROUTES. BUT YOU CAN'T CLAIM ASYLUM UNLESS YOU'RE IN THE COUNTRY.
YOU SEE THE PROBLEM.
THEY SAY THEY WANNA STOP THE SMUGGLERS WHILE MAKING THEM THE ONLY OPTION.
YOUR BOSSES TELL YOU ANY OF THIS?
NO.
THEY TOLD ME A LOT ABOUT CHANGES TO EQUALITY IN BRITISH LAW. IN SOCIETY.
ANYONE WITH EYES COULD SEE IT'S NOT PERFECT, BUT...SO MANY THINGS DO SEEM BETTER.
THAT'S WHAT THEY LOVE TO DO. TELL YOU THE GOOD STUFF, NOT EVEN MENTION THE BAD.
I COULD NAME EVERY KING AND QUEEN SINCE 1066, BUT YOU KNOW WHAT THEY TAUGHT ME ABOUT THE BRITISH EMPIRE AT SCHOOL? NOT A THING.
DID THEY EVEN TELL YOU HOW THE EMPIRE ENDED?

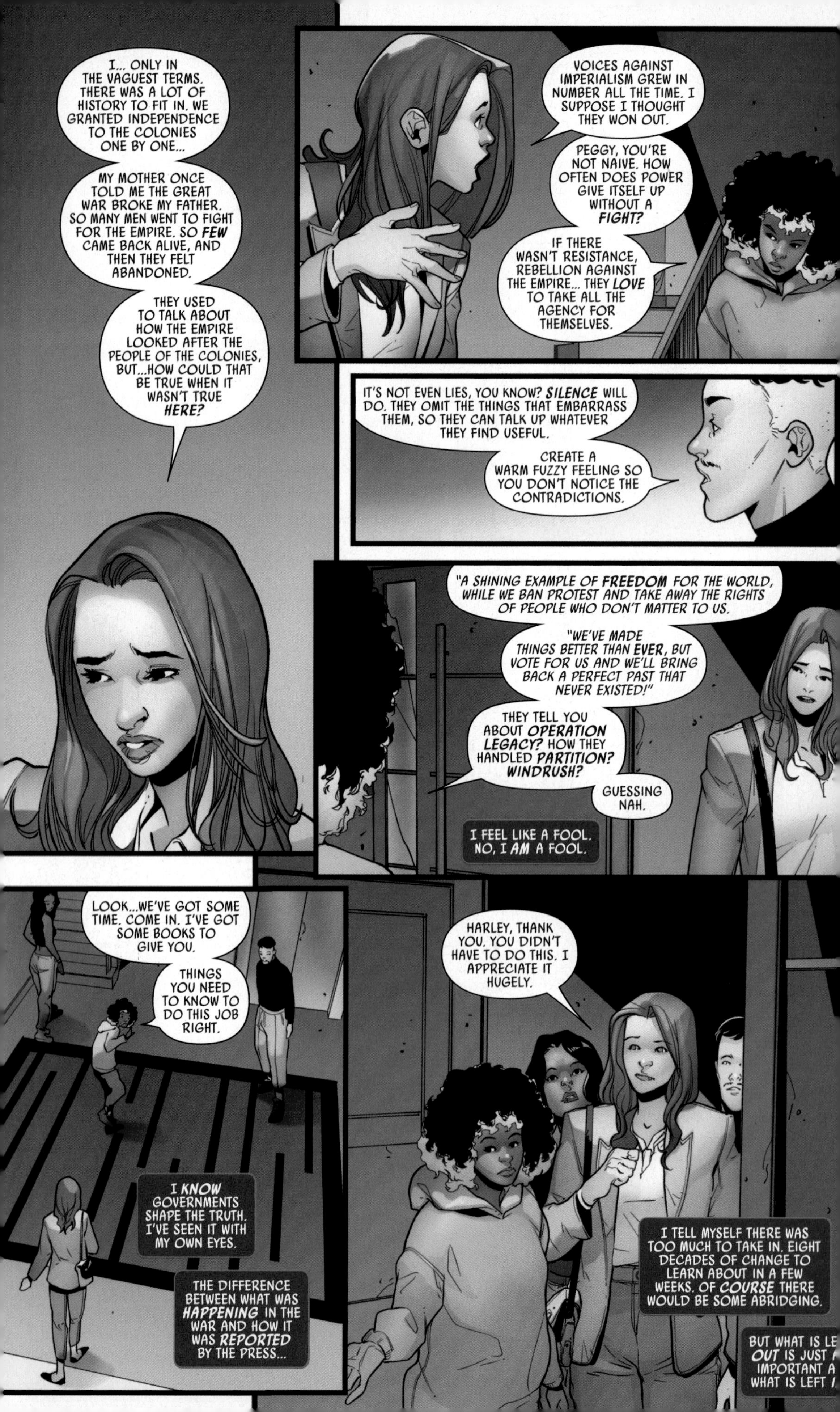
I... ONLY IN THE VAGUEST TERMS. THERE WAS A LOT OF HISTORY TO FIT IN. WE GRANTED INDEPENDENCE TO THE COLONIES ONE BY ONE...
MY MOTHER ONCE TOLD ME THE GREAT WAR BROKE MY FATHER. SO MANY MEN WENT TO FIGHT FOR THE EMPIRE. SO FEW CAME BACK ALIVE, AND THEN THEY FELT ABANDONED.
THEY USED TO TALK ABOUT HOW THE EMPIRE LOOKED AFTER THE PEOPLE OF THE COLONIES, BUT...HOW COULD THAT BE TRUE WHEN IT WASN'T TRUE HERE?
VOICES AGAINST IMPERIALISM GREW IN NUMBER ALL THE TIME. I SUPPOSE I THOUGHT THEY WON OUT.
PEGGY, YOU'RE NOT NAIVE. HOW OFTEN DOES POWER GIVE ITSELF UP WITHOUT A FIGHT?
IF THERE WASN'T RESISTANCE, REBELLION AGAINST THE EMPIRE... THEY LOVE TO TAKE ALL THE AGENCY FOR THEMSELVES.
IT'S NOT EVEN LIES, YOU KNOW? SILENCE WILL DO. THEY OMIT THE THINGS THAT EMBARRASS THEM, SO THEY CAN TALK UP WHATEVER THEY FIND USEFUL.
CREATE A WARM FUZZY FEELING SO YOU DON'T NOTICE THE CONTRADICTIONS.
"A SHINING EXAMPLE OF FREEDOM FOR THE WORLD, WHILE WE BAN PROTEST AND TAKE AWAY THE RIGHTS OF PEOPLE WHO DON'T MATTER TO US.
"WE'VE MADE THINGS BETTER THAN EVER, BUT VOTE FOR US AND WE'LL BRING BACK A PERFECT PAST THAT NEVER EXISTED!"
THEY TELL YOU ABOUT OPERATION LEGACY? HOW THEY HANDLED PARTITION? WINDRUSH?
GUESSING NAH.
I FEEL LIKE A FOOL. NO, I AM A FOOL.
LOOK...WE'VE GOT SOME TIME. COME IN. I'VE GOT SOME BOOKS TO GIVE YOU.
THINGS YOU NEED TO KNOW TO DO THIS JOB RIGHT.
I KNOW GOVERNMENTS SHAPE THE TRUTH. I'VE SEEN IT WITH MY OWN EYES.
THE DIFFERENCE BETWEEN WHAT WAS HAPPENING IN THE WAR AND HOW IT WAS REPORTED BY THE PRESS...
HARLEY, THANK YOU. YOU DIDN'T HAVE TO DO THIS. I APPRECIATE IT HUGELY.
I TELL MYSELF THERE WAS TOO MUCH TO TAKE IN. EIGHT DECADES OF CHANGE TO LEARN ABOUT IN A FEW WEEKS. OF COURSE THERE WOULD BE SOME ABRIDGING.

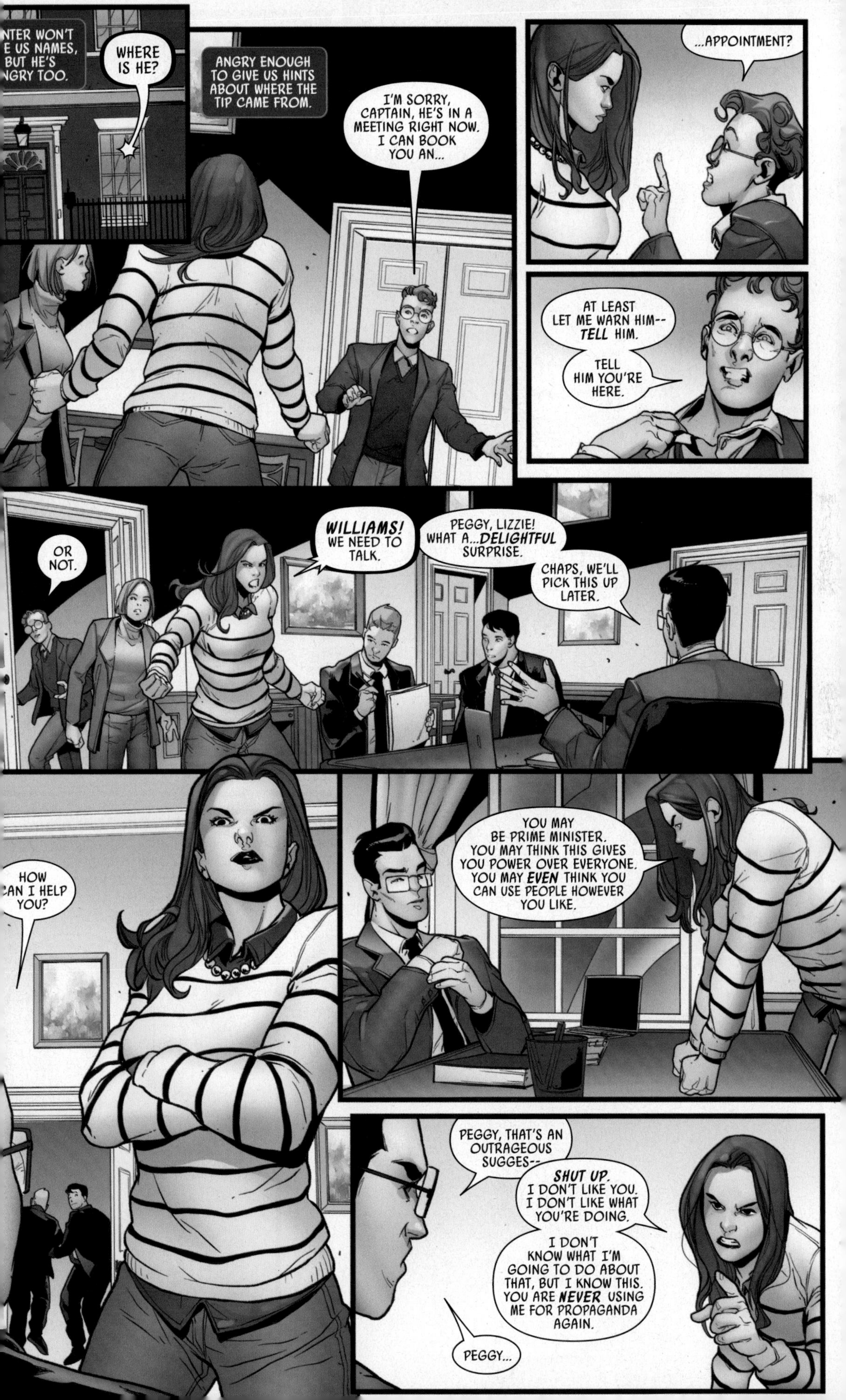

NTER WON'T
E US NAMES,
BUT HE'S
NGRY TOO.
WHERE IS HE?
ANGRY ENOUGH TO GIVE US HINTS ABOUT WHERE THE TIP CAME FROM.
I'M SORRY, CAPTAIN, HE'S IN A MEETING RIGHT NOW. I CAN BOOK YOU AN...
...APPOINTMENT?
AT LEAST LET ME WARN HIM-- TELL HIM.
TELL HIM YOU'RE HERE.
OR NOT.
WILLIAMS! WE NEED TO TALK.
PEGGY, LIZZIE! WHAT A...DELIGHTFUL SURPRISE.
CHAPS, WE'LL PICK THIS UP LATER.
HOW
CAN I HELP
YOU?
YOU MAY BE PRIME MINISTER. YOU MAY THINK THIS GIVES YOU POWER OVER EVERYONE. YOU MAY EVEN THINK YOU CAN USE PEOPLE HOWEVER YOU LIKE.
PEGGY, THAT'S AN OUTRAGEOUS SUGGES--
SHUT UP. I DON'T LIKE YOU. I DON'T LIKE WHAT YOU'RE DOING.
I DON'T KNOW WHAT I'M GOING TO DO ABOUT THAT, BUT I KNOW THIS. YOU ARE NEVER USING ME FOR PROPAGANDA AGAIN.
PEGGY...

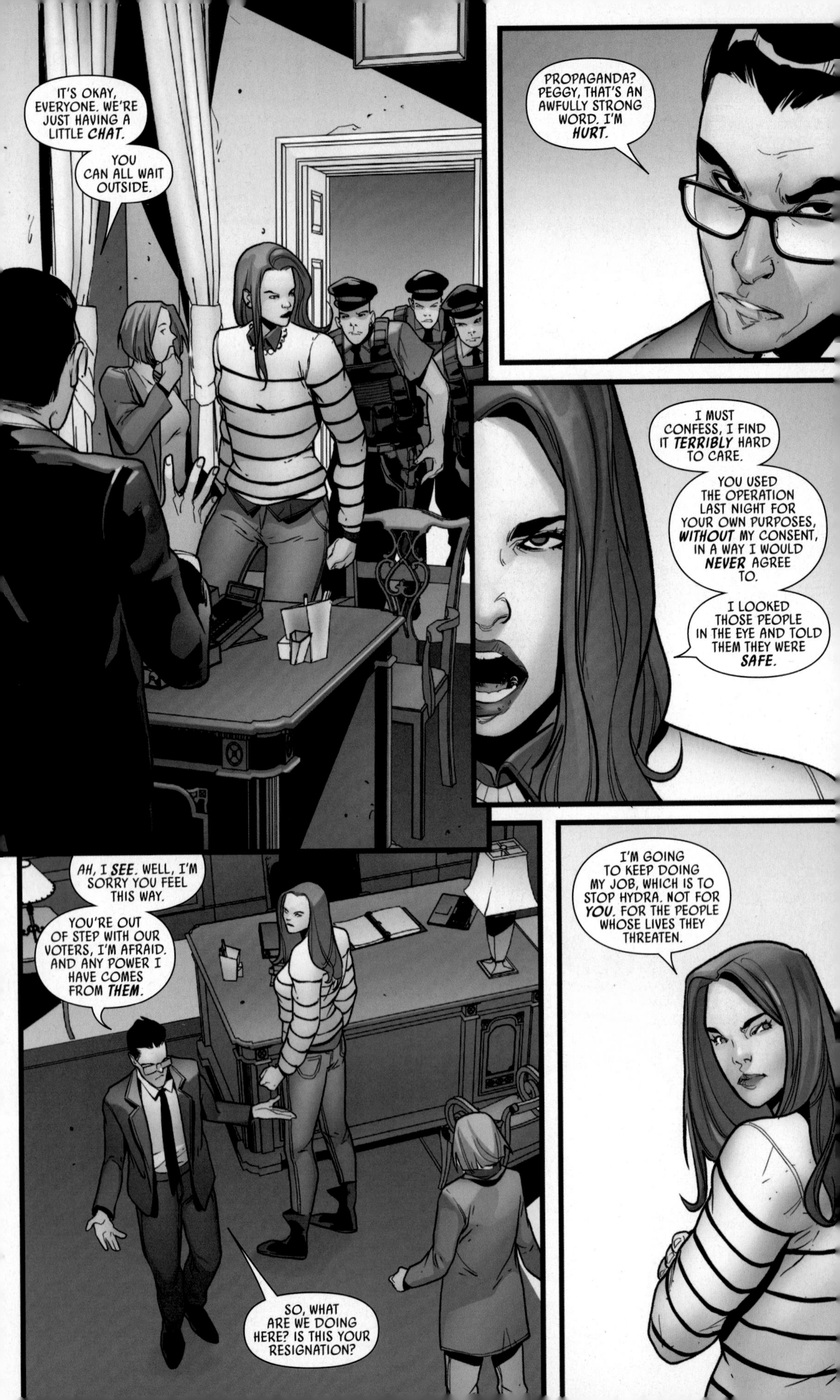
IT'S OKAY, EVERYONE. WE'RE JUST HAVING A LITTLE *CHAT*.
YOU CAN ALL WAIT OUTSIDE.
PROPAGANDA? PEGGY, THAT'S AN AWFULLY STRONG WORD. I'M *HURT*.
I MUST CONFESS, I FIND IT *TERRIBLY* HARD TO CARE.
YOU USED THE OPERATION LAST NIGHT FOR YOUR OWN PURPOSES, *WITHOUT* MY CONSENT, IN A WAY I WOULD *NEVER* AGREE TO.
I LOOKED THOSE PEOPLE IN THE EYE AND TOLD THEM THEY WERE *SAFE*.
AH, I *SEE*. WELL, I'M SORRY YOU FEEL THIS WAY.
YOU'RE OUT OF STEP WITH OUR VOTERS, I'M AFRAID. AND ANY POWER I HAVE COMES FROM *THEM*.
SO, WHAT ARE WE DOING HERE? IS THIS YOUR RESIGNATION?
I'M GOING TO KEEP DOING MY JOB, WHICH IS TO STOP HYDRA. NOT FOR *YOU*. FOR THE PEOPLE WHOSE LIVES THEY THREATEN.

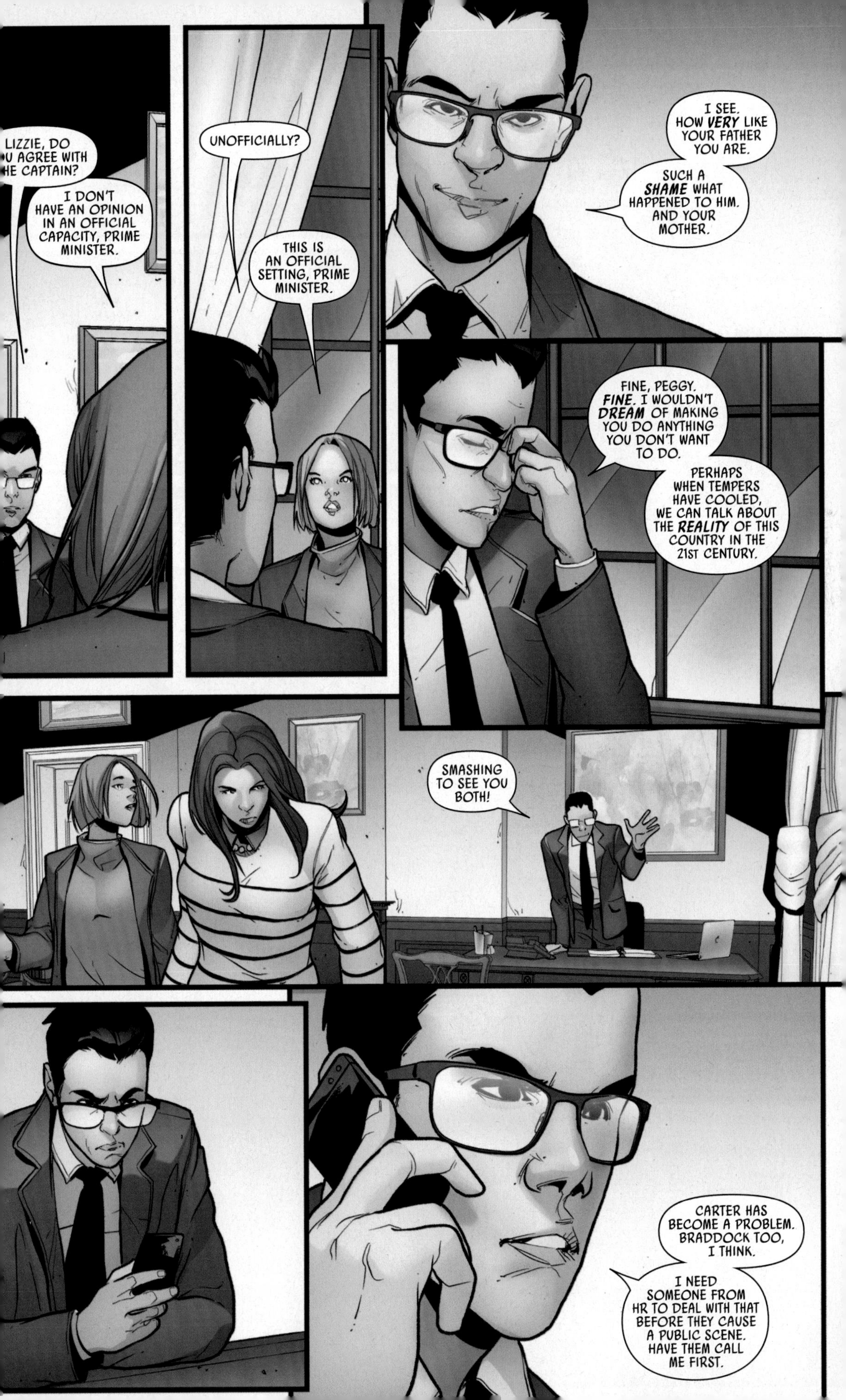

LIZZIE, DO
U AGREE WITH
HE CAPTAIN?
I DON'T HAVE AN OPINION IN AN OFFICIAL CAPACITY, PRIME MINISTER.
UNOFFICIALLY?
THIS IS AN OFFICIAL SETTING, PRIME MINISTER.
I SEE. HOW VERY LIKE YOUR FATHER YOU ARE.
SUCH A SHAME WHAT HAPPENED TO HIM. AND YOUR MOTHER.
FINE, PEGGY. FINE. I WOULDN'T DREAM OF MAKING YOU DO ANYTHING YOU DON'T WANT TO DO.
PERHAPS WHEN TEMPERS HAVE COOLED, WE CAN TALK ABOUT THE REALITY OF THIS COUNTRY IN THE 21ST CENTURY.
SMASHING TO SEE YOU BOTH!
CARTER HAS BECOME A PROBLEM. BRADDOCK TOO, I THINK.
I NEED SOMEONE FROM HR TO DEAL WITH THAT BEFORE THEY CAUSE A PUBLIC SCENE. HAVE THEM CALL ME FIRST.

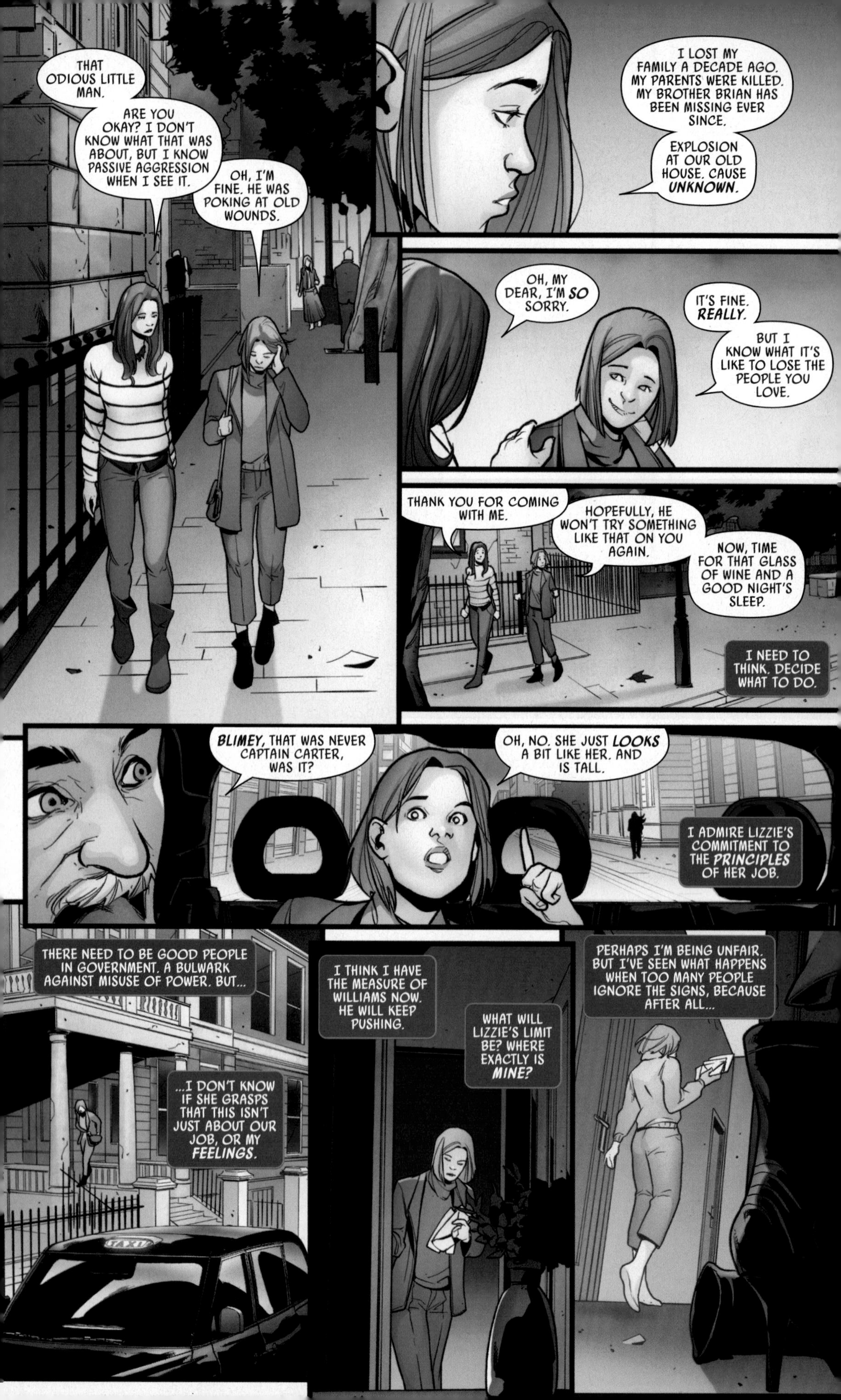
THAT ODIOUS LITTLE MAN.
ARE YOU OKAY? I DON'T KNOW WHAT THAT WAS ABOUT, BUT I KNOW PASSIVE AGGRESSION WHEN I SEE IT.
OH, I'M FINE. HE WAS POKING AT OLD WOUNDS.
I LOST MY FAMILY A DECADE AGO. MY PARENTS WERE KILLED. MY BROTHER BRIAN HAS BEEN MISSING EVER SINCE.
EXPLOSION AT OUR OLD HOUSE. CAUSE UNKNOWN.
OH, MY DEAR, I'M SO SORRY.
IT'S FINE. REALLY.
BUT I KNOW WHAT IT'S LIKE TO LOSE THE PEOPLE YOU LOVE.
THANK YOU FOR COMING WITH ME.
HOPEFULLY, HE WON'T TRY SOMETHING LIKE THAT ON YOU AGAIN.
NOW, TIME FOR THAT GLASS OF WINE AND A GOOD NIGHT'S SLEEP.
I NEED TO THINK. DECIDE WHAT TO DO.
BLIMEY, THAT WAS NEVER CAPTAIN CARTER, WAS IT?
OH, NO. SHE JUST LOOKS A BIT LIKE HER. AND IS TALL.
I ADMIRE LIZZIE'S COMMITMENT TO THE PRINCIPLES OF HER JOB.
THERE NEED TO BE GOOD PEOPLE IN GOVERNMENT. A BULWARK AGAINST MISUSE OF POWER. BUT...
...I DON'T KNOW IF SHE GRASPS THAT THIS ISN'T JUST ABOUT OUR JOB, OR MY FEELINGS.
TAXI
I THINK I HAVE THE MEASURE OF WILLIAMS NOW. HE WILL KEEP PUSHING.
WHAT WILL LIZZIE'S LIMIT BE? WHERE EXACTLY IS MINE?
PERHAPS I'M BEING UNFAIR. BUT I'VE SEEN WHAT HAPPENS WHEN TOO MANY PEOPLE IGNORE THE SIGNS, BECAUSE AFTER ALL...

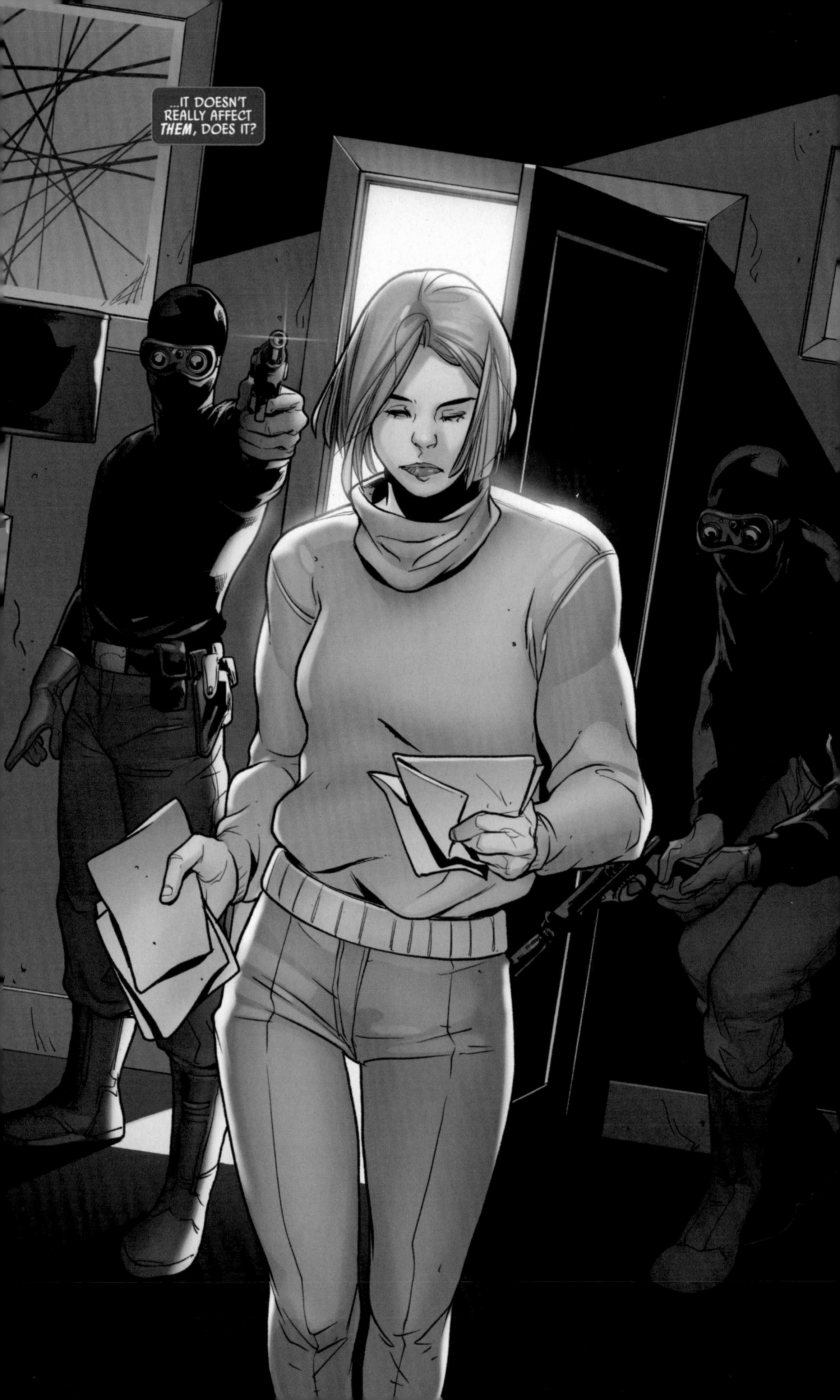
...IT DOESN'T REALLY AFFECT *THEM*, DOES IT?

#3

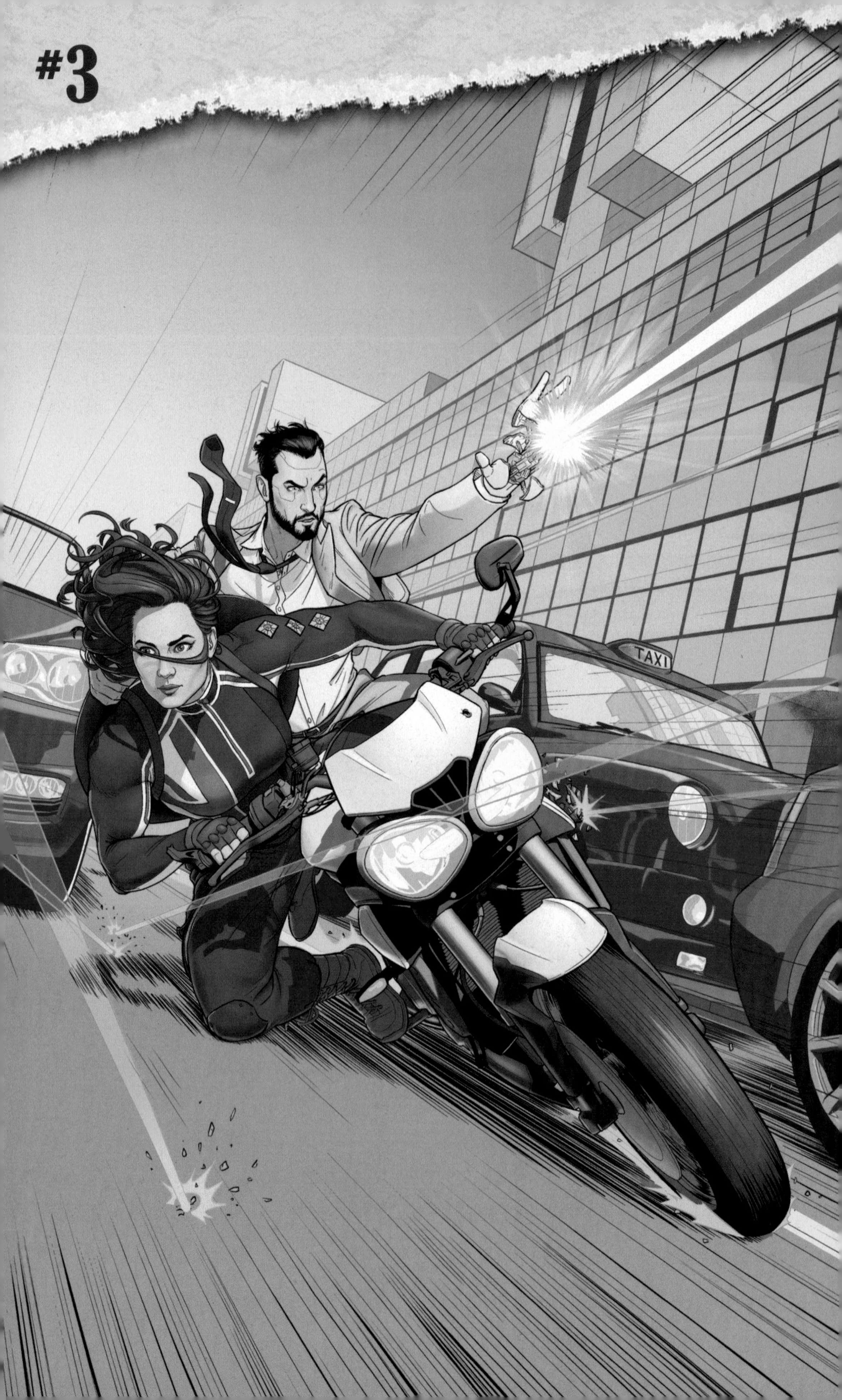
TAXI

LONDON

The capital's premier free newspaper

...E. STOPS TERRORISTS AT EASTPARK SHOPPING CENTRE, BUT NOT BEFORE...

3 KILLED IN YDRA MA
ATTACK

- Questions asked
- security services
- Home Secreta
in S.T.R.I.K.E. le

Wednesday, May 18, 2022

NEWSPAPER OF THE PEOPLE   70p

- CARTER TAKES DOWN ILLEG
IMMIGRANT SMUGGLING RING

CAPTAIN PE
PROTECTS
BORDER

---

en of synth-pop is back!
ere has she been? Page 42

Daniel Jackson Policing our borders:
a legitimate role for a super hero - or a
political stunt too far? Page 27

10 easy
vegan
recipes
for any
budget

The Morning Sentinel
£2.00

ydra Bill 'certain' to become law
s majority of MPs vote aye

DAILY Herald

Thursday May 19, 2022

Telling it like it is

- SHOUTING HEARD AT No. 10 • PM'S OFFICE DENIES R

CARTER IN
SHOWDOWN
WITH PM

UK £5 Channel Islands £3.10 Republic of Ireland £3.60

THURSDAY 19 May 2022

utant debate
greement grows over the rights -
dangers - of mutants — PAGE 5

BUSINESS TIMES

Cost of living crisis grows
With bills spiralling out of control, what can YOU
do to save money? Expert panel advice — PAGE 18

£

Reese Richards
How the Fantastic Five founder turned
Doom from rival to teammate — PAGE 34

lice did not breach rights of
ested protesters, court rules

allenge to recent change in protest law fails to convince High C

reach the rights
the officers
demonstration
restrictions
High Court

of last year,
protesters
ey claimed
police to use
protesters
medical
s tha

News in brief

Hydra terroris
The terror
pre

lient

£2.25 £1.50 to subscribers

No 73862

The Morning Chronicle

9 2022

aspers named as new spy chief

d as Director General of MI5 following Kenneth Turner's fatal heart attack

---

Tony Stark
The tech heir rebuilt
himself. Can he
rebuild his family's
company?

FUT

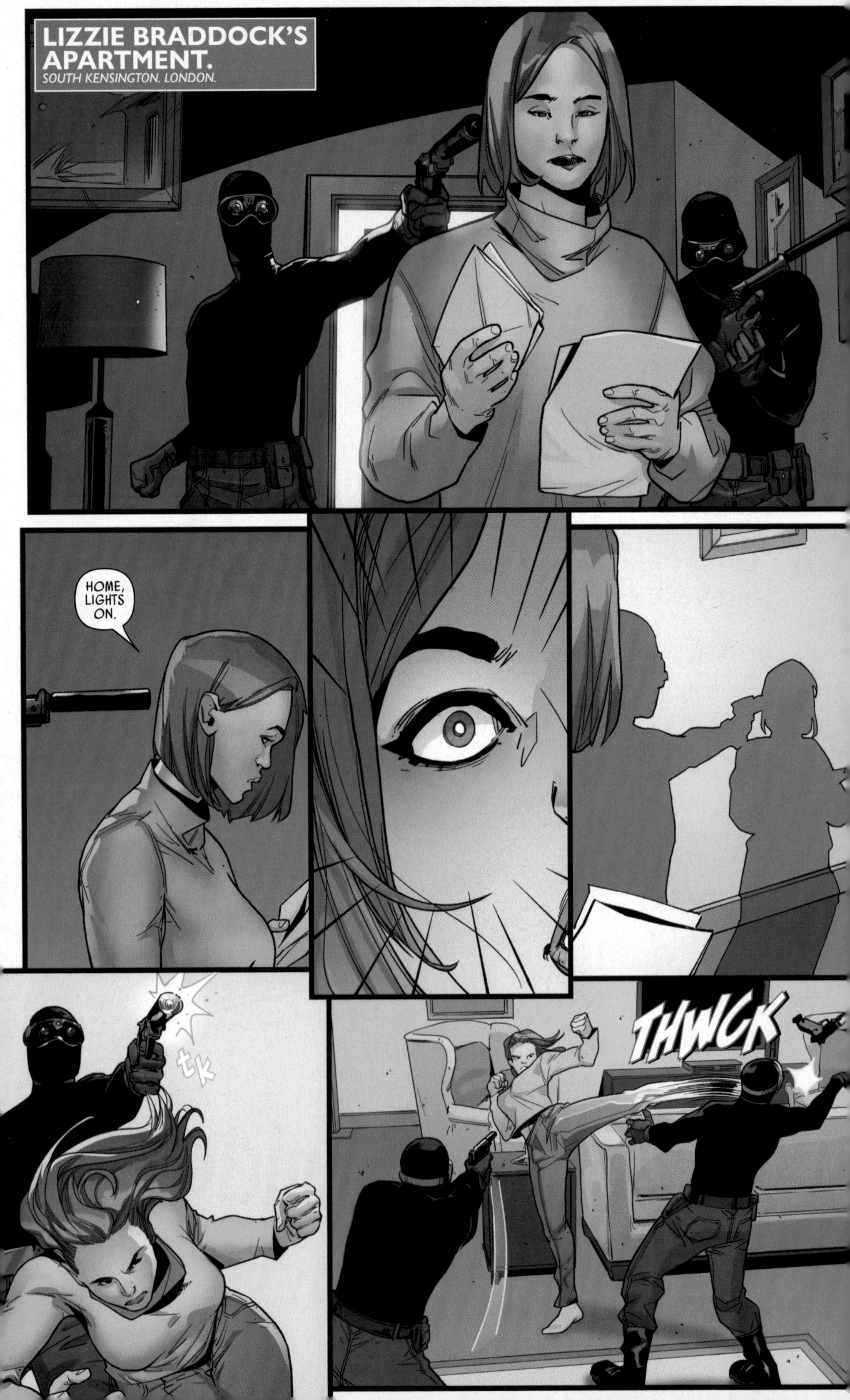
LIZZIE BRADDOCK'S APARTMENT.
SOUTH KENSINGTON. LONDON.
HOME, LIGHTS ON.
tk
THWCK

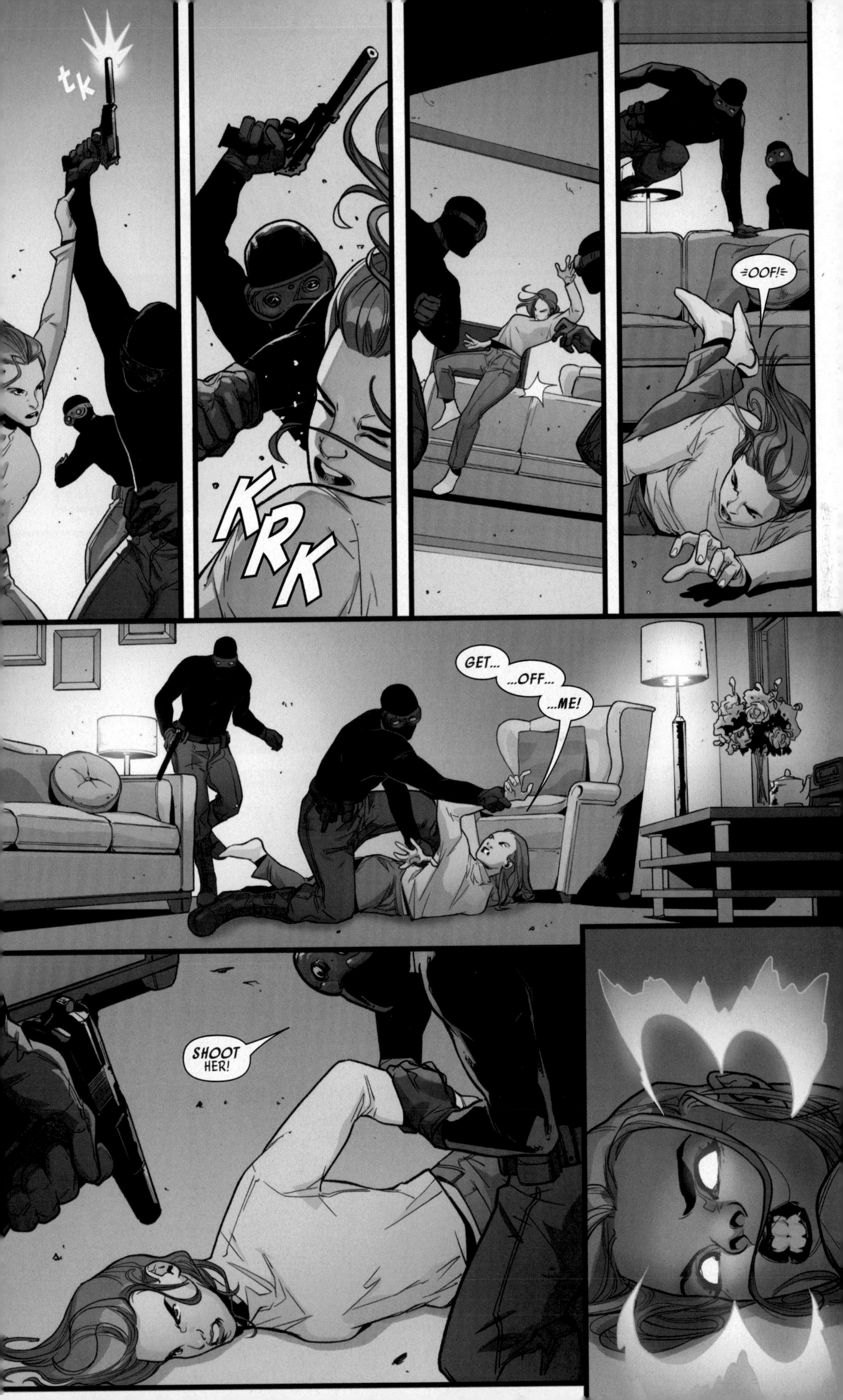
tk
KRK
OOF!
GET...
...OFF...
...ME!
SHOOT HER!

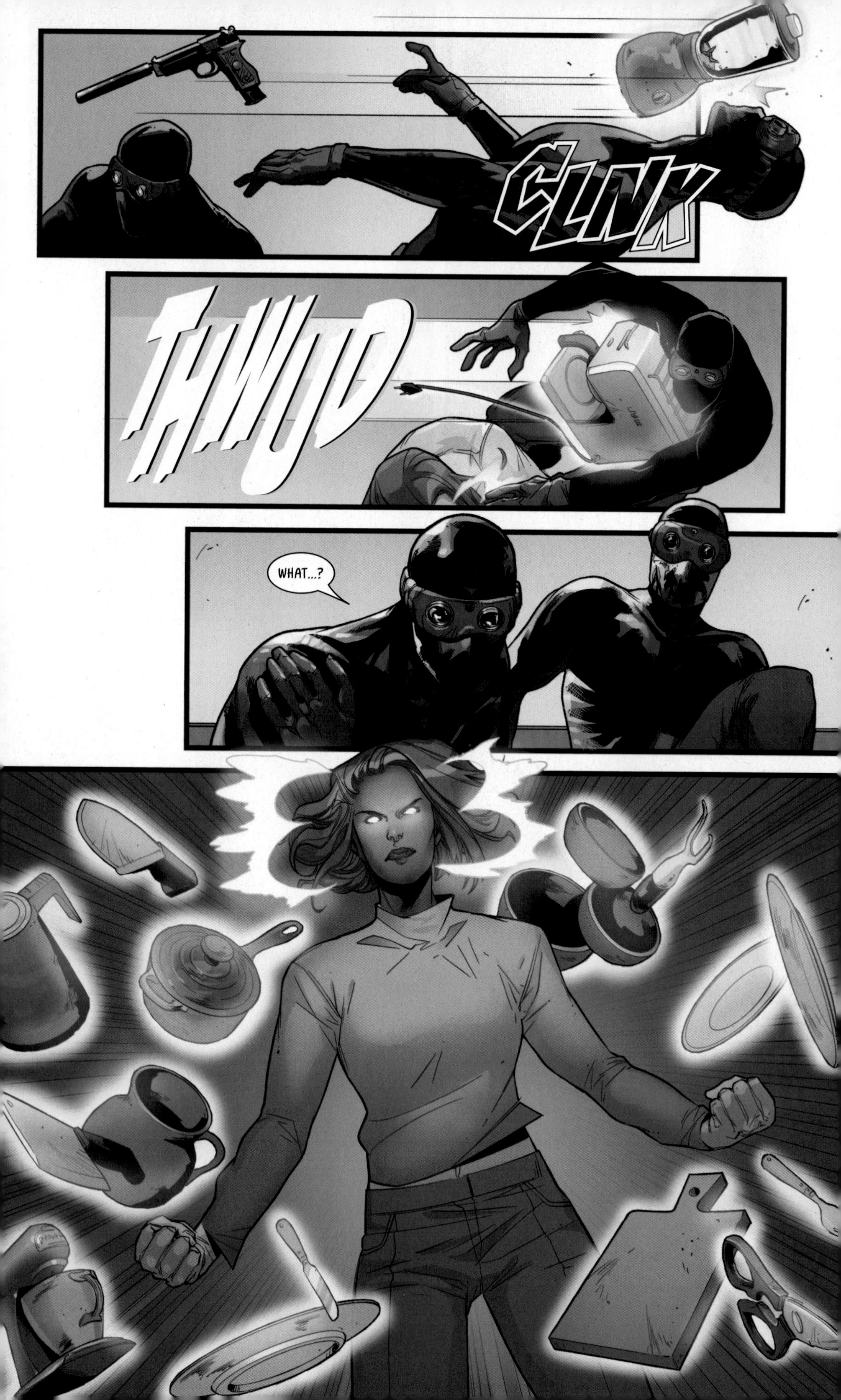
CLINK
THWUD
WHAT...?

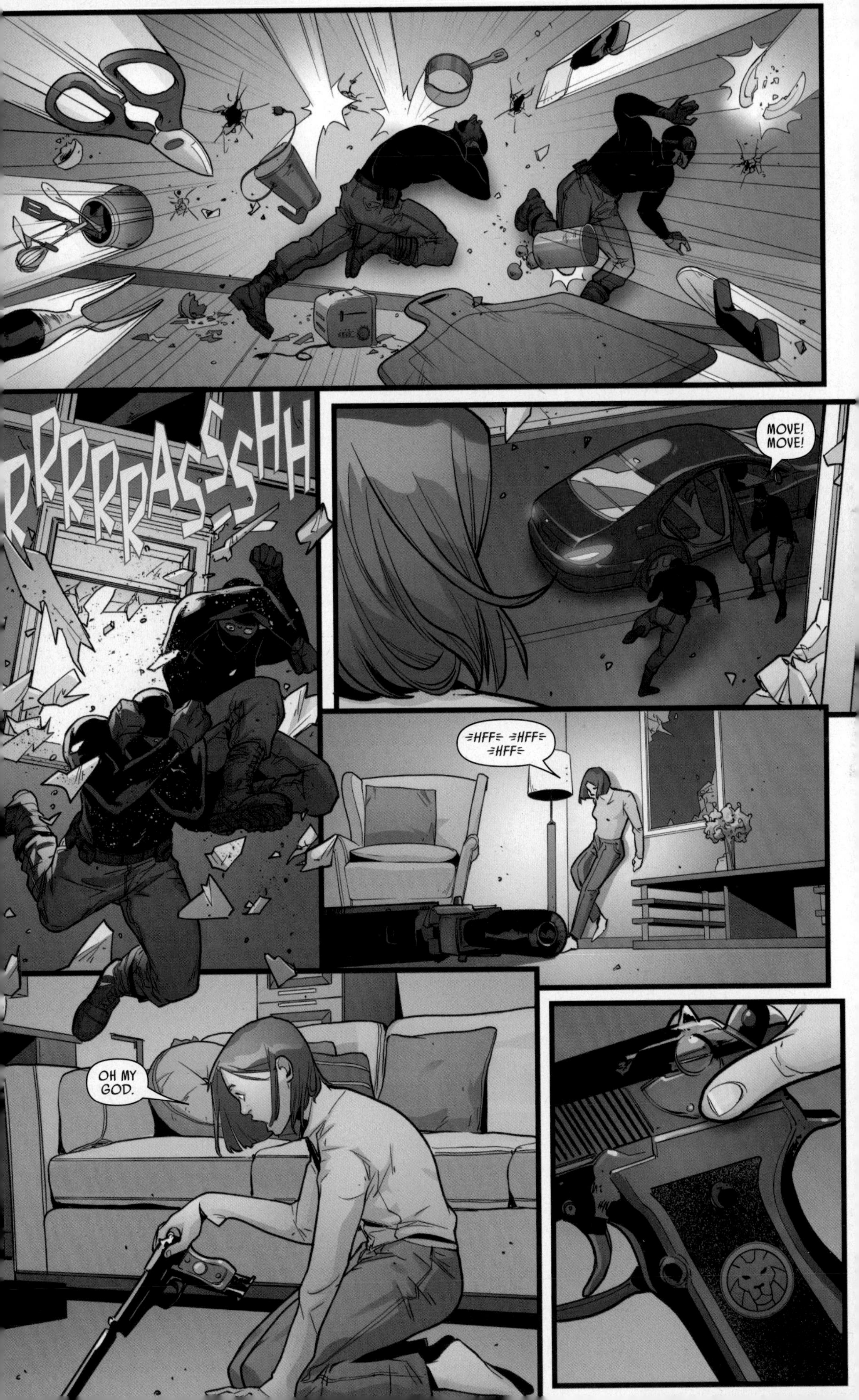
RRRRRASSSHH
MOVE! MOVE!
HFF HFF HFF
OH MY GOD.

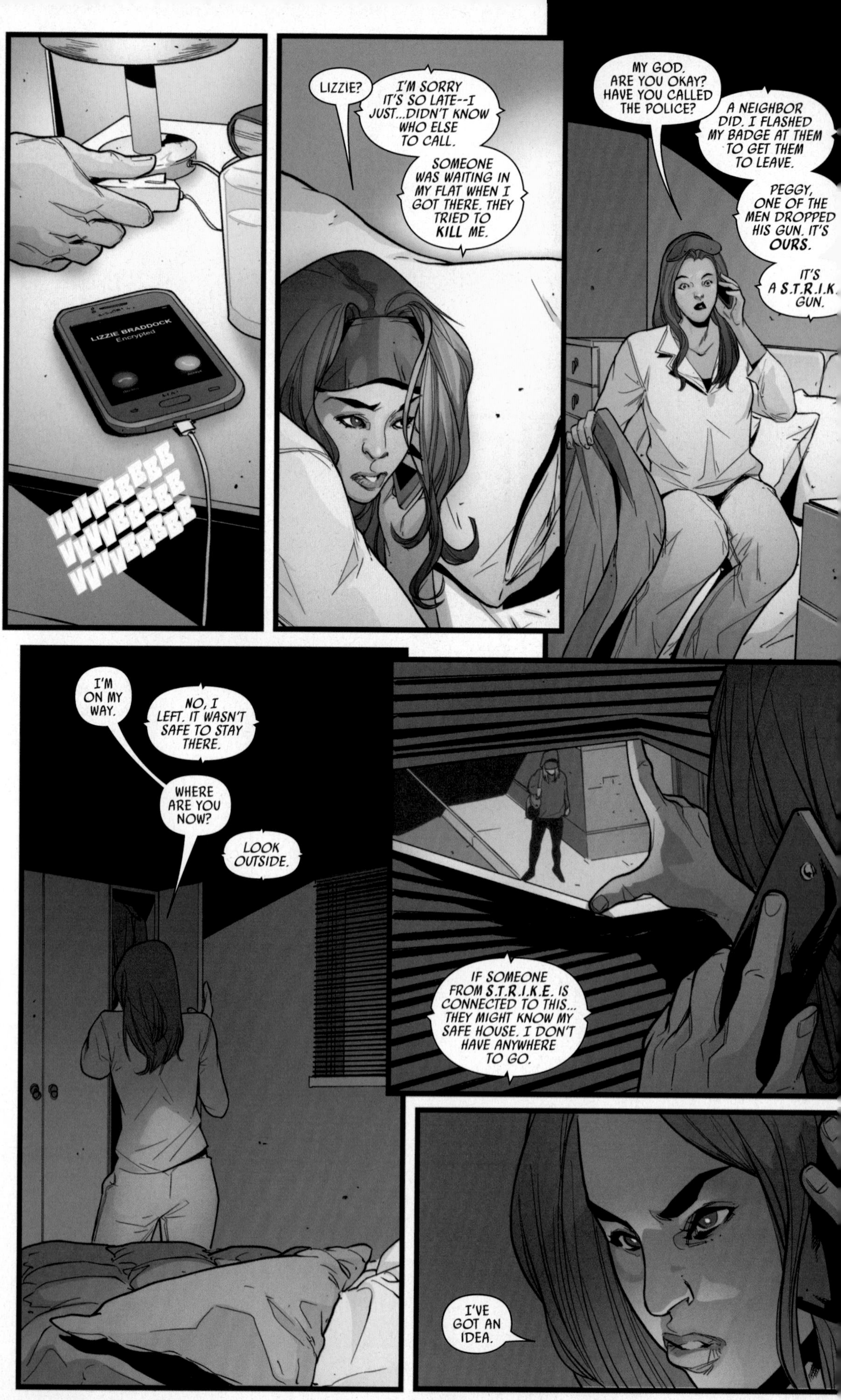
LIZZIE BRADDOCK
Encrypted
VVVVBBBBB
VVVVBBBBB
VVVVBBBBB
LIZZIE?
I'M SORRY IT'S SO LATE--I JUST...DIDN'T KNOW WHO ELSE TO CALL.
SOMEONE WAS WAITING IN MY FLAT WHEN I GOT THERE. THEY TRIED TO KILL ME.
MY GOD. ARE YOU OKAY? HAVE YOU CALLED THE POLICE?
A NEIGHBOR DID. I FLASHED MY BADGE AT THEM TO GET THEM TO LEAVE.
PEGGY, ONE OF THE MEN DROPPED HIS GUN. IT'S OURS.
IT'S A S.T.R.I.K. GUN.
I'M ON MY WAY.
NO, I LEFT. IT WASN'T SAFE TO STAY THERE.
WHERE ARE YOU NOW?
LOOK OUTSIDE.
IF SOMEONE FROM S.T.R.I.K.E. IS CONNECTED TO THIS... THEY MIGHT KNOW MY SAFE HOUSE. I DON'T HAVE ANYWHERE TO GO.
I'VE GOT AN IDEA.

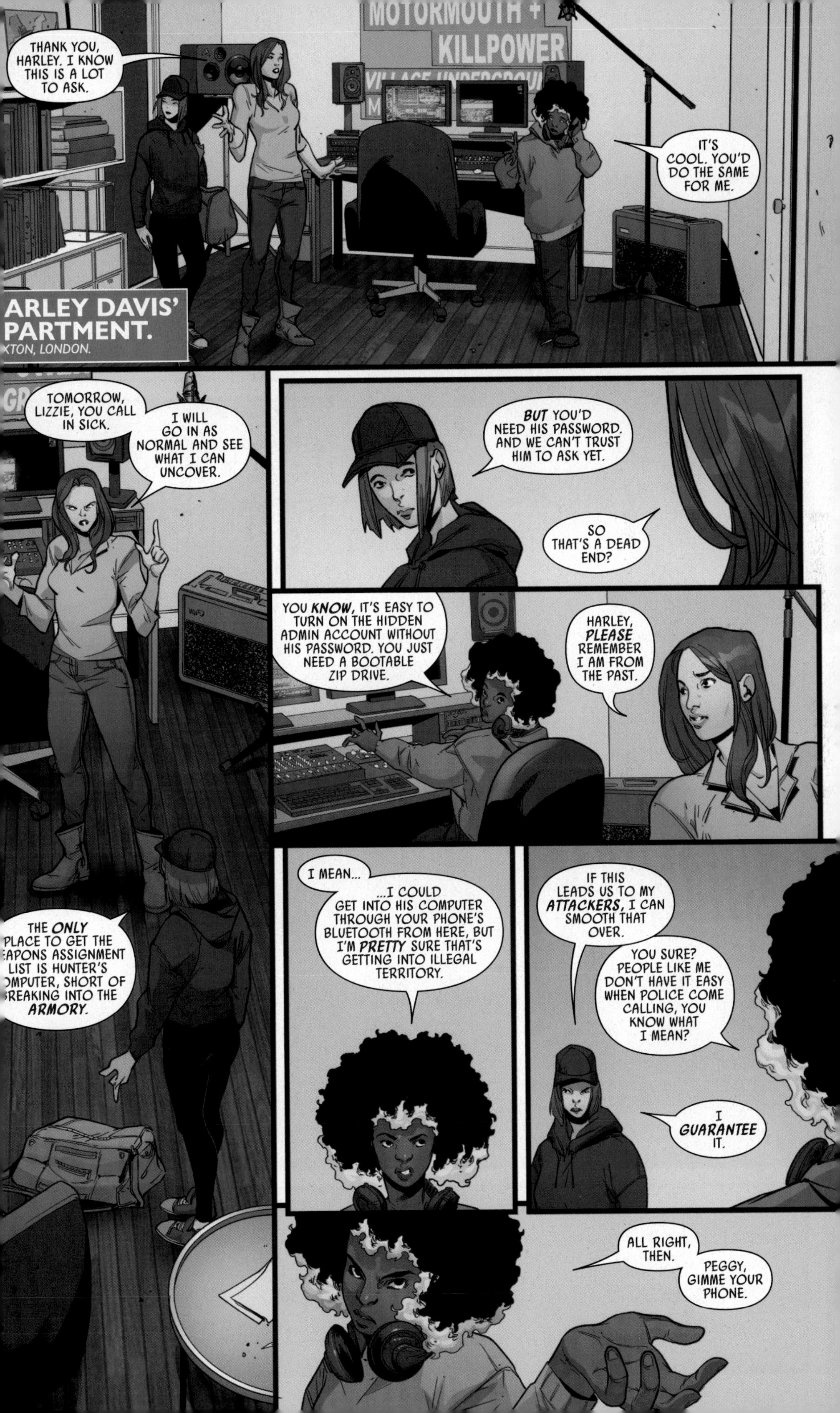
MOTORMOUTH + KILLPOWER
THANK YOU, HARLEY. I KNOW THIS IS A LOT TO ASK.
IT'S COOL. YOU'D DO THE SAME FOR ME.
ARLEY DAVIS' PARTMENT.
XTON, LONDON.
TOMORROW, LIZZIE, YOU CALL IN SICK.
I WILL GO IN AS NORMAL AND SEE WHAT I CAN UNCOVER.
BUT YOU'D NEED HIS PASSWORD. AND WE CAN'T TRUST HIM TO ASK YET.
SO THAT'S A DEAD END?
YOU KNOW, IT'S EASY TO TURN ON THE HIDDEN ADMIN ACCOUNT WITHOUT HIS PASSWORD. YOU JUST NEED A BOOTABLE ZIP DRIVE.
HARLEY, PLEASE REMEMBER I AM FROM THE PAST.
THE ONLY PLACE TO GET THE EAPONS ASSIGNMENT LIST IS HUNTER'S OMPUTER, SHORT OF REAKING INTO THE ARMORY.
I MEAN...
...I COULD GET INTO HIS COMPUTER THROUGH YOUR PHONE'S BLUETOOTH FROM HERE, BUT I'M PRETTY SURE THAT'S GETTING INTO ILLEGAL TERRITORY.
IF THIS LEADS US TO MY ATTACKERS, I CAN SMOOTH THAT OVER.
YOU SURE? PEOPLE LIKE ME DON'T HAVE IT EASY WHEN POLICE COME CALLING, YOU KNOW WHAT I MEAN?
I GUARANTEE IT.
ALL RIGHT, THEN.
PEGGY, GIMME YOUR PHONE.

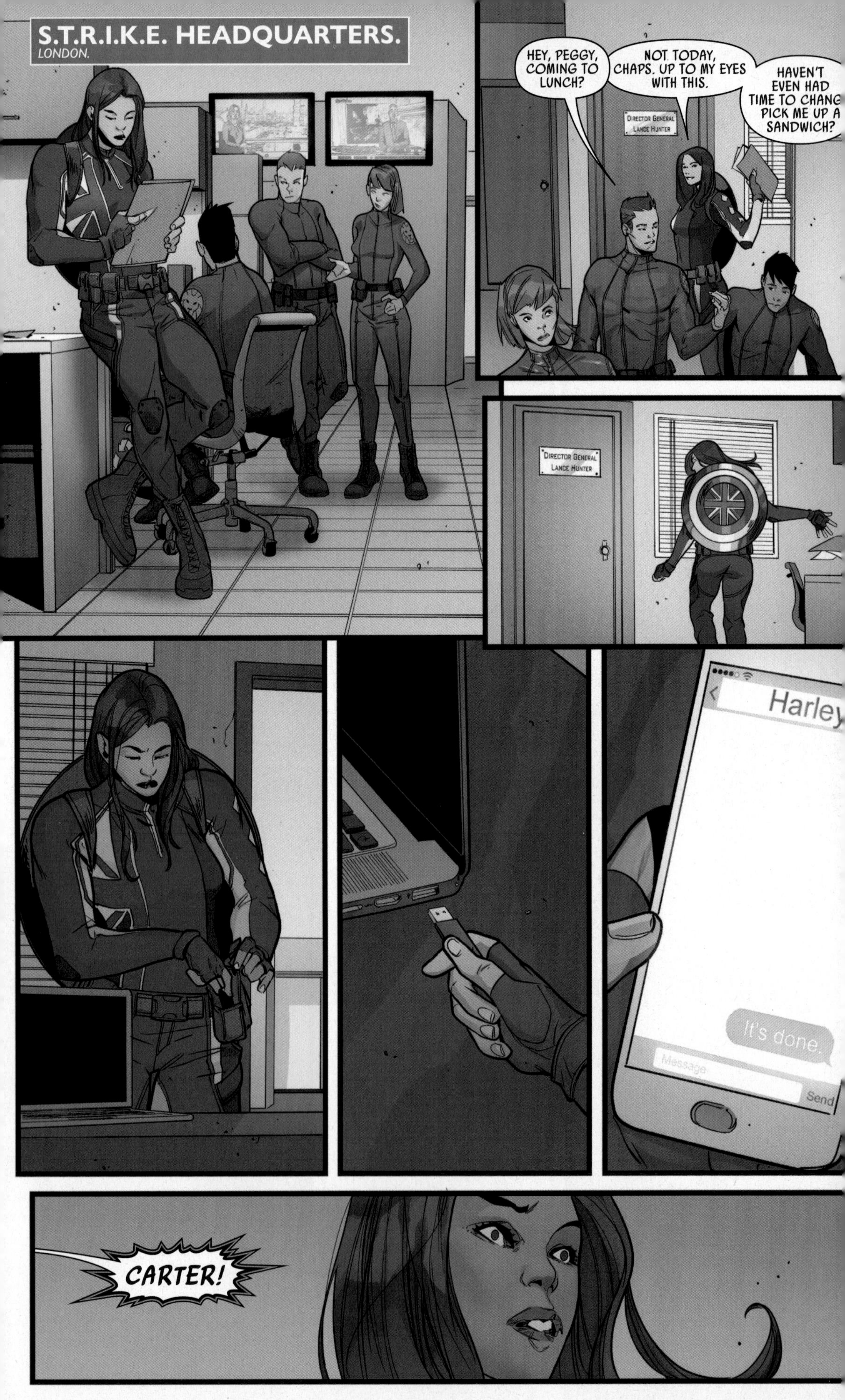

S.T.R.I.K.E. HEADQUARTERS.
LONDON.
HEY, PEGGY, COMING TO LUNCH?
NOT TODAY, CHAPS. UP TO MY EYES WITH THIS.
HAVEN'T EVEN HAD TIME TO CHANG PICK ME UP A SANDWICH?
DIRECTOR GENERAL LANCE HUNTER
DIRECTOR GENERAL LANCE HUNTER
Harley
It's done.
Message
Send
CARTER!

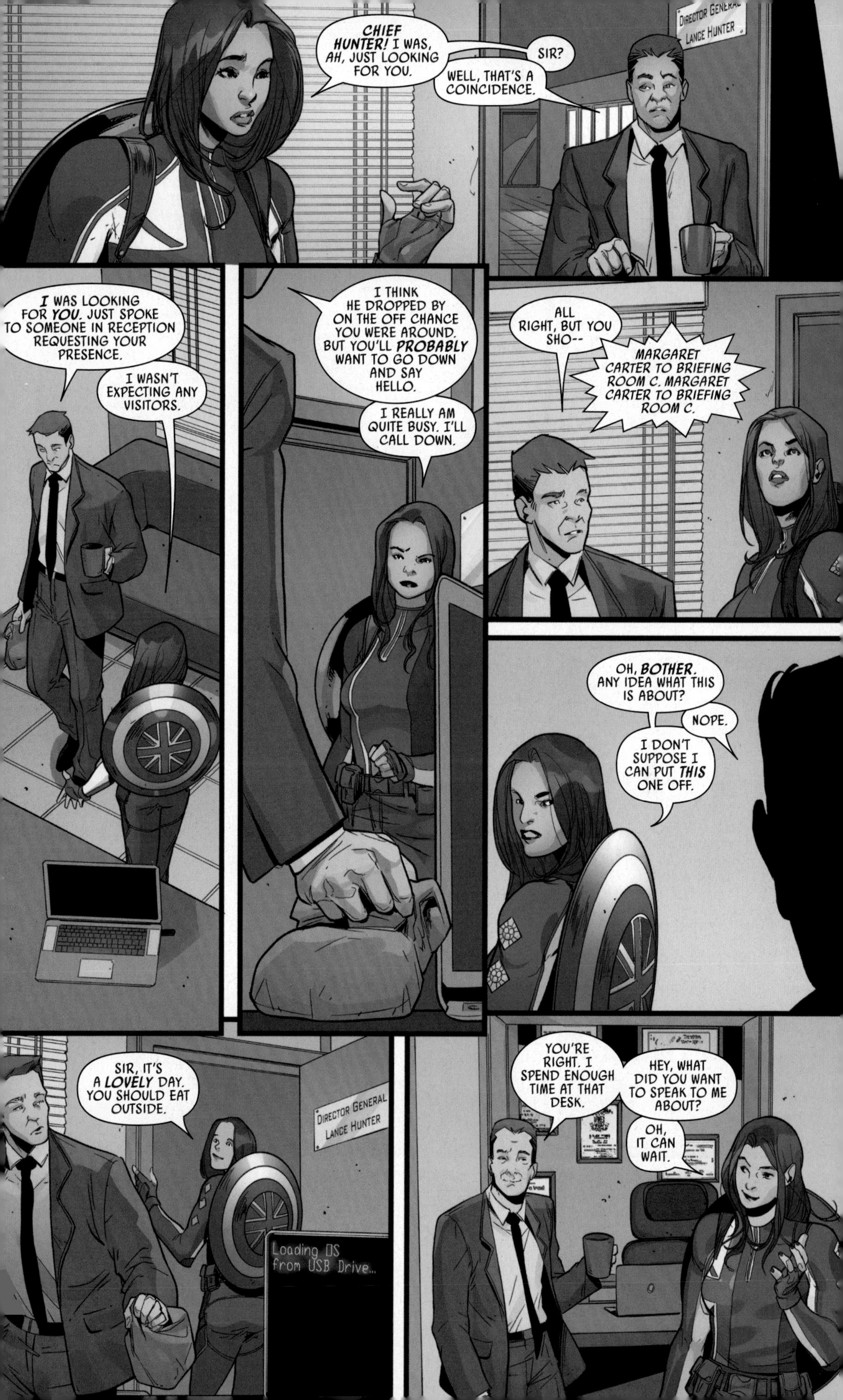
DIRECTOR GENERAL LANCE HUNTER
CHIEF HUNTER! I WAS, AH, JUST LOOKING FOR YOU.
SIR?
WELL, THAT'S A COINCIDENCE.
I WAS LOOKING FOR ***YOU.*** JUST SPOKE TO SOMEONE IN RECEPTION REQUESTING YOUR PRESENCE.
I WASN'T EXPECTING ANY VISITORS.
I THINK HE DROPPED BY ON THE OFF CHANCE YOU WERE AROUND. BUT YOU'LL ***PROBABLY*** WANT TO GO DOWN AND SAY HELLO.
I REALLY AM QUITE BUSY. I'LL CALL DOWN.
ALL RIGHT, BUT YOU SHO--
MARGARET CARTER TO BRIEFING ROOM C. MARGARET CARTER TO BRIEFING ROOM C.
OH, ***BOTHER.*** ANY IDEA WHAT THIS IS ABOUT?
NOPE.
I DON'T SUPPOSE I CAN PUT ***THIS*** ONE OFF.
SIR, IT'S A ***LOVELY*** DAY. YOU SHOULD EAT OUTSIDE.
DIRECTOR GENERAL LANCE HUNTER
Loading OS from USB Drive...
YOU'RE RIGHT. I SPEND ENOUGH TIME AT THAT DESK.
HEY, WHAT DID YOU WANT TO SPEAK TO ME ABOUT?
OH, IT CAN WAIT.

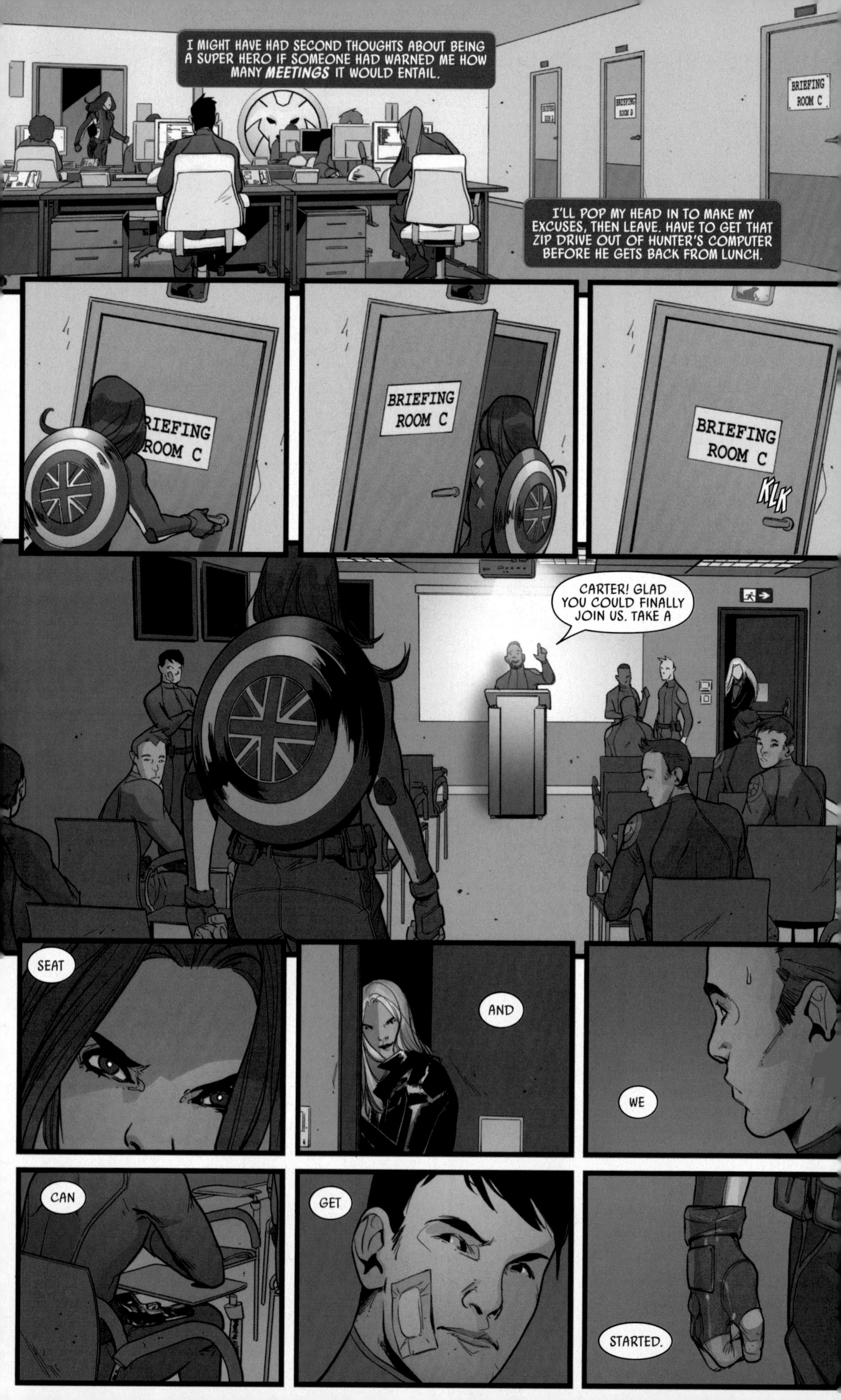

I MIGHT HAVE HAD SECOND THOUGHTS ABOUT BEING A SUPER HERO IF SOMEONE HAD WARNED ME HOW MANY MEETINGS IT WOULD ENTAIL.
BRIEFING ROOM B
BRIEFING ROOM C
I'LL POP MY HEAD IN TO MAKE MY EXCUSES, THEN LEAVE. HAVE TO GET THAT ZIP DRIVE OUT OF HUNTER'S COMPUTER BEFORE HE GETS BACK FROM LUNCH.
BRIEFING ROOM C
BRIEFING ROOM C
BRIEFING ROOM C
KLK
CARTER! GLAD YOU COULD FINALLY JOIN US. TAKE A
SEAT
AND
WE
CAN
GET
STARTED.

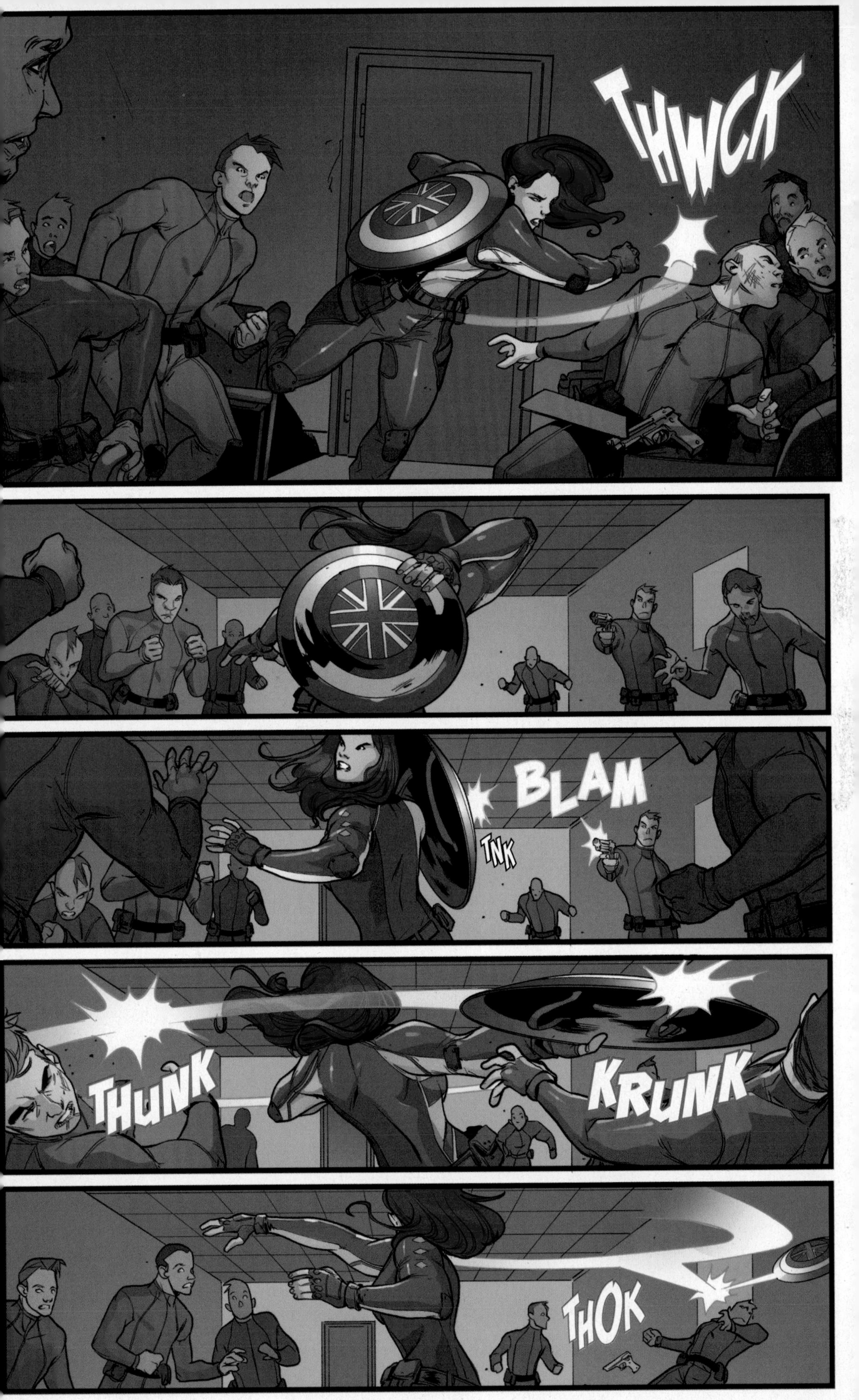
THWCK
BLAM
TNK
THUNK
KRUNK
THOK

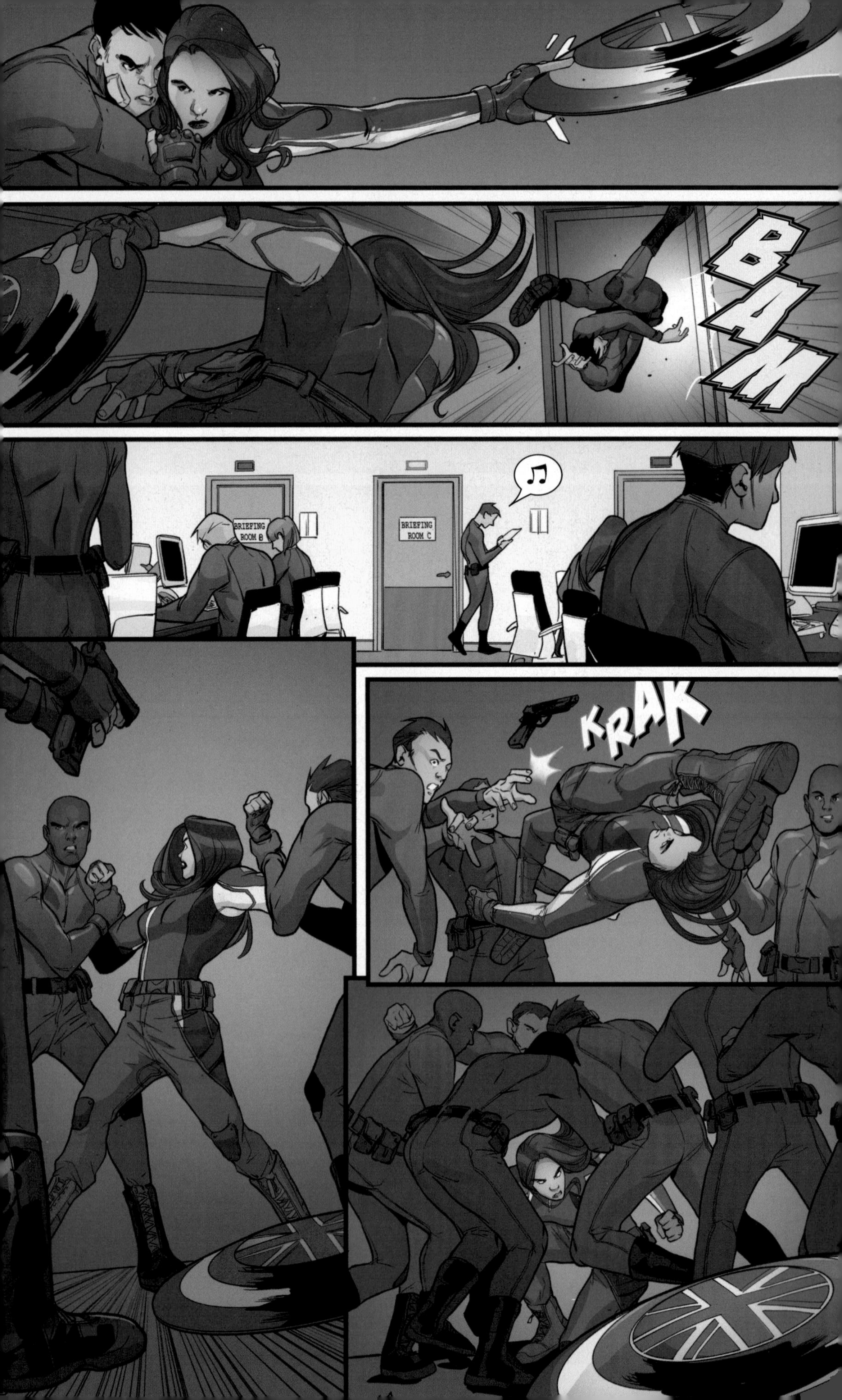

BAM
BRIEFING ROOM B
BRIEFING ROOM C
♫
KRAK

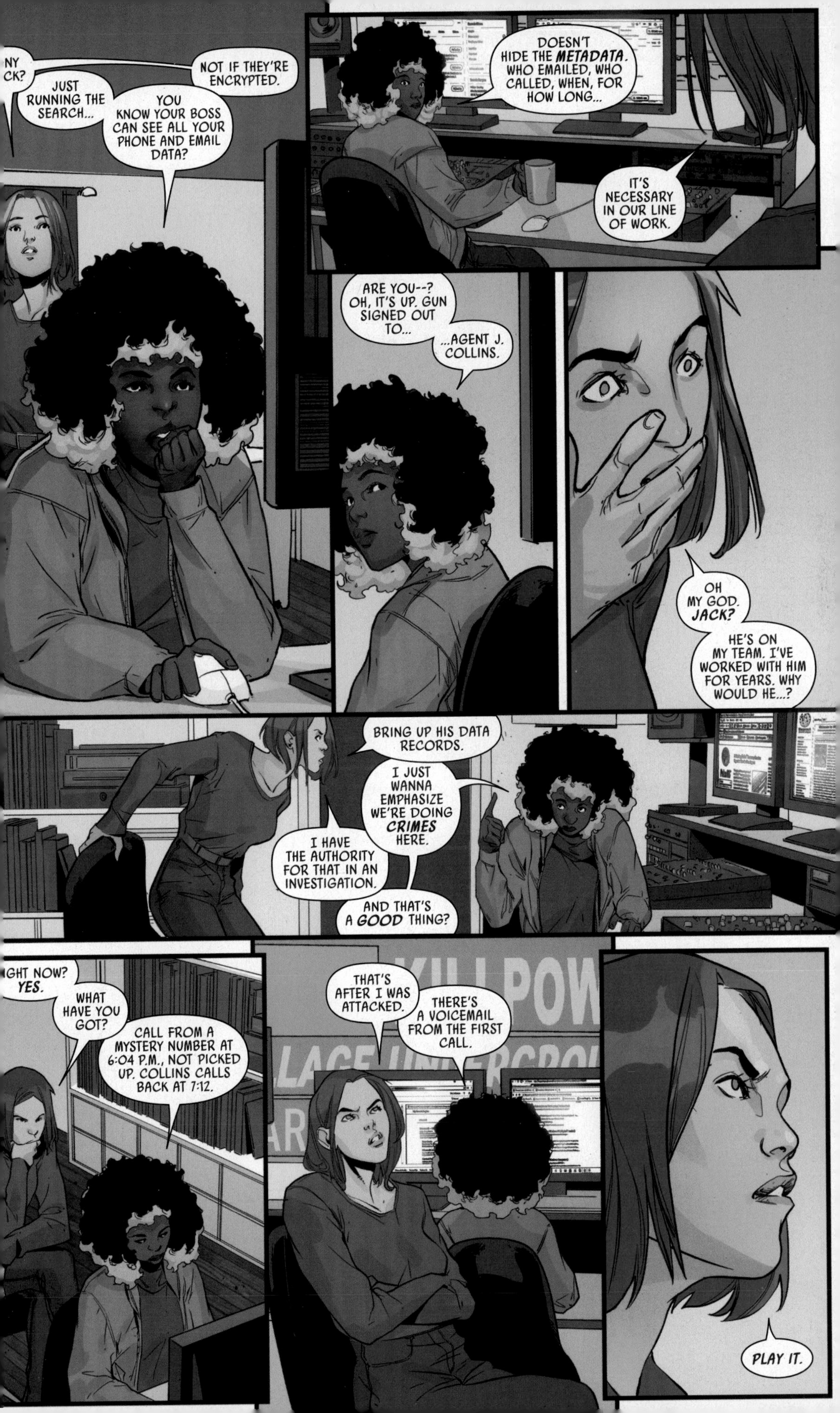
NY
CK?
JUST RUNNING THE SEARCH...
NOT IF THEY'RE ENCRYPTED.
YOU KNOW YOUR BOSS CAN SEE ALL YOUR PHONE AND EMAIL DATA?
DOESN'T HIDE THE METADATA. WHO EMAILED, WHO CALLED, WHEN, FOR HOW LONG...
IT'S NECESSARY IN OUR LINE OF WORK.
ARE YOU--? OH, IT'S UP. GUN SIGNED OUT TO...
...AGENT J. COLLINS.
OH MY GOD. JACK?
HE'S ON MY TEAM. I'VE WORKED WITH HIM FOR YEARS. WHY WOULD HE...?
BRING UP HIS DATA RECORDS.
I JUST WANNA EMPHASIZE WE'RE DOING CRIMES HERE.
I HAVE THE AUTHORITY FOR THAT IN AN INVESTIGATION.
AND THAT'S A GOOD THING?
GHT NOW? YES.
WHAT HAVE YOU GOT?
CALL FROM A MYSTERY NUMBER AT 6:04 P.M., NOT PICKED UP. COLLINS CALLS BACK AT 7:12.
THAT'S AFTER I WAS ATTACKED.
THERE'S A VOICEMAIL FROM THE FIRST CALL.
PLAY IT.

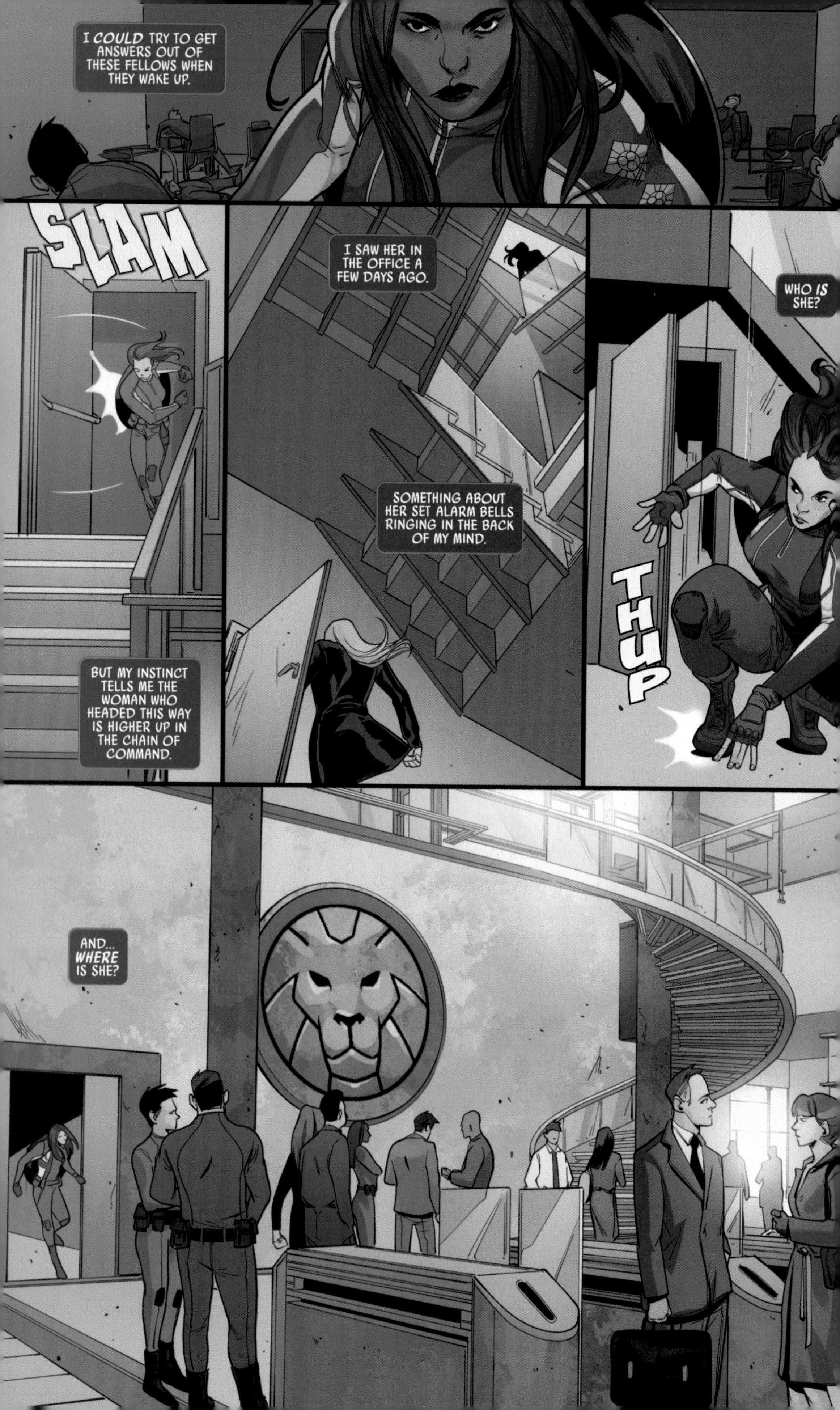
I COULD TRY TO GET ANSWERS OUT OF THESE FELLOWS WHEN THEY WAKE UP.
SLAM
BUT MY INSTINCT TELLS ME THE WOMAN WHO HEADED THIS WAY IS HIGHER UP IN THE CHAIN OF COMMAND.
I SAW HER IN THE OFFICE A FEW DAYS AGO.
SOMETHING ABOUT HER SET ALARM BELLS RINGING IN THE BACK OF MY MIND.
WHO IS SHE?
THUP
AND... WHERE IS SHE?

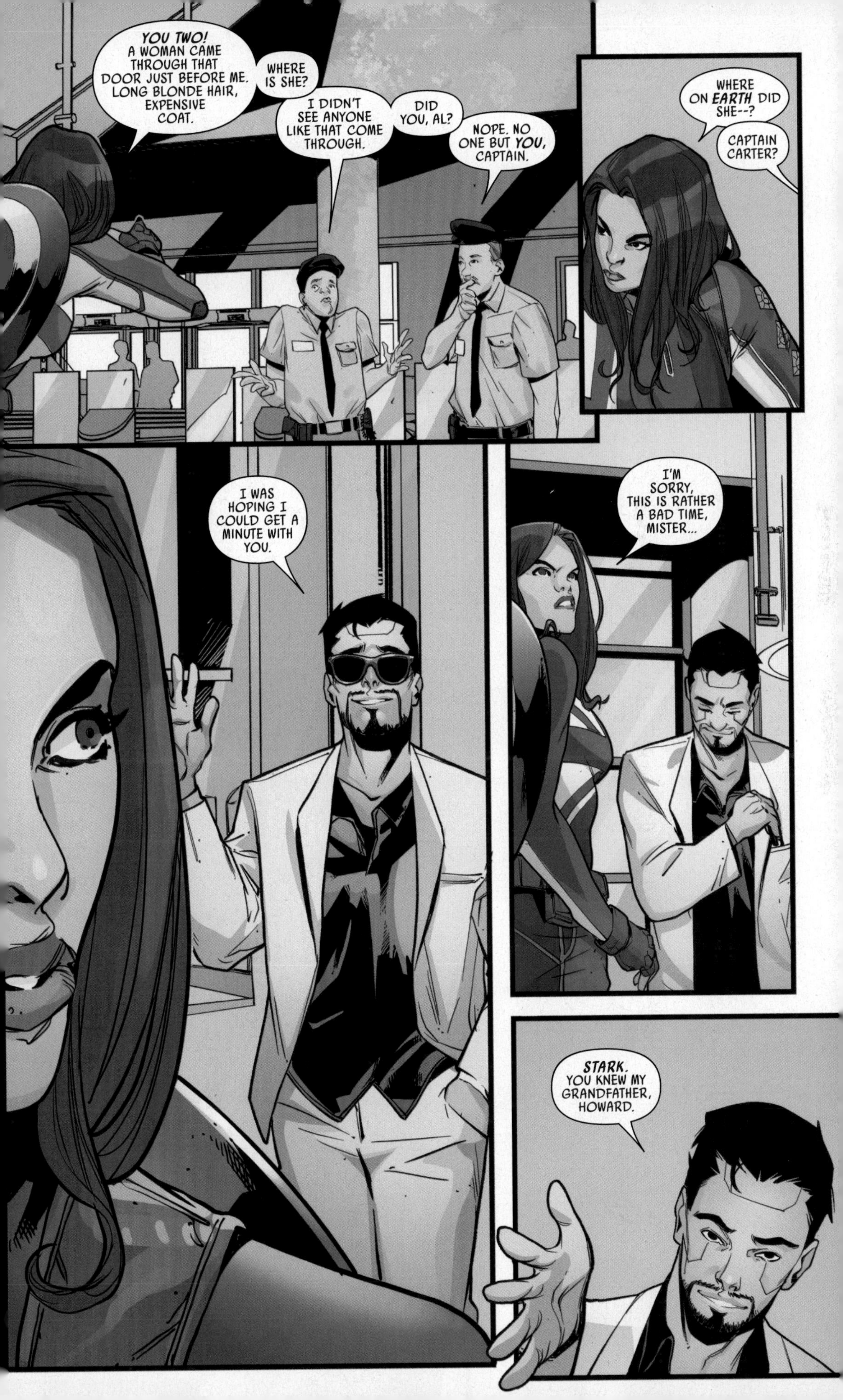
YOU TWO! A WOMAN CAME THROUGH THAT DOOR JUST BEFORE ME. LONG BLONDE HAIR, EXPENSIVE COAT.
WHERE IS SHE?
I DIDN'T SEE ANYONE LIKE THAT COME THROUGH.
DID YOU, AL?
NOPE. NO ONE BUT YOU, CAPTAIN.
WHERE ON EARTH DID SHE--?
CAPTAIN CARTER?
I WAS HOPING I COULD GET A MINUTE WITH YOU.
I'M SORRY, THIS IS RATHER A BAD TIME, MISTER...
STARK. YOU KNEW MY GRANDFATHER, HOWARD.

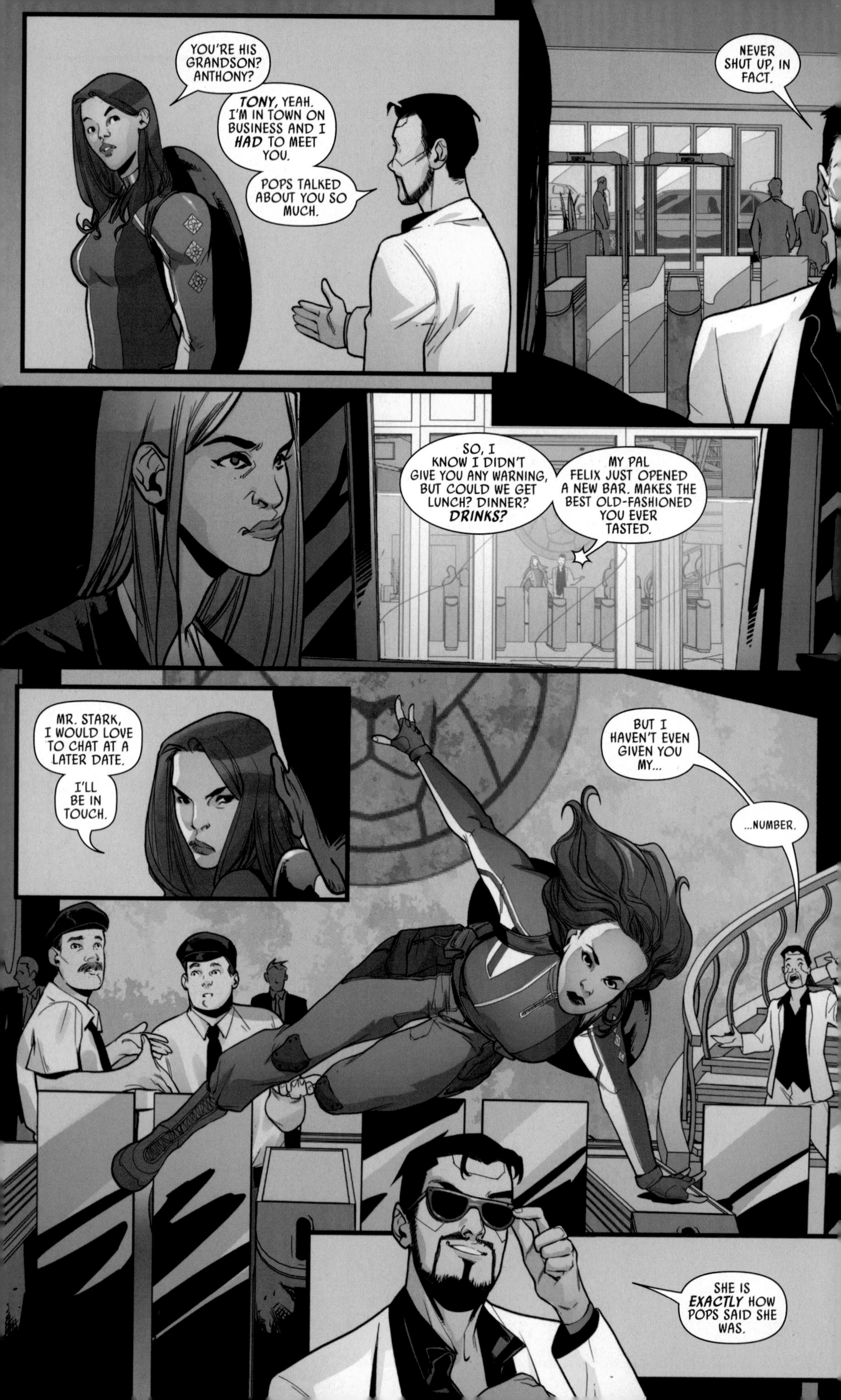
YOU'RE HIS GRANDSON? ANTHONY?
TONY, YEAH. I'M IN TOWN ON BUSINESS AND I HAD TO MEET YOU.
POPS TALKED ABOUT YOU SO MUCH.
NEVER SHUT UP, IN FACT.
SO, I KNOW I DIDN'T GIVE YOU ANY WARNING, BUT COULD WE GET LUNCH? DINNER? DRINKS?
MY PAL FELIX JUST OPENED A NEW BAR. MAKES THE BEST OLD-FASHIONED YOU EVER TASTED.
MR. STARK, I WOULD LOVE TO CHAT AT A LATER DATE.
I'LL BE IN TOUCH.
BUT I HAVEN'T EVEN GIVEN YOU MY...
...NUMBER.
SHE IS EXACTLY HOW POPS SAID SHE WAS.

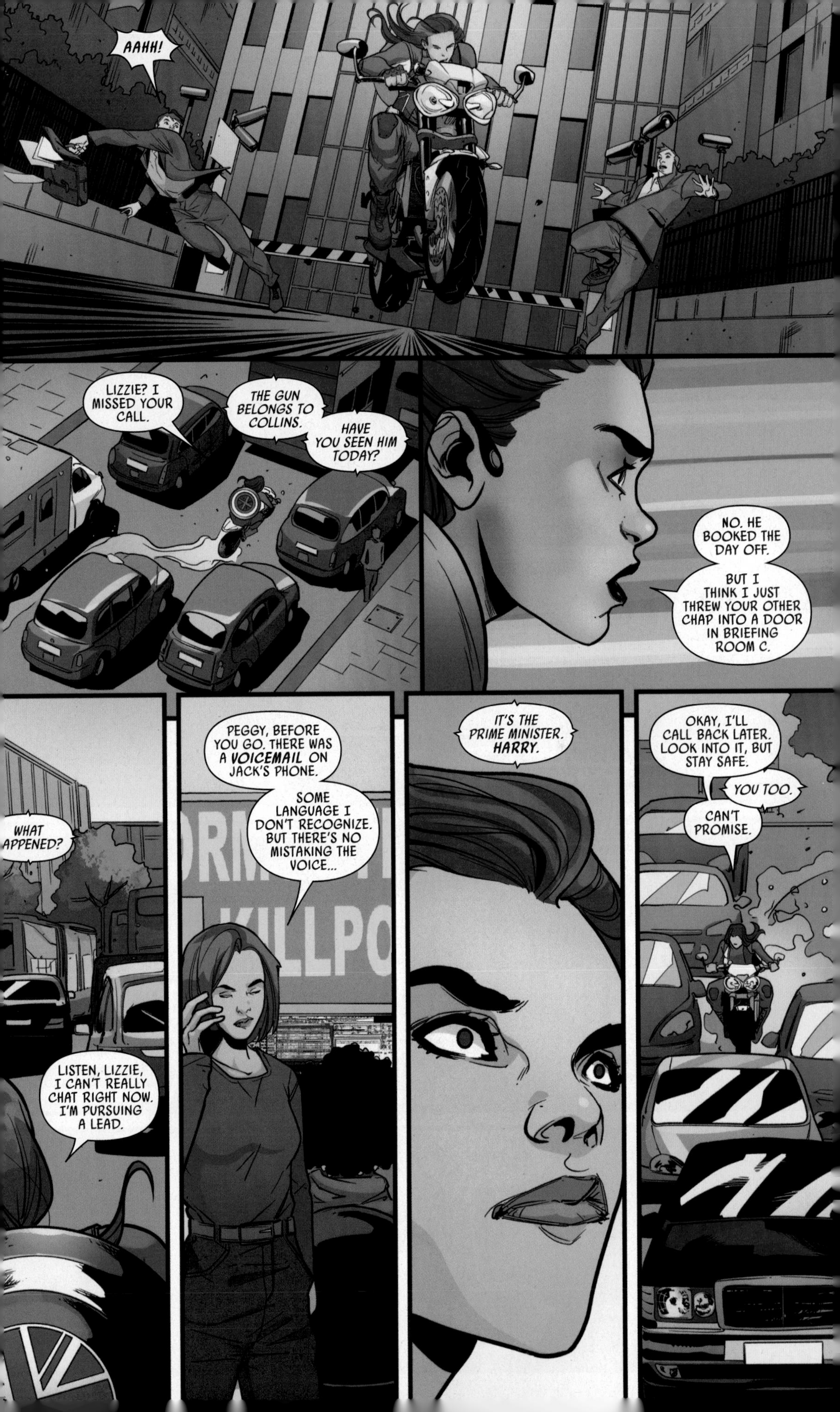

AAHH!
LIZZIE? I MISSED YOUR CALL.
THE GUN BELONGS TO COLLINS.
HAVE YOU SEEN HIM TODAY?
NO. HE BOOKED THE DAY OFF.
BUT I THINK I JUST THREW YOUR OTHER CHAP INTO A DOOR IN BRIEFING ROOM C.
WHAT APPENED?
LISTEN, LIZZIE, I CAN'T REALLY CHAT RIGHT NOW. I'M PURSUING A LEAD.
PEGGY, BEFORE YOU GO. THERE WAS A VOICEMAIL ON JACK'S PHONE.
SOME LANGUAGE I DON'T RECOGNIZE. BUT THERE'S NO MISTAKING THE VOICE...
ORM
KILLPO
IT'S THE PRIME MINISTER. HARRY.
OKAY, I'LL CALL BACK LATER. LOOK INTO IT, BUT STAY SAFE.
YOU TOO.
CAN'T PROMISE.

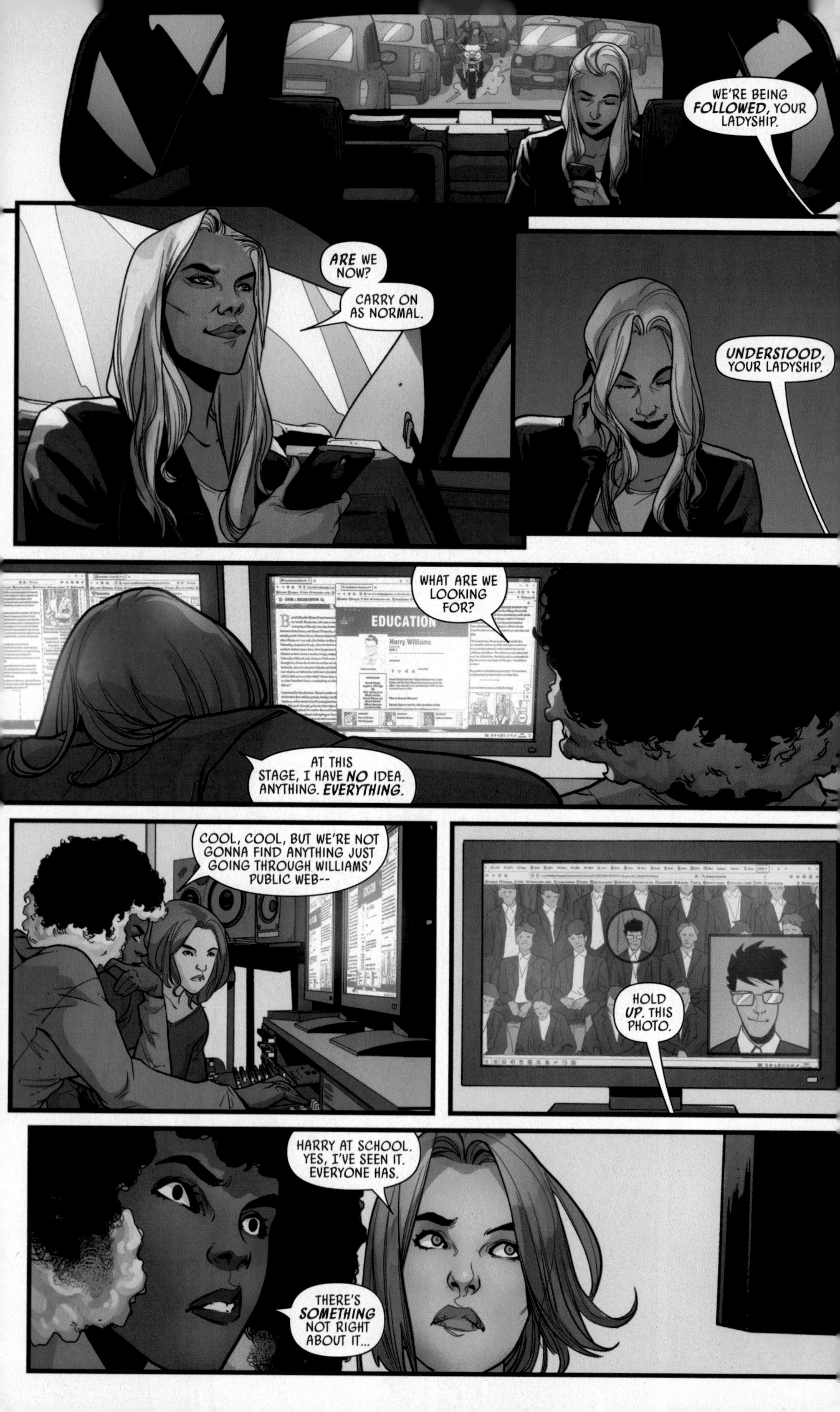
WE'RE BEING FOLLOWED, YOUR LADYSHIP.
ARE WE NOW?
CARRY ON AS NORMAL.
UNDERSTOOD, YOUR LADYSHIP.
WHAT ARE WE LOOKING FOR?
AT THIS STAGE, I HAVE NO IDEA. ANYTHING. EVERYTHING.
EDUCATION
Harry Williams
COOL, COOL, BUT WE'RE NOT GONNA FIND ANYTHING JUST GOING THROUGH WILLIAMS' PUBLIC WEB--
HOLD UP. THIS PHOTO.
HARRY AT SCHOOL. YES, I'VE SEEN IT. EVERYONE HAS.
THERE'S SOMETHING NOT RIGHT ABOUT IT...

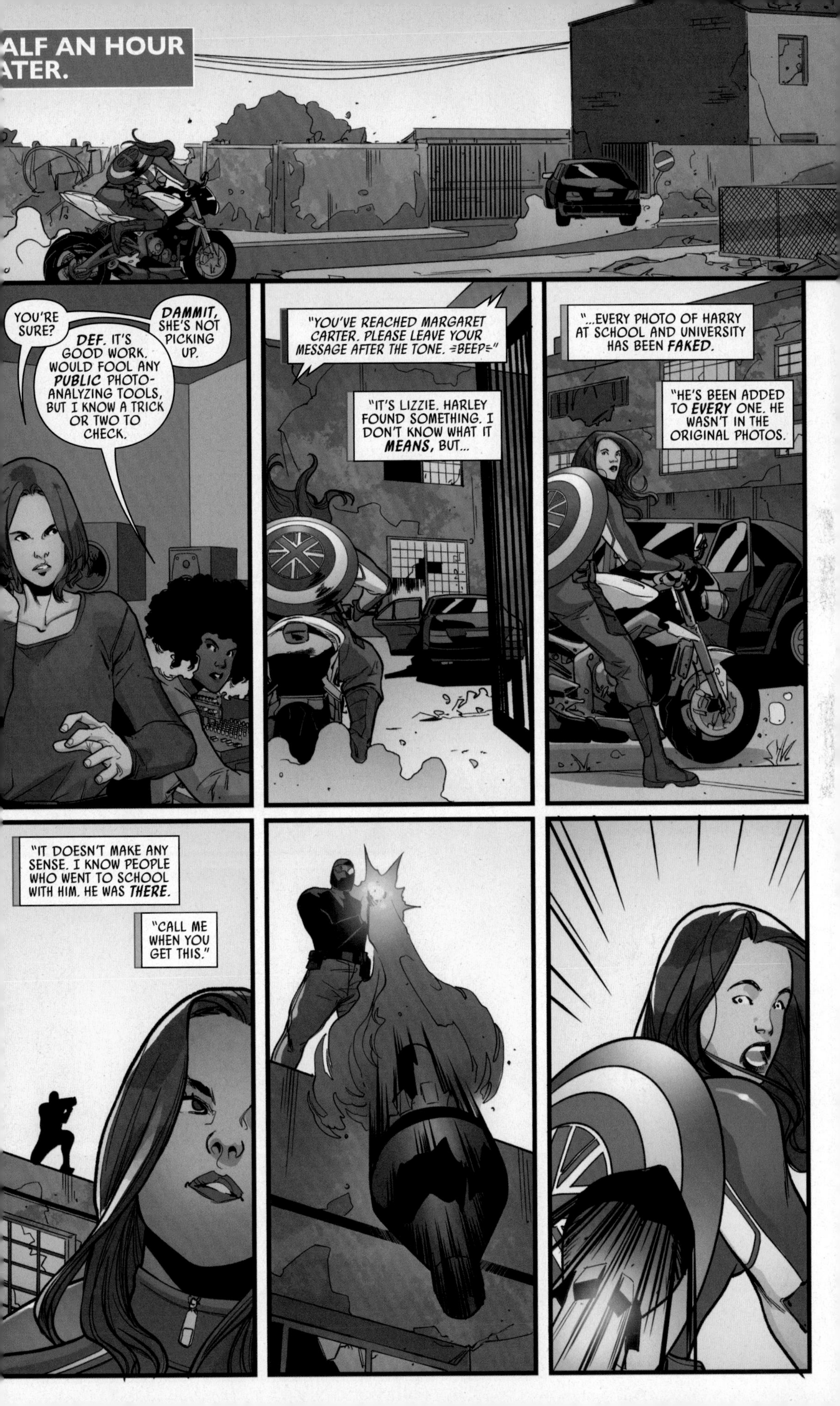
ALF AN HOUR
ATER.
YOU'RE SURE?
DAMMIT, SHE'S NOT PICKING UP.
DEF. IT'S GOOD WORK. WOULD FOOL ANY PUBLIC PHOTO-ANALYZING TOOLS, BUT I KNOW A TRICK OR TWO TO CHECK.
"YOU'VE REACHED MARGARET CARTER. PLEASE LEAVE YOUR MESSAGE AFTER THE TONE. =BEEP="
"IT'S LIZZIE. HARLEY FOUND SOMETHING. I DON'T KNOW WHAT IT MEANS, BUT...
"...EVERY PHOTO OF HARRY AT SCHOOL AND UNIVERSITY HAS BEEN FAKED.
"HE'S BEEN ADDED TO EVERY ONE. HE WASN'T IN THE ORIGINAL PHOTOS.
"IT DOESN'T MAKE ANY SENSE. I KNOW PEOPLE WHO WENT TO SCHOOL WITH HIM. HE WAS THERE.
"CALL ME WHEN YOU GET THIS."

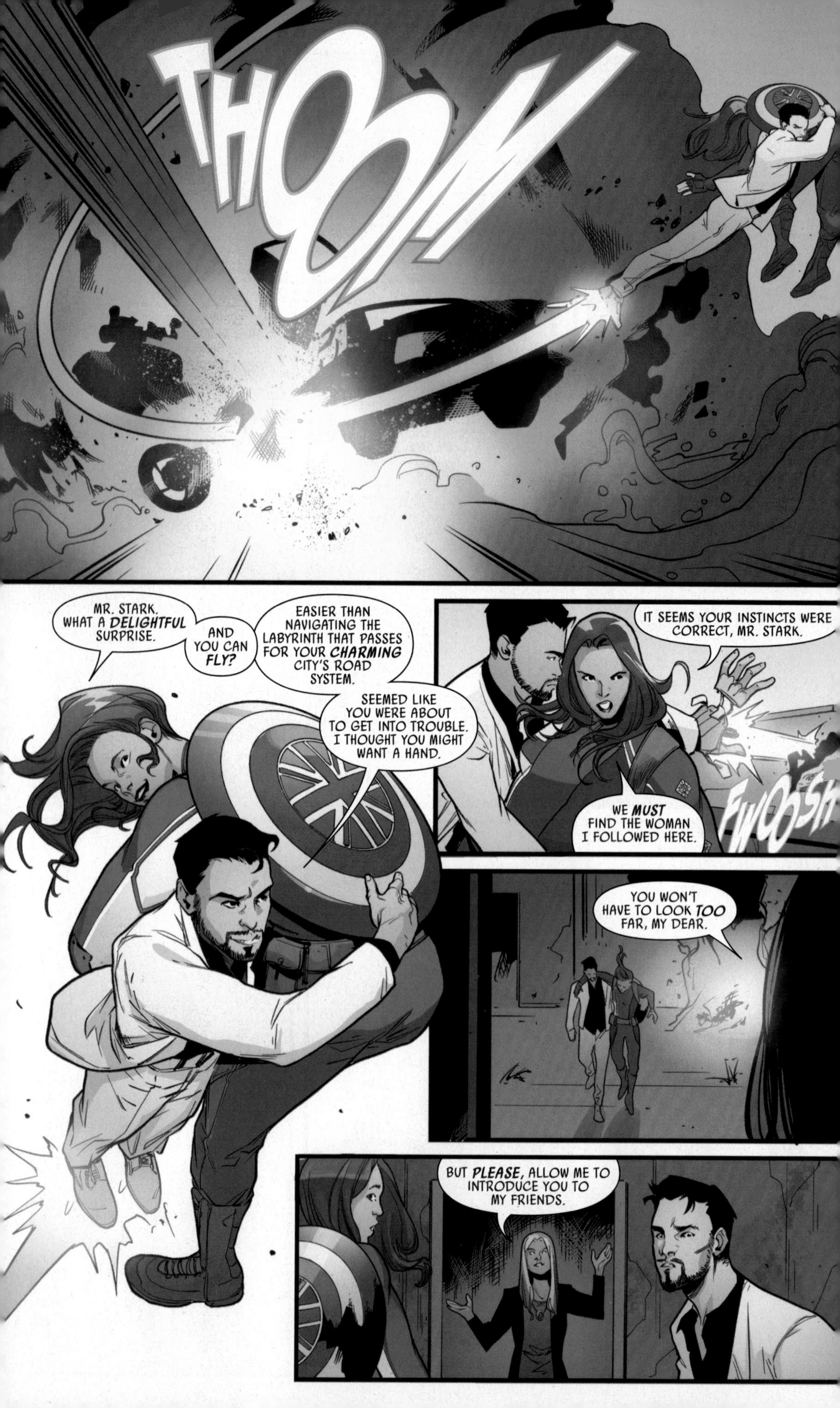

THOOM
MR. STARK. WHAT A DELIGHTFUL SURPRISE.
AND YOU CAN FLY?
EASIER THAN NAVIGATING THE LABYRINTH THAT PASSES FOR YOUR CHARMING CITY'S ROAD SYSTEM.
SEEMED LIKE YOU WERE ABOUT TO GET INTO TROUBLE. I THOUGHT YOU MIGHT WANT A HAND.
IT SEEMS YOUR INSTINCTS WERE CORRECT, MR. STARK.
WE MUST FIND THE WOMAN I FOLLOWED HERE.
FWOOSH
YOU WON'T HAVE TO LOOK TOO FAR, MY DEAR.
BUT PLEASE, ALLOW ME TO INTRODUCE YOU TO MY FRIENDS.

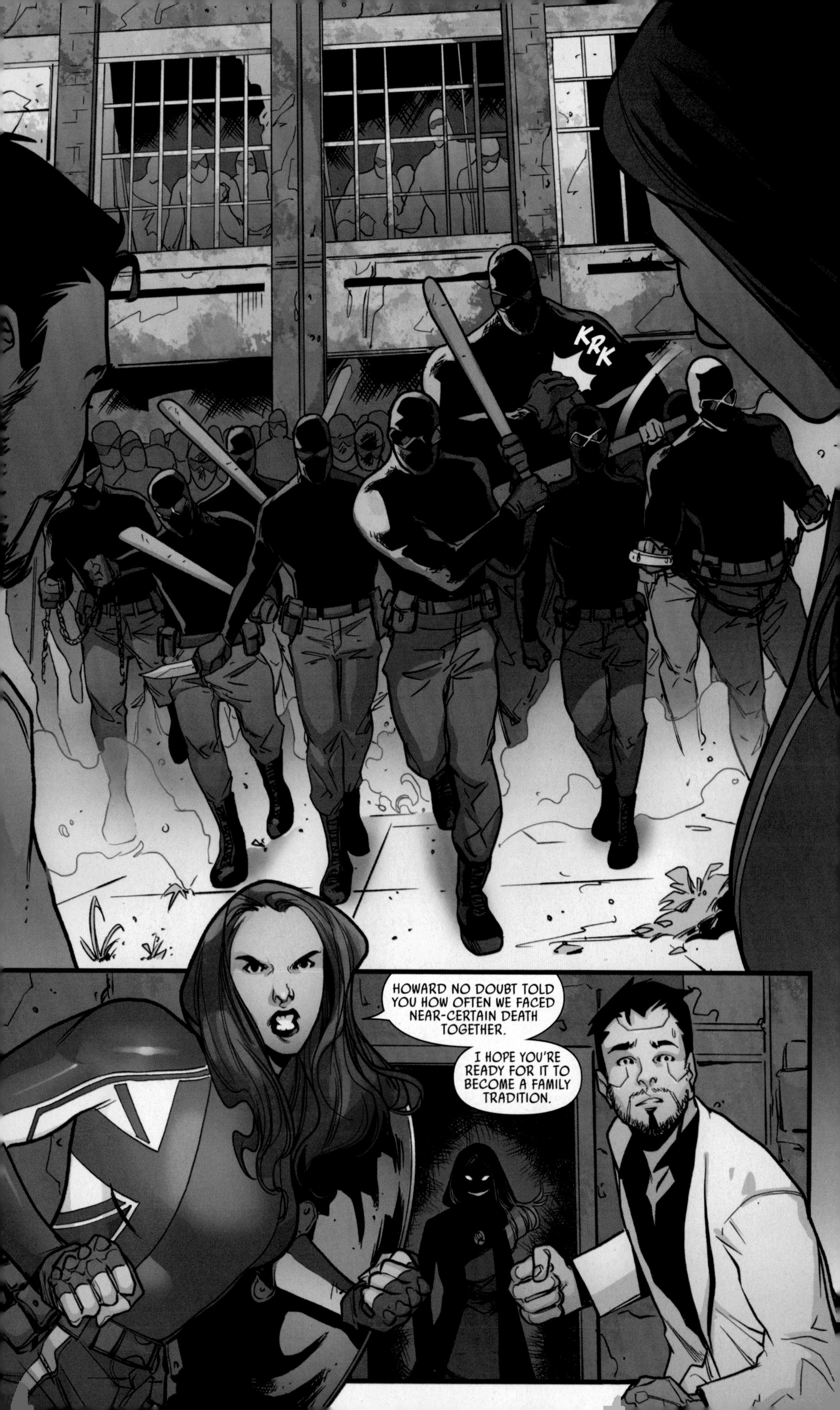

KRK
HOWARD NO DOUBT TOLD YOU HOW OFTEN WE FACED NEAR-CERTAIN DEATH TOGETHER.
I HOPE YOU'RE READY FOR IT TO BECOME A FAMILY TRADITION.

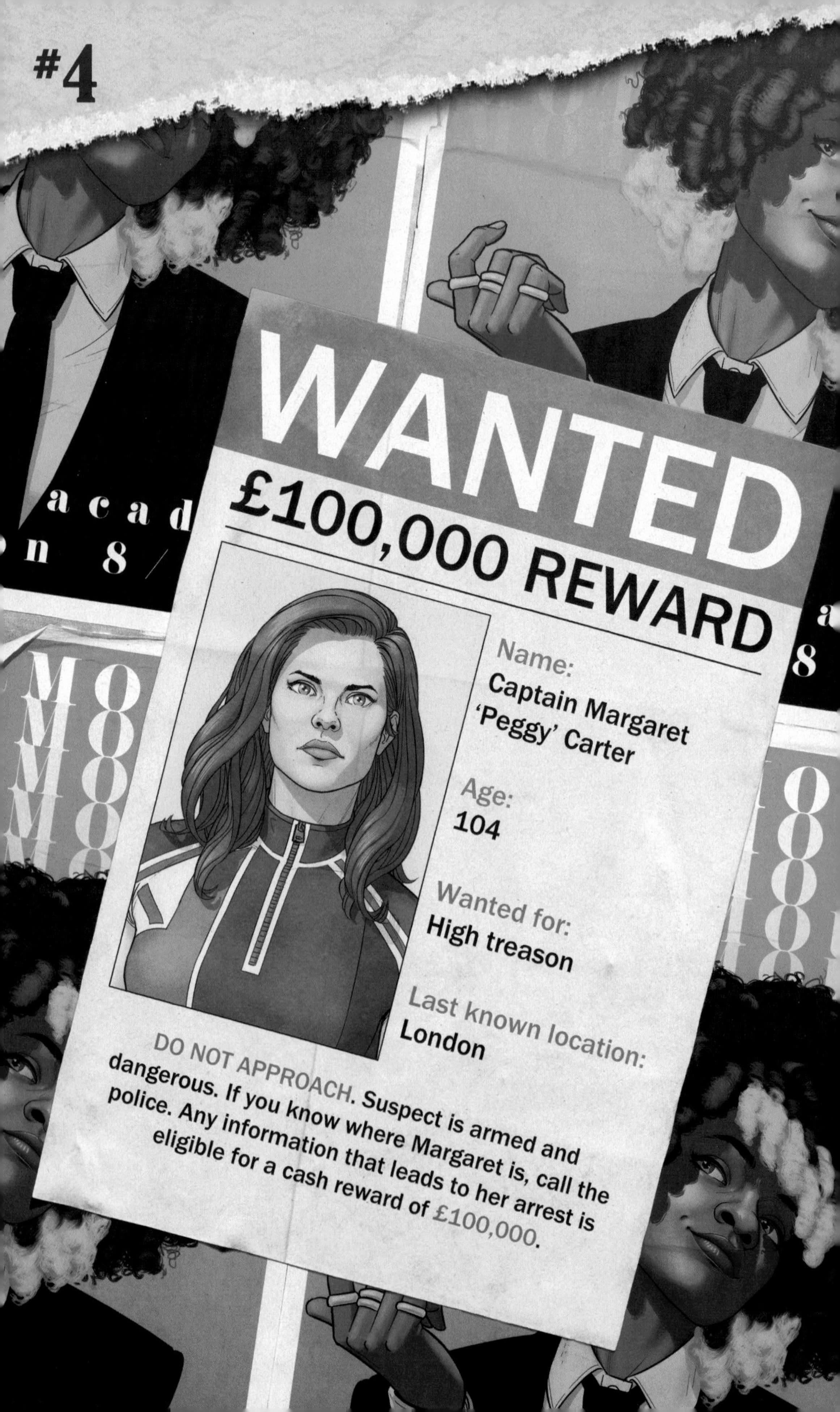
#4
WANTED
£100,000 REWARD
Name:
Captain Margaret 'Peggy' Carter
Age:
104
Wanted for:
High treason
Last known location:
London
DO NOT APPROACH. Suspect is armed and dangerous. If you know where Margaret is, call the police. Any information that leads to her arrest is eligible for a cash reward of £100,000.

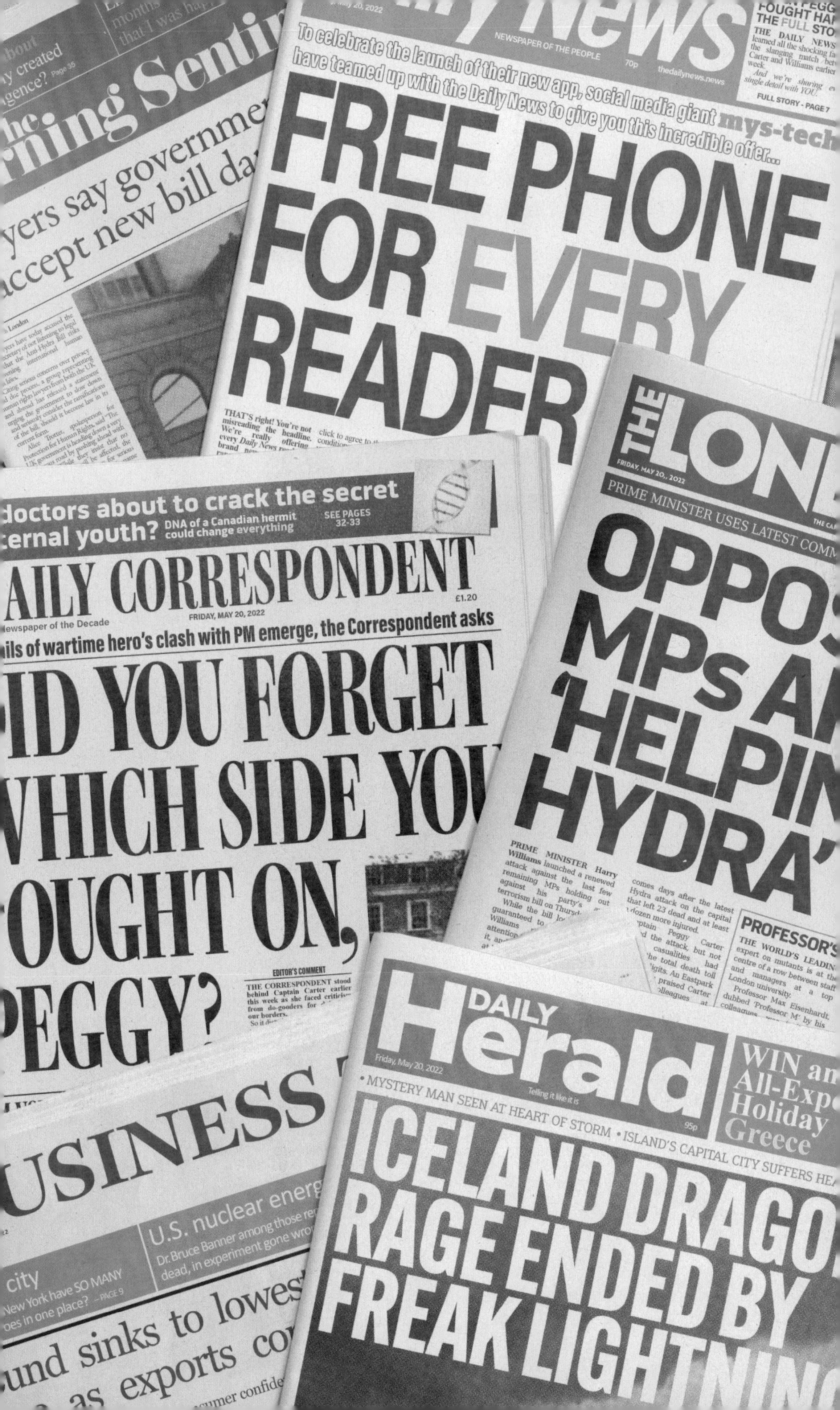

FOUGHT HA
THE FULL STO
THE DAILY NEWS learned all the shocking fa the slanging match betw Carter and Williams earlie week.
And we're sharing e single detail with YOU.
FULL STORY - PAGE 7
NEWSPAPER OF THE PEOPLE
70p
thedailynews.news
To celebrate the launch of their new app, social media giant mys-tech have teamed up with the Daily News to give you this incredible offer...
FREE PHONE FOR EVERY READER
THAT'S right! You're not misreading the headline. We're really offering every Daily News read
yers say governme accept new bill da
y created gence? Page 35
doctors about to crack the secret ernal youth?
DNA of a Canadian hermit could change everything
SEE PAGES 32-33
AILY CORRESPONDENT
£1.20
FRIDAY, MAY 20, 2022
Newspaper of the Decade
ils of wartime hero's clash with PM emerge, the Correspondent asks
ID YOU FORGET WHICH SIDE YOU OUGHT ON, PEGGY?
EDITOR'S COMMENT
THE CORRESPONDENT stood behind Captain Carter earlier this week as she faced criticism from do-gooders for our borders.
THE LON
FRIDAY, MAY 20., 2022
PRIME MINISTER USES LATEST COMM
OPPOS MPs A 'HELPIN HYDRA'
PRIME MINISTER Harry Williams launched a renewed attack against the last few remaining MPs holding out against his party's terrorism bill on Thursd
comes days after the latest Hydra attack on the capital that left 23 dead and at least dozen more injured.
PROFESSOR'S
THE WORLD'S LEADIN expert on mutants is at the centre of a row between staff and managers at a top London university.
Professor Max Eisenhardt, dubbed 'Professor M' by his colleagues
USINESS
U.S. nuclear energ
Dr. Bruce Banner among those re dead, in experiment gone wro
city
New York have SO MANY oes in one place? —PAGE 9
und sinks to lowes as exports co
DAILY Herald
Friday, May 20, 2022
Telling it like it is
95p
WIN an All-Exp Holiday Greece
• MYSTERY MAN SEEN AT HEART OF STORM • ISLAND'S CAPITAL CITY SUFFERS HE
ICELAND DRAGO RAGE ENDED BY FREAK LIGHTNIN

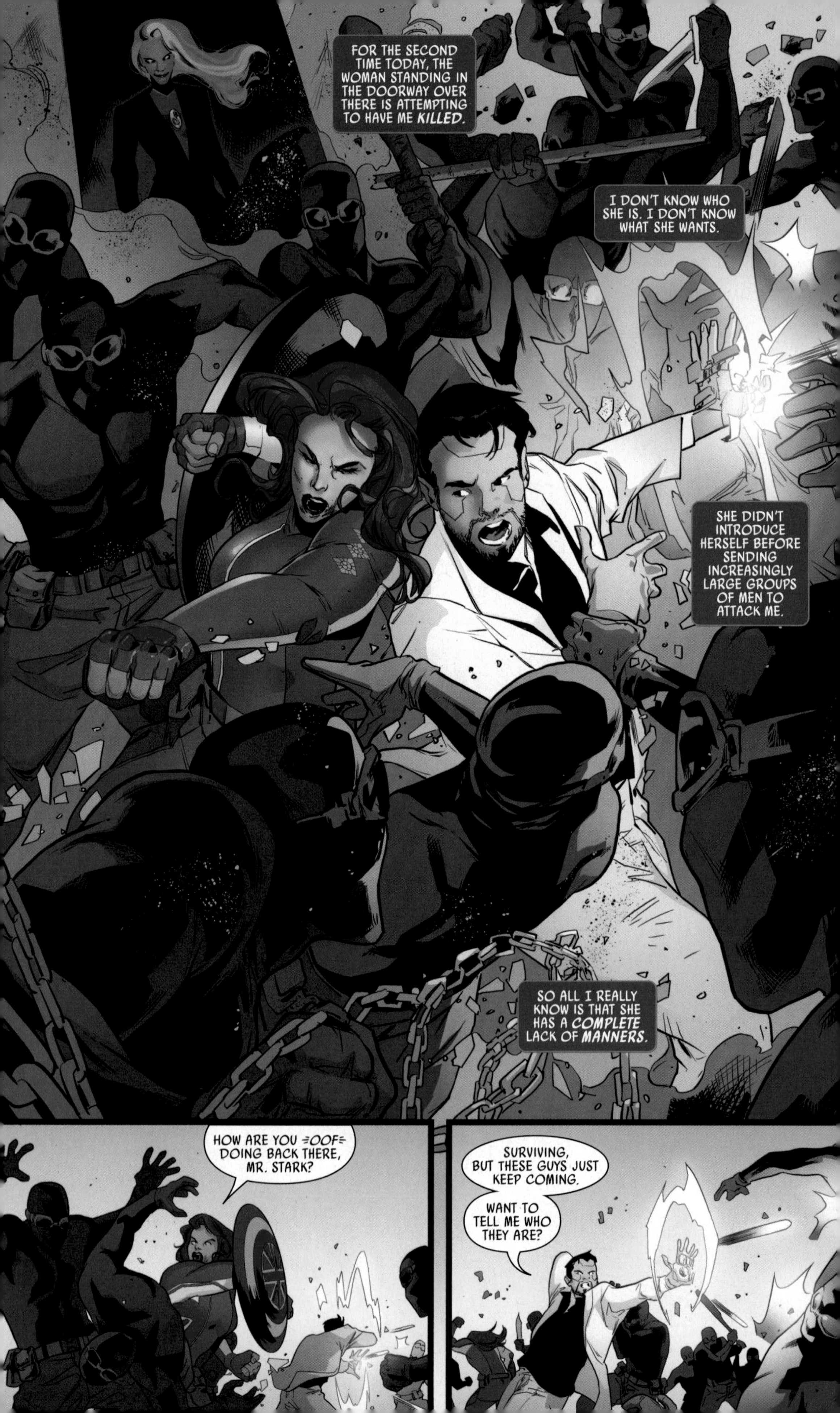
FOR THE SECOND TIME TODAY, THE WOMAN STANDING IN THE DOORWAY OVER THERE IS ATTEMPTING TO HAVE ME KILLED.
I DON'T KNOW WHO SHE IS. I DON'T KNOW WHAT SHE WANTS.
SHE DIDN'T INTRODUCE HERSELF BEFORE SENDING INCREASINGLY LARGE GROUPS OF MEN TO ATTACK ME.
SO ALL I REALLY KNOW IS THAT SHE HAS A COMPLETE LACK OF MANNERS.
HOW ARE YOU =OOF= DOING BACK THERE, MR. STARK?
SURVIVING, BUT THESE GUYS JUST KEEP COMING.
WANT TO TELL ME WHO THEY ARE?

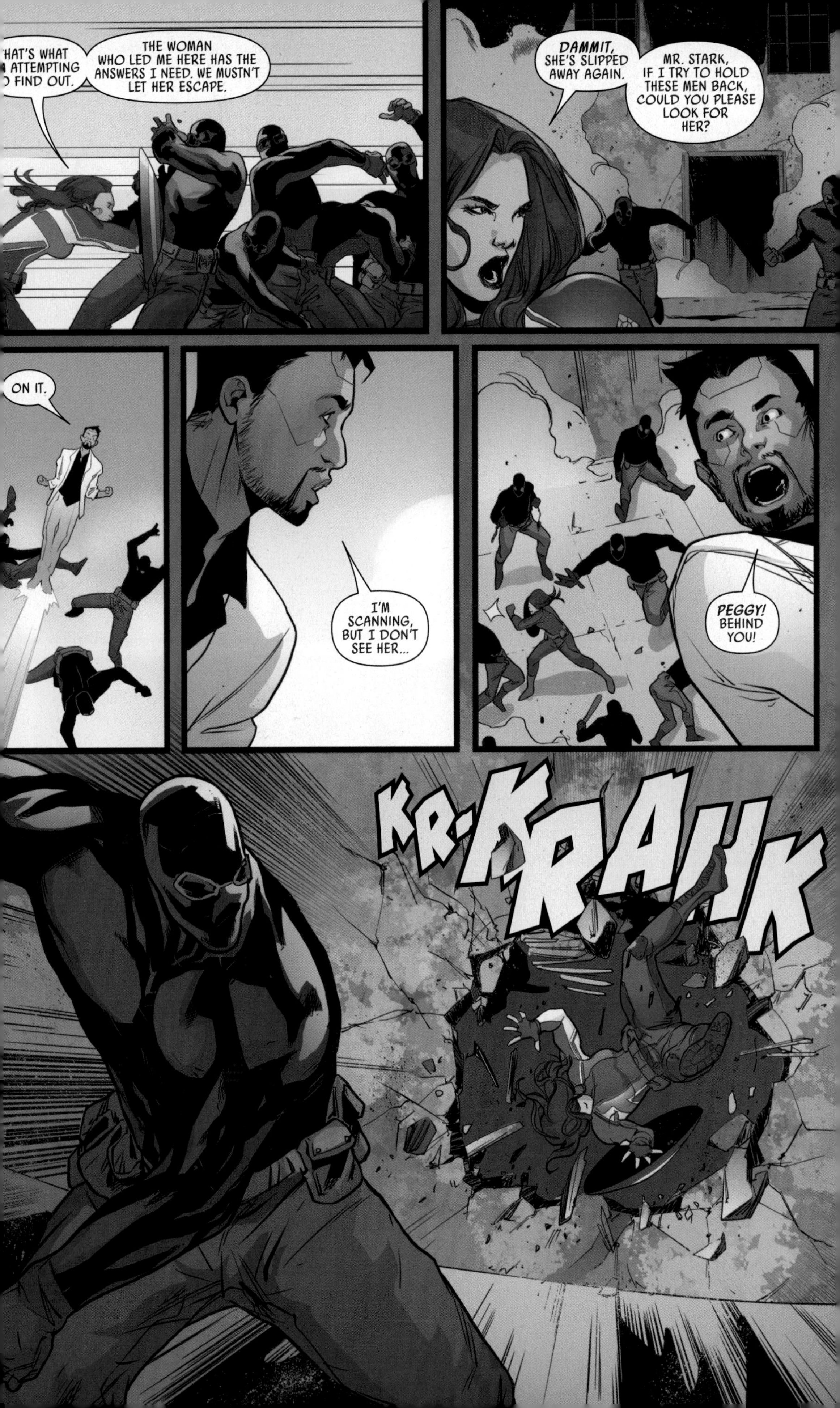

HAT'S WHAT
ATTEMPTING
FIND OUT.
THE WOMAN WHO LED ME HERE HAS THE ANSWERS I NEED. WE MUSTN'T LET HER ESCAPE.
DAMMIT, SHE'S SLIPPED AWAY AGAIN.
MR. STARK, IF I TRY TO HOLD THESE MEN BACK, COULD YOU PLEASE LOOK FOR HER?
ON IT.
I'M SCANNING, BUT I DON'T SEE HER...
PEGGY! BEHIND YOU!
KR-KRAKK

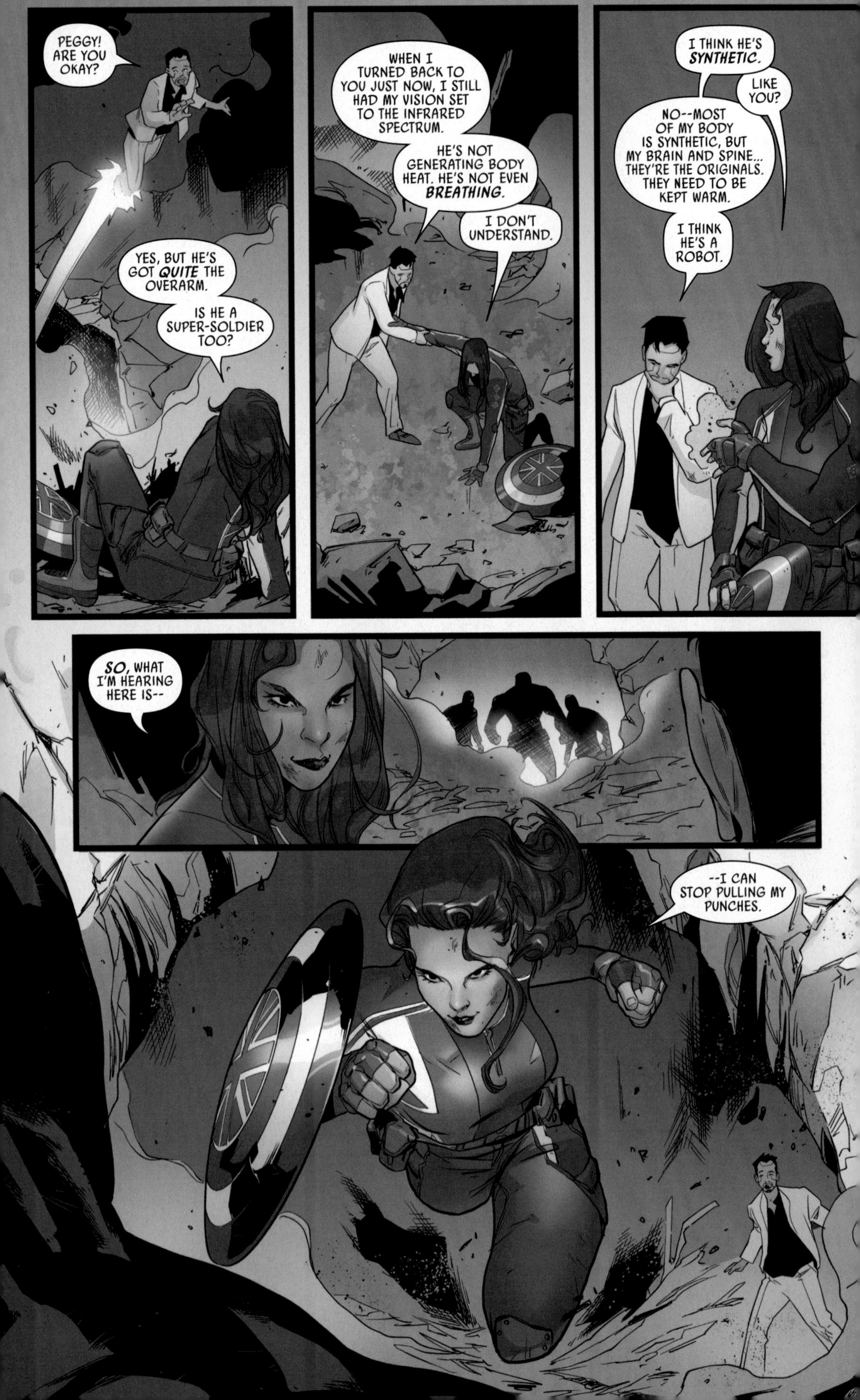
PEGGY! ARE YOU OKAY?
YES, BUT HE'S GOT QUITE THE OVERARM.
IS HE A SUPER-SOLDIER TOO?
WHEN I TURNED BACK TO YOU JUST NOW, I STILL HAD MY VISION SET TO THE INFRARED SPECTRUM.
HE'S NOT GENERATING BODY HEAT. HE'S NOT EVEN BREATHING.
I DON'T UNDERSTAND.
I THINK HE'S SYNTHETIC.
LIKE YOU?
NO--MOST OF MY BODY IS SYNTHETIC, BUT MY BRAIN AND SPINE... THEY'RE THE ORIGINALS. THEY NEED TO BE KEPT WARM.
I THINK HE'S A ROBOT.
SO, WHAT I'M HEARING HERE IS--
--I CAN STOP PULLING MY PUNCHES.

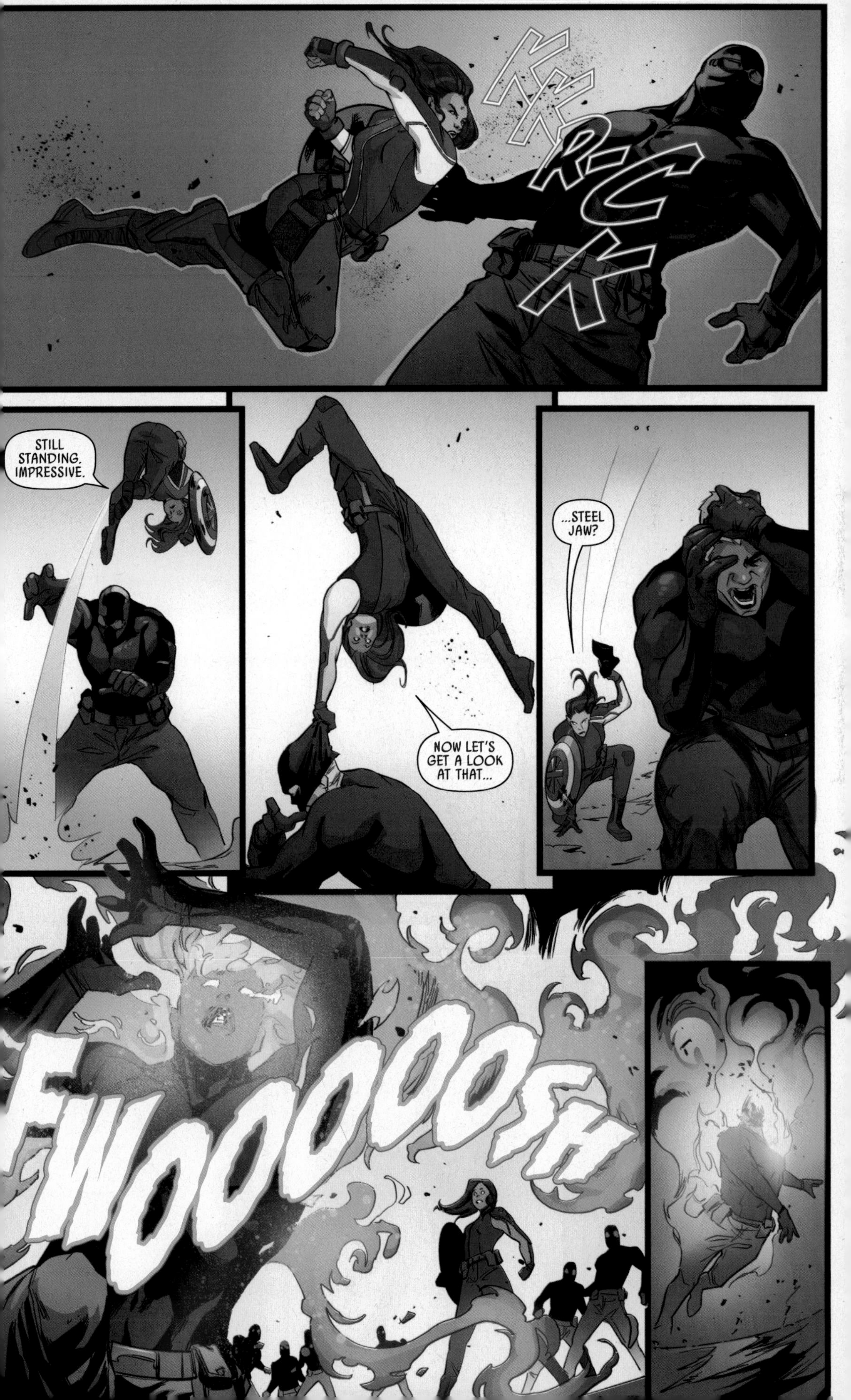

KR-RUCK
STILL STANDING. IMPRESSIVE.
NOW LET'S GET A LOOK AT THAT...
...STEEL JAW?
FWOOOOOSH

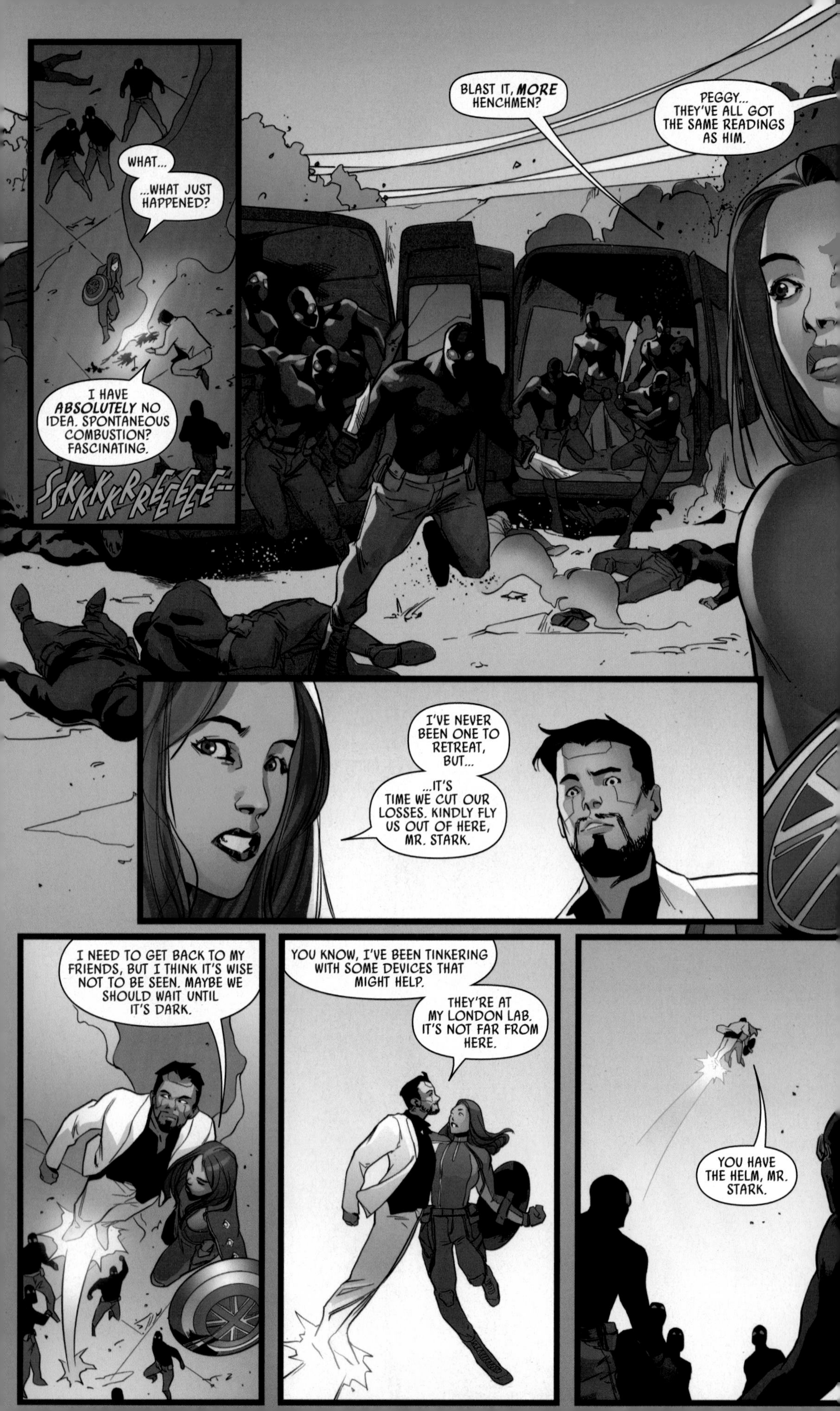
WHAT... ...WHAT JUST HAPPENED?
I HAVE ABSOLUTELY NO IDEA. SPONTANEOUS COMBUSTION? FASCINATING.
SSKKKKRREEEEEE--
BLAST IT, MORE HENCHMEN?
PEGGY... THEY'VE ALL GOT THE SAME READINGS AS HIM.
I'VE NEVER BEEN ONE TO RETREAT, BUT...
...IT'S TIME WE CUT OUR LOSSES. KINDLY FLY US OUT OF HERE, MR. STARK.
I NEED TO GET BACK TO MY FRIENDS, BUT I THINK IT'S WISE NOT TO BE SEEN. MAYBE WE SHOULD WAIT UNTIL IT'S DARK.
YOU KNOW, I'VE BEEN TINKERING WITH SOME DEVICES THAT MIGHT HELP.
THEY'RE AT MY LONDON LAB. IT'S NOT FAR FROM HERE.
YOU HAVE THE HELM, MR. STARK.

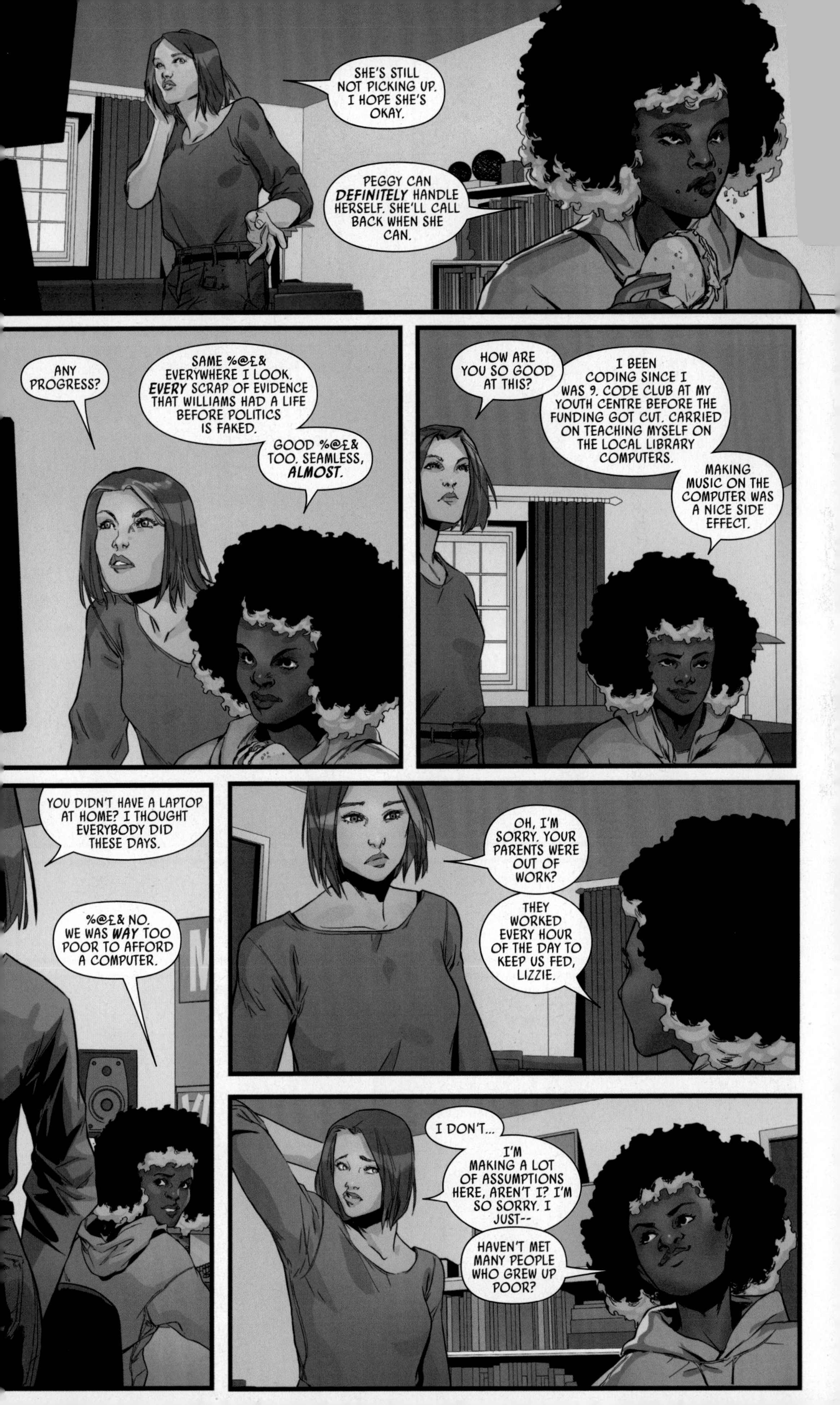

SHE'S STILL NOT PICKING UP. I HOPE SHE'S OKAY.
PEGGY CAN DEFINITELY HANDLE HERSELF. SHE'LL CALL BACK WHEN SHE CAN.
ANY PROGRESS?
SAME %@£& EVERYWHERE I LOOK. EVERY SCRAP OF EVIDENCE THAT WILLIAMS HAD A LIFE BEFORE POLITICS IS FAKED.
GOOD %@£& TOO. SEAMLESS, ALMOST.
HOW ARE YOU SO GOOD AT THIS?
I BEEN CODING SINCE I WAS 9. CODE CLUB AT MY YOUTH CENTRE BEFORE THE FUNDING GOT CUT. CARRIED ON TEACHING MYSELF ON THE LOCAL LIBRARY COMPUTERS.
MAKING MUSIC ON THE COMPUTER WAS A NICE SIDE EFFECT.
YOU DIDN'T HAVE A LAPTOP AT HOME? I THOUGHT EVERYBODY DID THESE DAYS.
%@£& NO. WE WAS WAY TOO POOR TO AFFORD A COMPUTER.
OH, I'M SORRY. YOUR PARENTS WERE OUT OF WORK?
THEY WORKED EVERY HOUR OF THE DAY TO KEEP US FED, LIZZIE.
I DON'T...
I'M MAKING A LOT OF ASSUMPTIONS HERE, AREN'T I? I'M SO SORRY. I JUST--
HAVEN'T MET MANY PEOPLE WHO GREW UP POOR?

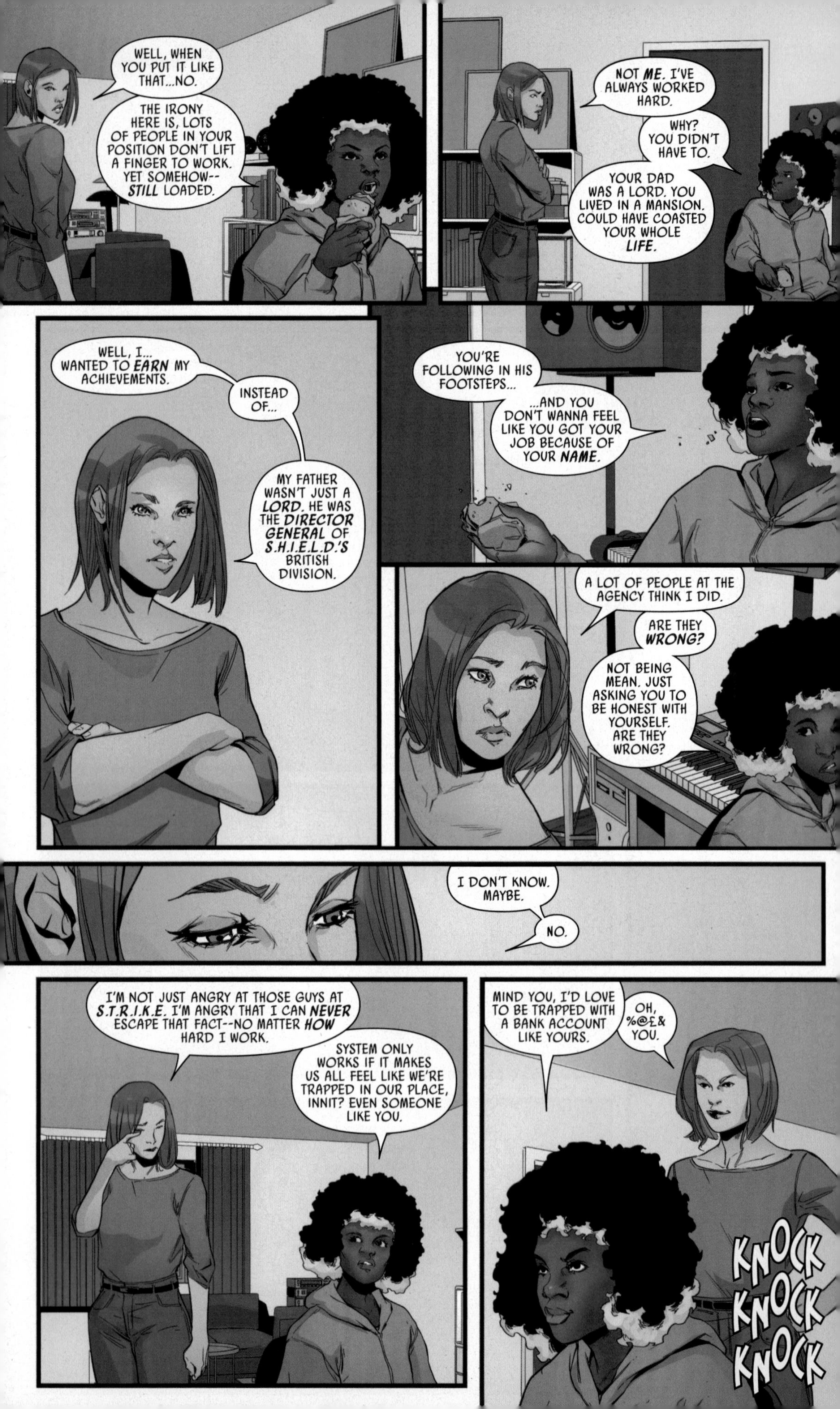

WELL, WHEN YOU PUT IT LIKE THAT...NO.
THE IRONY HERE IS, LOTS OF PEOPLE IN YOUR POSITION DON'T LIFT A FINGER TO WORK. YET SOMEHOW--STILL LOADED.
NOT ME. I'VE ALWAYS WORKED HARD.
WHY? YOU DIDN'T HAVE TO.
YOUR DAD WAS A LORD. YOU LIVED IN A MANSION. COULD HAVE COASTED YOUR WHOLE LIFE.
WELL, I... WANTED TO EARN MY ACHIEVEMENTS.
INSTEAD OF...
MY FATHER WASN'T JUST A LORD. HE WAS THE DIRECTOR GENERAL OF S.H.I.E.L.D.'S BRITISH DIVISION.
YOU'RE FOLLOWING IN HIS FOOTSTEPS...
...AND YOU DON'T WANNA FEEL LIKE YOU GOT YOUR JOB BECAUSE OF YOUR NAME.
A LOT OF PEOPLE AT THE AGENCY THINK I DID.
ARE THEY WRONG?
NOT BEING MEAN. JUST ASKING YOU TO BE HONEST WITH YOURSELF. ARE THEY WRONG?
I DON'T KNOW. MAYBE.
NO.
I'M NOT JUST ANGRY AT THOSE GUYS AT S.T.R.I.K.E. I'M ANGRY THAT I CAN NEVER ESCAPE THAT FACT--NO MATTER HOW HARD I WORK.
SYSTEM ONLY WORKS IF IT MAKES US ALL FEEL LIKE WE'RE TRAPPED IN OUR PLACE, INNIT? EVEN SOMEONE LIKE YOU.
MIND YOU, I'D LOVE TO BE TRAPPED WITH A BANK ACCOUNT LIKE YOURS.
OH, %@£& YOU.
KNOCK
KNOCK
KNOCK

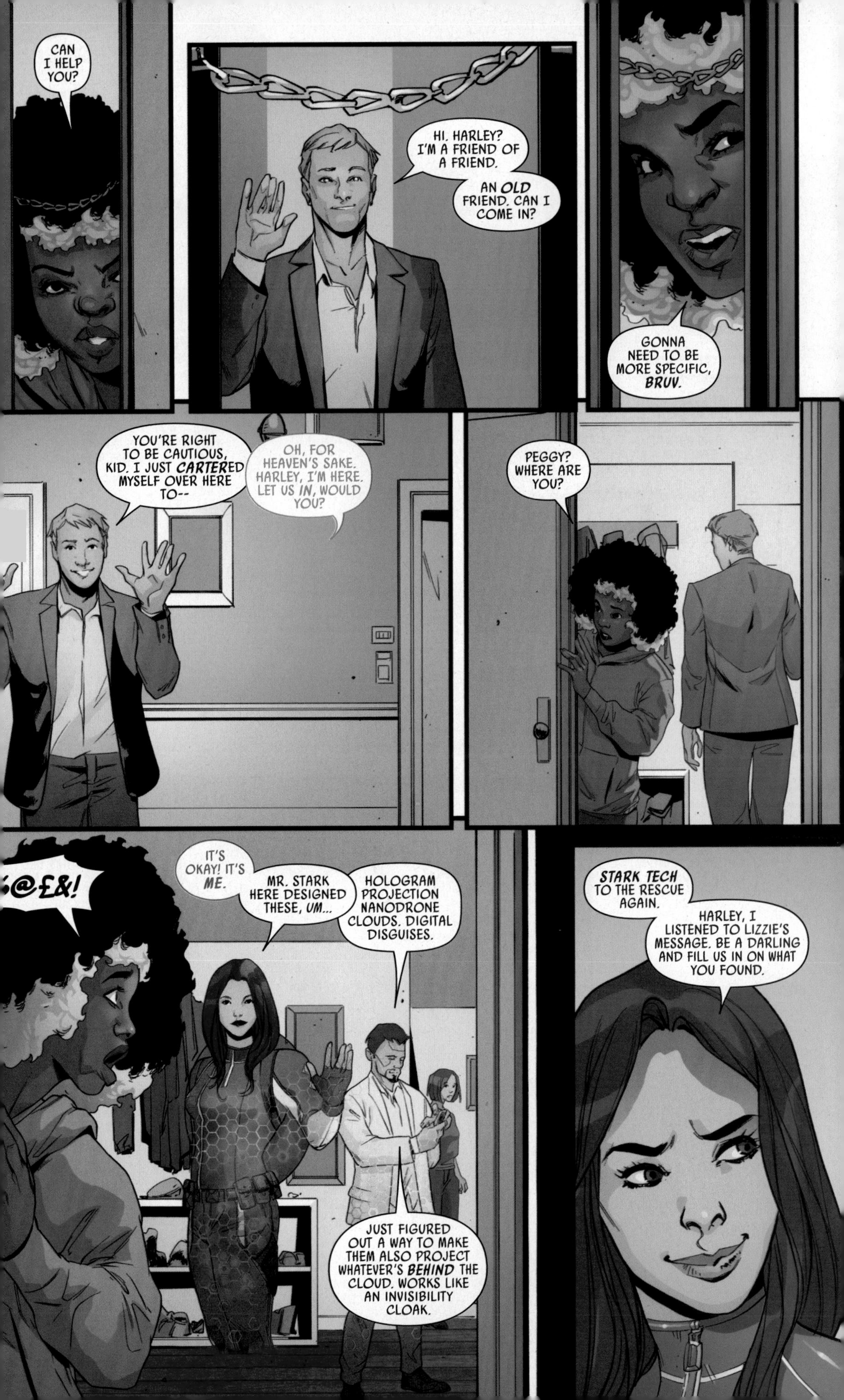
CAN I HELP YOU?
HI. HARLEY? I'M A FRIEND OF A FRIEND.
AN OLD FRIEND. CAN I COME IN?
GONNA NEED TO BE MORE SPECIFIC, BRUV.
YOU'RE RIGHT TO BE CAUTIOUS, KID. I JUST CARTERED MYSELF OVER HERE TO--
OH, FOR HEAVEN'S SAKE. HARLEY, I'M HERE. LET US IN, WOULD YOU?
PEGGY? WHERE ARE YOU?
$@£&!
IT'S OKAY! IT'S ME.
MR. STARK HERE DESIGNED THESE, UM...
HOLOGRAM PROJECTION NANODRONE CLOUDS. DIGITAL DISGUISES.
JUST FIGURED OUT A WAY TO MAKE THEM ALSO PROJECT WHATEVER'S BEHIND THE CLOUD. WORKS LIKE AN INVISIBILITY CLOAK.
STARK TECH TO THE RESCUE AGAIN.
HARLEY, I LISTENED TO LIZZIE'S MESSAGE. BE A DARLING AND FILL US IN ON WHAT YOU FOUND.

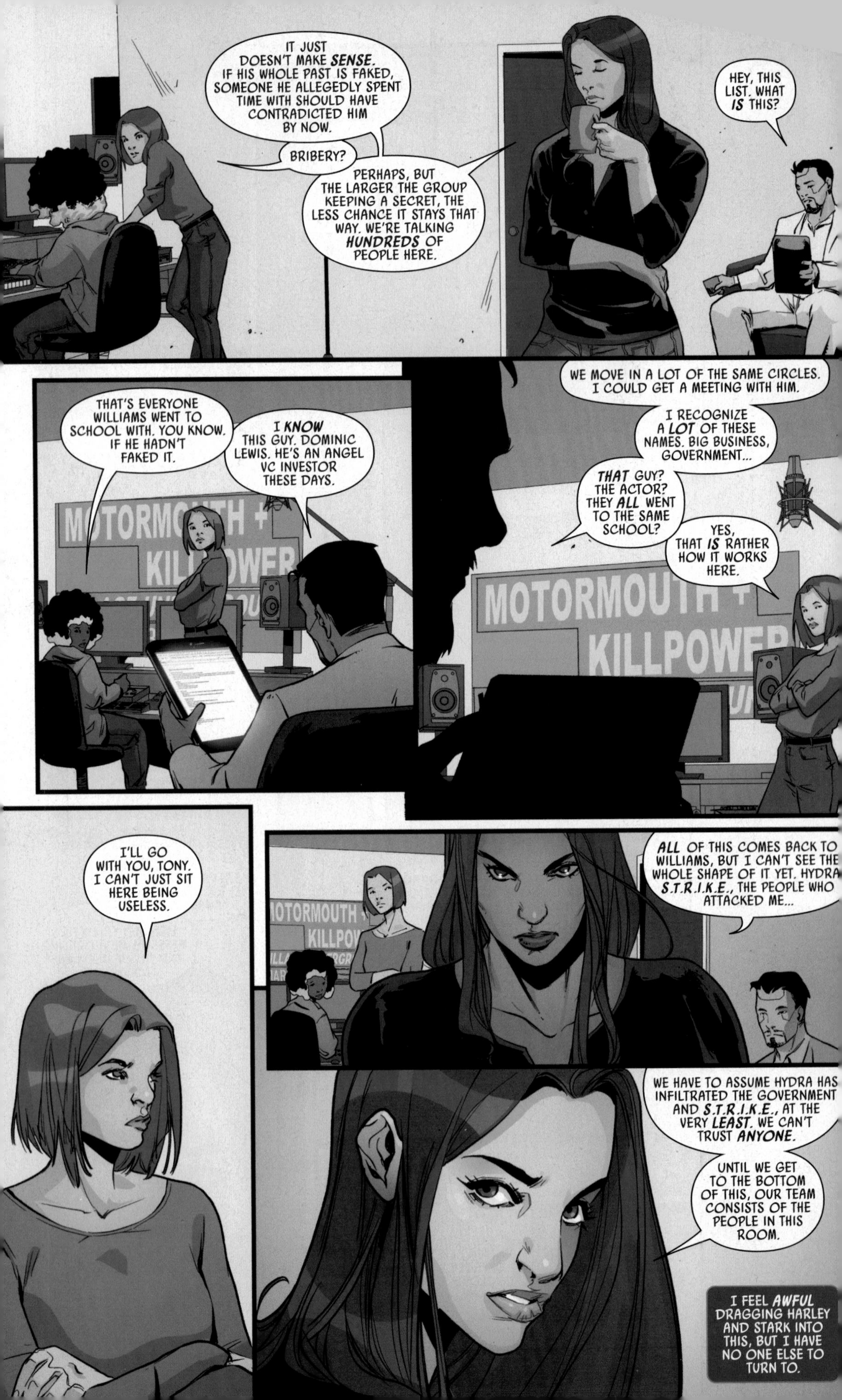
IT JUST DOESN'T MAKE SENSE. IF HIS WHOLE PAST IS FAKED, SOMEONE HE ALLEGEDLY SPENT TIME WITH SHOULD HAVE CONTRADICTED HIM BY NOW.
BRIBERY?
PERHAPS, BUT THE LARGER THE GROUP KEEPING A SECRET, THE LESS CHANCE IT STAYS THAT WAY. WE'RE TALKING HUNDREDS OF PEOPLE HERE.
HEY, THIS LIST. WHAT IS THIS?
THAT'S EVERYONE WILLIAMS WENT TO SCHOOL WITH. YOU KNOW. IF HE HADN'T FAKED IT.
I KNOW THIS GUY. DOMINIC LEWIS. HE'S AN ANGEL VC INVESTOR THESE DAYS.
MOTORMOUTH + KILLPOWER
WE MOVE IN A LOT OF THE SAME CIRCLES. I COULD GET A MEETING WITH HIM.
I RECOGNIZE A LOT OF THESE NAMES. BIG BUSINESS, GOVERNMENT...
THAT GUY? THE ACTOR? THEY ALL WENT TO THE SAME SCHOOL?
YES, THAT IS RATHER HOW IT WORKS HERE.
MOTORMOUTH + KILLPOWER
I'LL GO WITH YOU, TONY. I CAN'T JUST SIT HERE BEING USELESS.
ALL OF THIS COMES BACK TO WILLIAMS, BUT I CAN'T SEE THE WHOLE SHAPE OF IT YET. HYDRA, S.T.R.I.K.E., THE PEOPLE WHO ATTACKED ME...
WE HAVE TO ASSUME HYDRA HAS INFILTRATED THE GOVERNMENT AND S.T.R.I.K.E., AT THE VERY LEAST. WE CAN'T TRUST ANYONE.
UNTIL WE GET TO THE BOTTOM OF THIS, OUR TEAM CONSISTS OF THE PEOPLE IN THIS ROOM.
I FEEL AWFUL DRAGGING HARLEY AND STARK INTO THIS, BUT I HAVE NO ONE ELSE TO TURN TO.

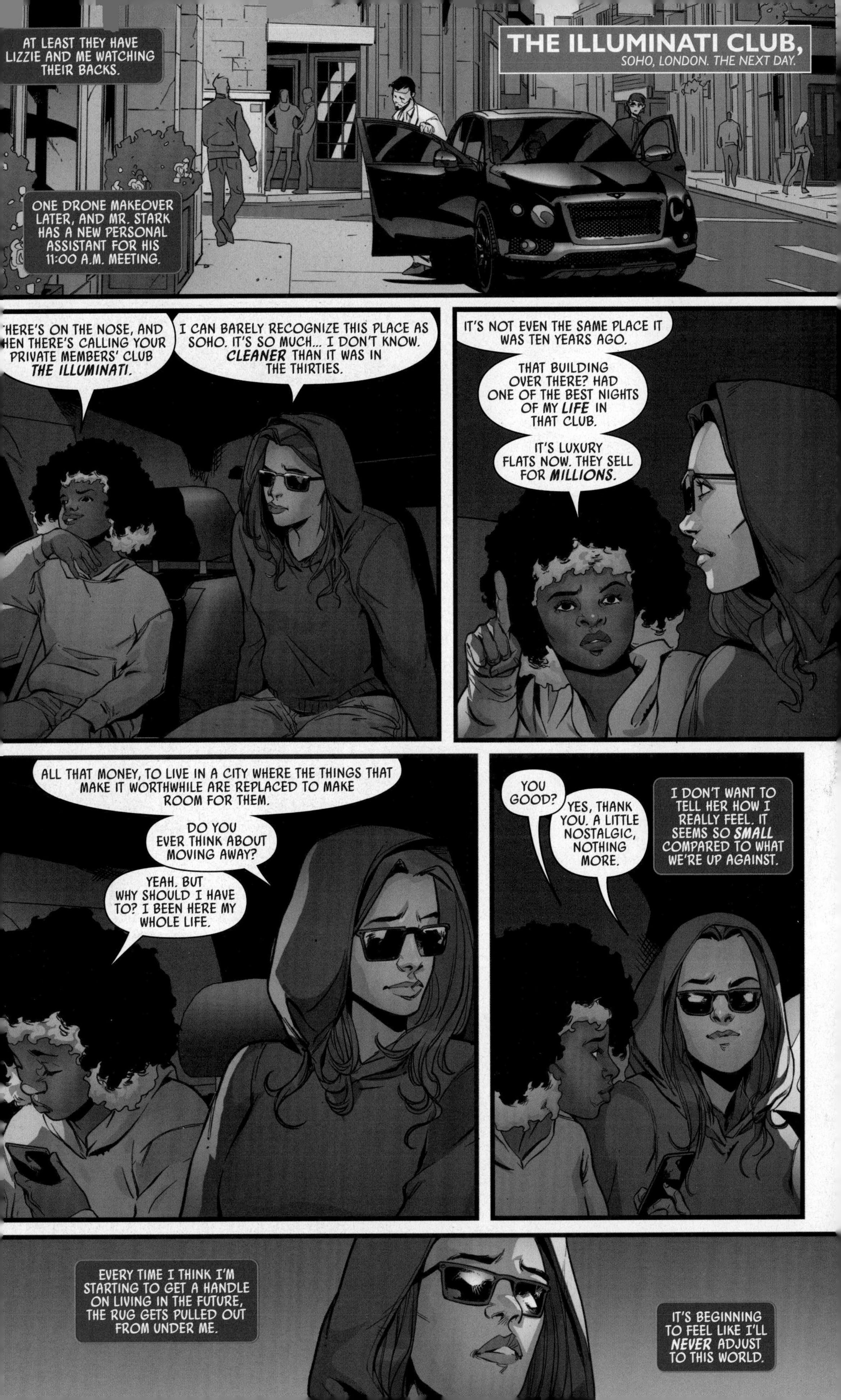
AT LEAST THEY HAVE LIZZIE AND ME WATCHING THEIR BACKS.
THE ILLUMINATI CLUB, SOHO, LONDON. THE NEXT DAY.
ONE DRONE MAKEOVER LATER, AND MR. STARK HAS A NEW PERSONAL ASSISTANT FOR HIS 11:00 A.M. MEETING.
THERE'S ON THE NOSE, AND THEN THERE'S CALLING YOUR PRIVATE MEMBERS' CLUB THE ILLUMINATI.
I CAN BARELY RECOGNIZE THIS PLACE AS SOHO. IT'S SO MUCH... I DON'T KNOW. CLEANER THAN IT WAS IN THE THIRTIES.
IT'S NOT EVEN THE SAME PLACE IT WAS TEN YEARS AGO.
THAT BUILDING OVER THERE? HAD ONE OF THE BEST NIGHTS OF MY LIFE IN THAT CLUB.
IT'S LUXURY FLATS NOW. THEY SELL FOR MILLIONS.
ALL THAT MONEY, TO LIVE IN A CITY WHERE THE THINGS THAT MAKE IT WORTHWHILE ARE REPLACED TO MAKE ROOM FOR THEM.
DO YOU EVER THINK ABOUT MOVING AWAY?
YEAH. BUT WHY SHOULD I HAVE TO? I BEEN HERE MY WHOLE LIFE.
YOU GOOD?
YES, THANK YOU. A LITTLE NOSTALGIC, NOTHING MORE.
I DON'T WANT TO TELL HER HOW I REALLY FEEL. IT SEEMS SO SMALL COMPARED TO WHAT WE'RE UP AGAINST.
EVERY TIME I THINK I'M STARTING TO GET A HANDLE ON LIVING IN THE FUTURE, THE RUG GETS PULLED OUT FROM UNDER ME.
IT'S BEGINNING TO FEEL LIKE I'LL NEVER ADJUST TO THIS WORLD.

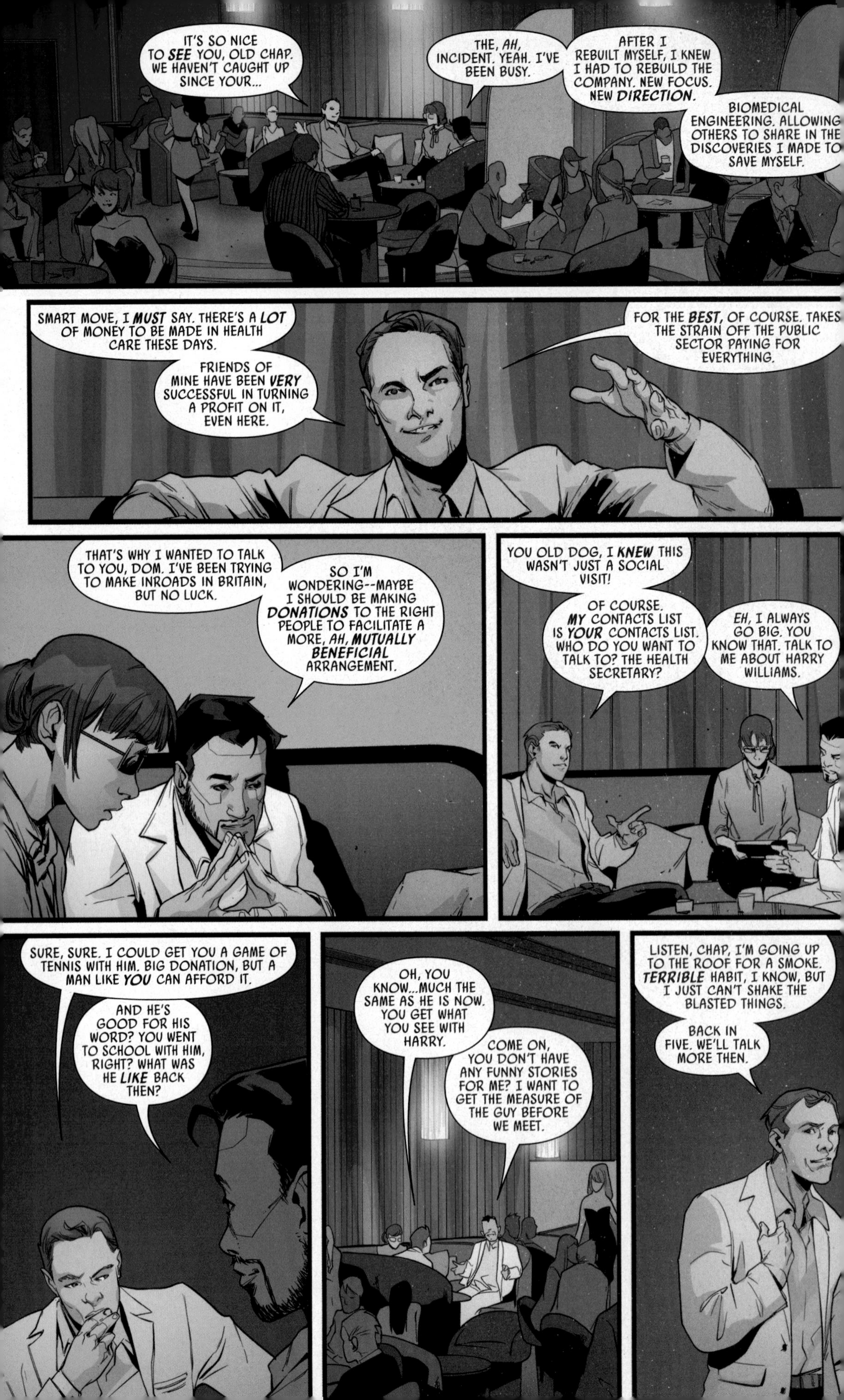
IT'S SO NICE TO SEE YOU, OLD CHAP. WE HAVEN'T CAUGHT UP SINCE YOUR...
THE, AH, INCIDENT. YEAH. I'VE BEEN BUSY.
AFTER I REBUILT MYSELF, I KNEW I HAD TO REBUILD THE COMPANY. NEW FOCUS. NEW DIRECTION.
BIOMEDICAL ENGINEERING. ALLOWING OTHERS TO SHARE IN THE DISCOVERIES I MADE TO SAVE MYSELF.
SMART MOVE, I MUST SAY. THERE'S A LOT OF MONEY TO BE MADE IN HEALTH CARE THESE DAYS.
FRIENDS OF MINE HAVE BEEN VERY SUCCESSFUL IN TURNING A PROFIT ON IT, EVEN HERE.
FOR THE BEST, OF COURSE. TAKES THE STRAIN OFF THE PUBLIC SECTOR PAYING FOR EVERYTHING.
THAT'S WHY I WANTED TO TALK TO YOU, DOM. I'VE BEEN TRYING TO MAKE INROADS IN BRITAIN, BUT NO LUCK.
SO I'M WONDERING--MAYBE I SHOULD BE MAKING DONATIONS TO THE RIGHT PEOPLE TO FACILITATE A MORE, AH, MUTUALLY BENEFICIAL ARRANGEMENT.
YOU OLD DOG, I KNEW THIS WASN'T JUST A SOCIAL VISIT!
OF COURSE. MY CONTACTS LIST IS YOUR CONTACTS LIST. WHO DO YOU WANT TO TALK TO? THE HEALTH SECRETARY?
EH, I ALWAYS GO BIG. YOU KNOW THAT. TALK TO ME ABOUT HARRY WILLIAMS.
SURE, SURE. I COULD GET YOU A GAME OF TENNIS WITH HIM. BIG DONATION, BUT A MAN LIKE YOU CAN AFFORD IT.
AND HE'S GOOD FOR HIS WORD? YOU WENT TO SCHOOL WITH HIM, RIGHT? WHAT WAS HE LIKE BACK THEN?
OH, YOU KNOW...MUCH THE SAME AS HE IS NOW. YOU GET WHAT YOU SEE WITH HARRY.
COME ON, YOU DON'T HAVE ANY FUNNY STORIES FOR ME? I WANT TO GET THE MEASURE OF THE GUY BEFORE WE MEET.
LISTEN, CHAP, I'M GOING UP TO THE ROOF FOR A SMOKE. TERRIBLE HABIT, I KNOW, BUT I JUST CAN'T SHAKE THE BLASTED THINGS.
BACK IN FIVE. WE'LL TALK MORE THEN.

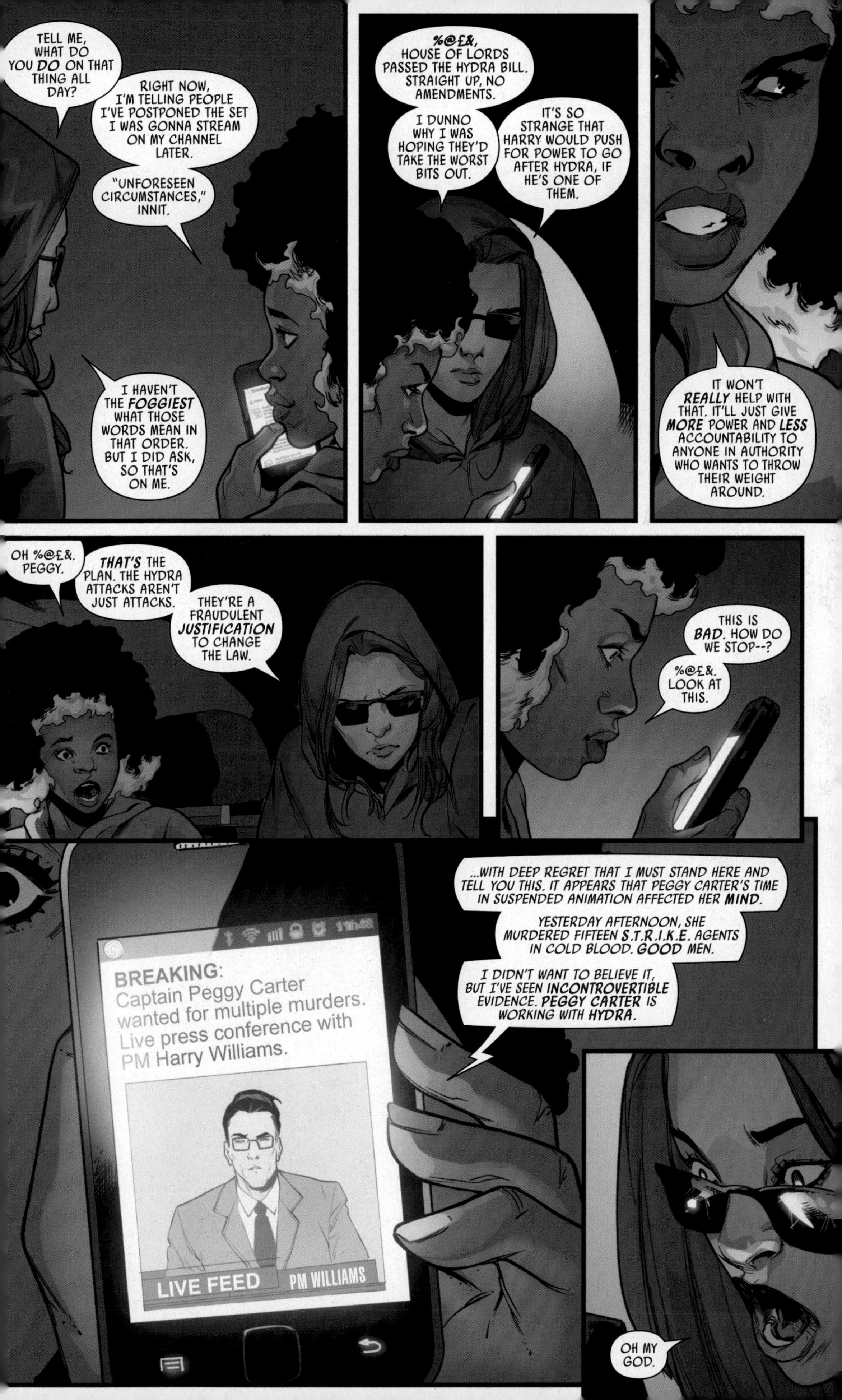

TELL ME, WHAT DO YOU DO ON THAT THING ALL DAY?
RIGHT NOW, I'M TELLING PEOPLE I'VE POSTPONED THE SET I WAS GONNA STREAM ON MY CHANNEL LATER.
"UNFORESEEN CIRCUMSTANCES," INNIT.
I HAVEN'T THE FOGGIEST WHAT THOSE WORDS MEAN IN THAT ORDER. BUT I DID ASK, SO THAT'S ON ME.
%@£&, HOUSE OF LORDS PASSED THE HYDRA BILL. STRAIGHT UP, NO AMENDMENTS.
I DUNNO WHY I WAS HOPING THEY'D TAKE THE WORST BITS OUT.
IT'S SO STRANGE THAT HARRY WOULD PUSH FOR POWER TO GO AFTER HYDRA, IF HE'S ONE OF THEM.
IT WON'T REALLY HELP WITH THAT. IT'LL JUST GIVE MORE POWER AND LESS ACCOUNTABILITY TO ANYONE IN AUTHORITY WHO WANTS TO THROW THEIR WEIGHT AROUND.
OH %@£&. PEGGY.
THAT'S THE PLAN. THE HYDRA ATTACKS AREN'T JUST ATTACKS.
THEY'RE A FRAUDULENT JUSTIFICATION TO CHANGE THE LAW.
THIS IS BAD. HOW DO WE STOP--?
%@£&. LOOK AT THIS.
BREAKING: Captain Peggy Carter wanted for multiple murders. Live press conference with PM Harry Williams.
LIVE FEED
PM WILLIAMS
...WITH DEEP REGRET THAT I MUST STAND HERE AND TELL YOU THIS. IT APPEARS THAT PEGGY CARTER'S TIME IN SUSPENDED ANIMATION AFFECTED HER MIND.
YESTERDAY AFTERNOON, SHE MURDERED FIFTEEN S.T.R.I.K.E. AGENTS IN COLD BLOOD. GOOD MEN.
I DIDN'T WANT TO BELIEVE IT, BUT I'VE SEEN INCONTROVERTIBLE EVIDENCE. PEGGY CARTER IS WORKING WITH HYDRA.
OH MY GOD.

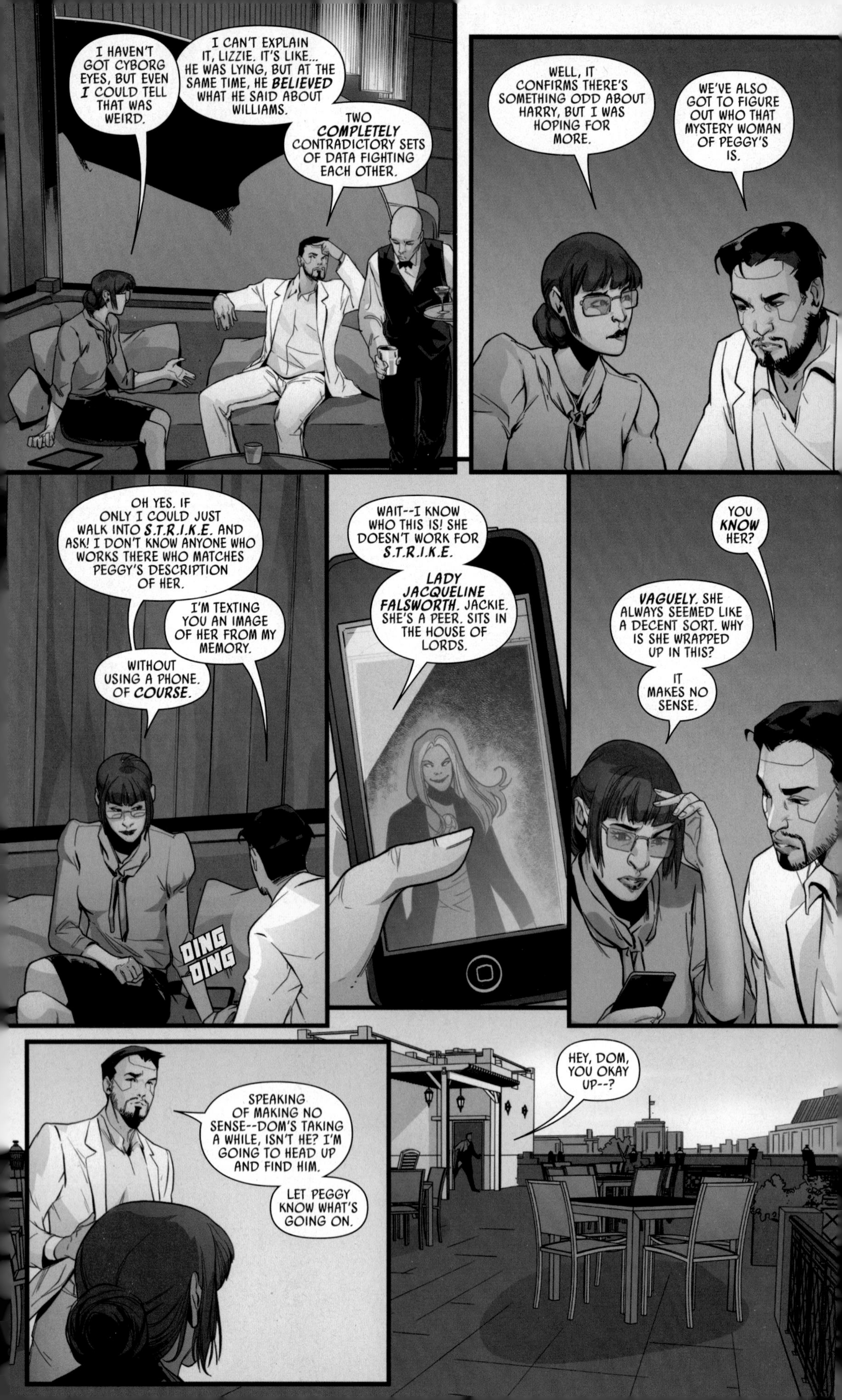

I HAVEN'T GOT CYBORG EYES, BUT EVEN I COULD TELL THAT WAS WEIRD.
I CAN'T EXPLAIN IT, LIZZIE. IT'S LIKE... HE WAS LYING, BUT AT THE SAME TIME, HE BELIEVED WHAT HE SAID ABOUT WILLIAMS.
TWO COMPLETELY CONTRADICTORY SETS OF DATA FIGHTING EACH OTHER.
WELL, IT CONFIRMS THERE'S SOMETHING ODD ABOUT HARRY, BUT I WAS HOPING FOR MORE.
WE'VE ALSO GOT TO FIGURE OUT WHO THAT MYSTERY WOMAN OF PEGGY'S IS.
OH YES. IF ONLY I COULD JUST WALK INTO S.T.R.I.K.E. AND ASK! I DON'T KNOW ANYONE WHO WORKS THERE WHO MATCHES PEGGY'S DESCRIPTION OF HER.
I'M TEXTING YOU AN IMAGE OF HER FROM MY MEMORY.
WITHOUT USING A PHONE. OF COURSE.
DING DING
WAIT--I KNOW WHO THIS IS! SHE DOESN'T WORK FOR S.T.R.I.K.E.
LADY JACQUELINE FALSWORTH. JACKIE. SHE'S A PEER. SITS IN THE HOUSE OF LORDS.
YOU KNOW HER?
VAGUELY. SHE ALWAYS SEEMED LIKE A DECENT SORT. WHY IS SHE WRAPPED UP IN THIS?
IT MAKES NO SENSE.
SPEAKING OF MAKING NO SENSE--DOM'S TAKING A WHILE, ISN'T HE? I'M GOING TO HEAD UP AND FIND HIM.
LET PEGGY KNOW WHAT'S GOING ON.
HEY, DOM, YOU OKAY UP--?

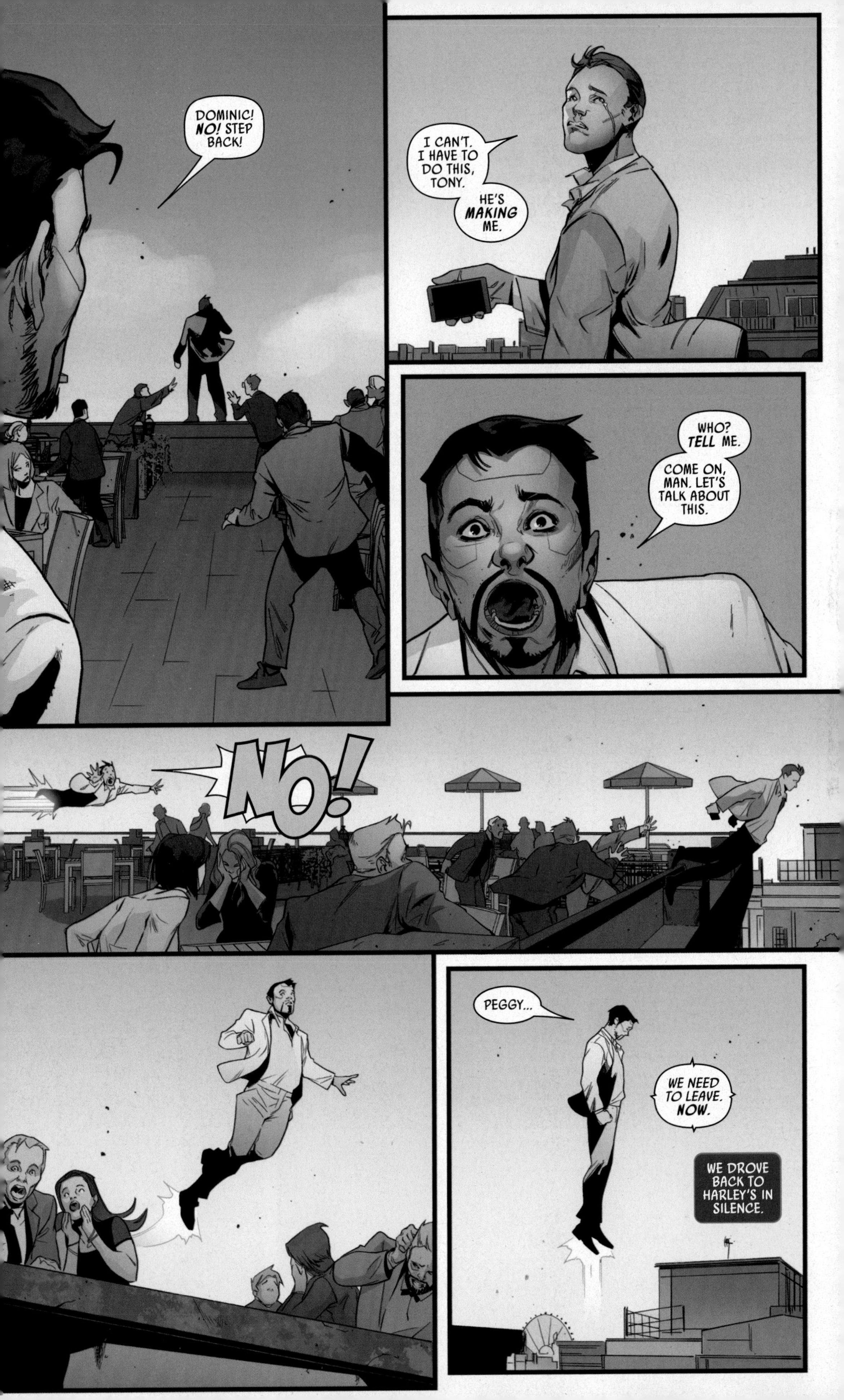
DOMINIC! NO! STEP BACK!
I CAN'T. I HAVE TO DO THIS, TONY.
HE'S MAKING ME.
WHO? TELL ME.
COME ON, MAN. LET'S TALK ABOUT THIS.
NO!
PEGGY...
WE NEED TO LEAVE. NOW.
WE DROVE BACK TO HARLEY'S IN SILENCE.

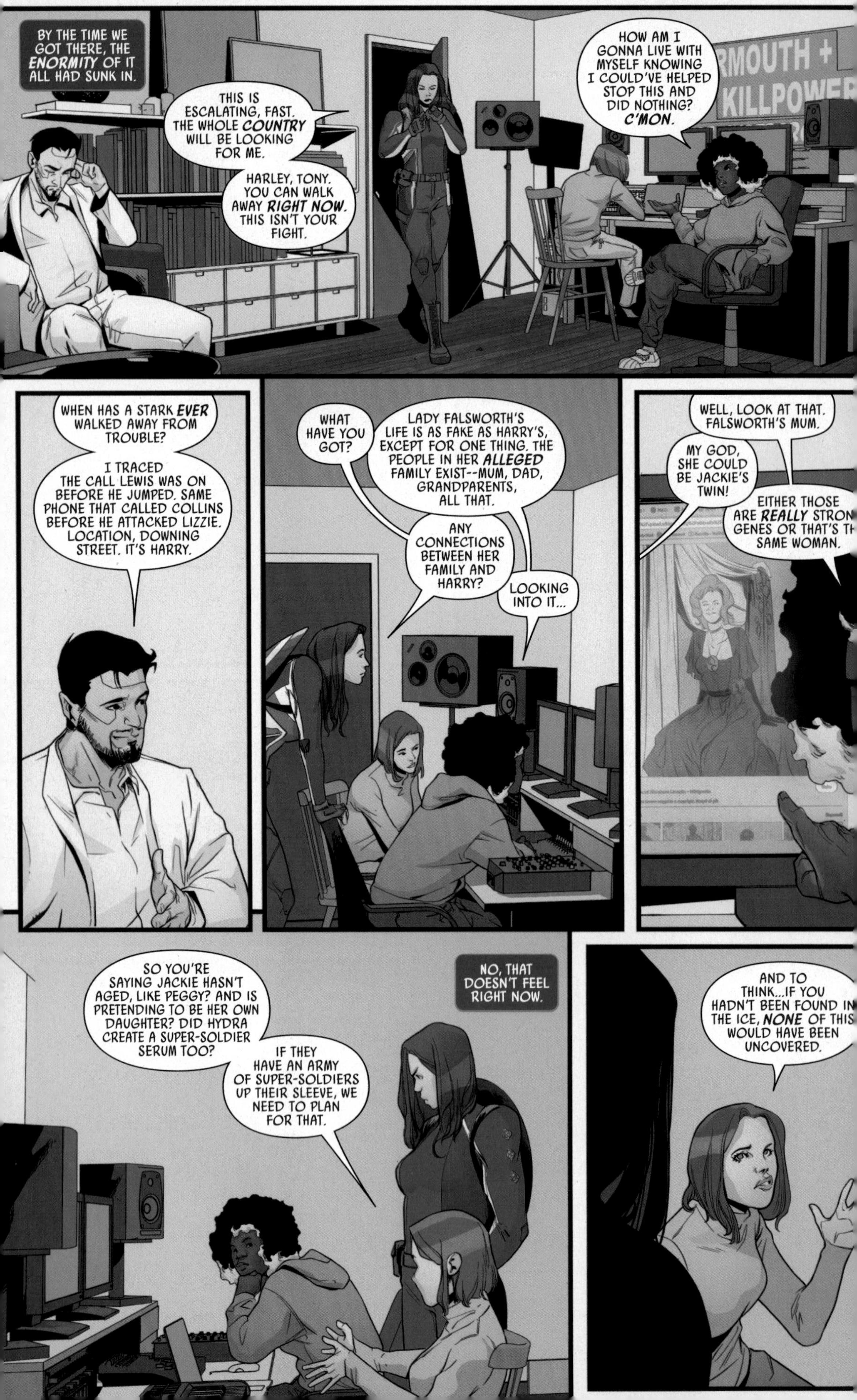
BY THE TIME WE GOT THERE, THE *ENORMITY* OF IT ALL HAD SUNK IN.
THIS IS ESCALATING, FAST. THE WHOLE *COUNTRY* WILL BE LOOKING FOR ME.
HARLEY, TONY. YOU CAN WALK AWAY *RIGHT NOW.* THIS ISN'T YOUR FIGHT.
HOW AM I GONNA LIVE WITH MYSELF KNOWING I COULD'VE HELPED STOP THIS AND DID NOTHING? *C'MON.*
WHEN HAS A STARK *EVER* WALKED AWAY FROM TROUBLE?
I TRACED THE CALL LEWIS WAS ON BEFORE HE JUMPED. SAME PHONE THAT CALLED COLLINS BEFORE HE ATTACKED LIZZIE. LOCATION, DOWNING STREET. IT'S HARRY.
WHAT HAVE YOU GOT?
LADY FALSWORTH'S LIFE IS AS FAKE AS HARRY'S, EXCEPT FOR ONE THING. THE PEOPLE IN HER *ALLEGED* FAMILY EXIST--MUM, DAD, GRANDPARENTS, ALL THAT.
ANY CONNECTIONS BETWEEN HER FAMILY AND HARRY?
LOOKING INTO IT...
WELL, LOOK AT THAT. FALSWORTH'S MUM.
MY GOD, SHE COULD BE JACKIE'S TWIN!
EITHER THOSE ARE *REALLY* STRON GENES OR THAT'S TH SAME WOMAN.
SO YOU'RE SAYING JACKIE HASN'T AGED, LIKE PEGGY? AND IS PRETENDING TO BE HER OWN DAUGHTER? DID HYDRA CREATE A SUPER-SOLDIER SERUM TOO?
IF THEY HAVE AN ARMY OF SUPER-SOLDIERS UP THEIR SLEEVE, WE NEED TO PLAN FOR THAT.
NO, THAT DOESN'T FEEL RIGHT NOW.
AND TO THINK...IF YOU HADN'T BEEN FOUND IN THE ICE, *NONE* OF THIS WOULD HAVE BEEN UNCOVERED.

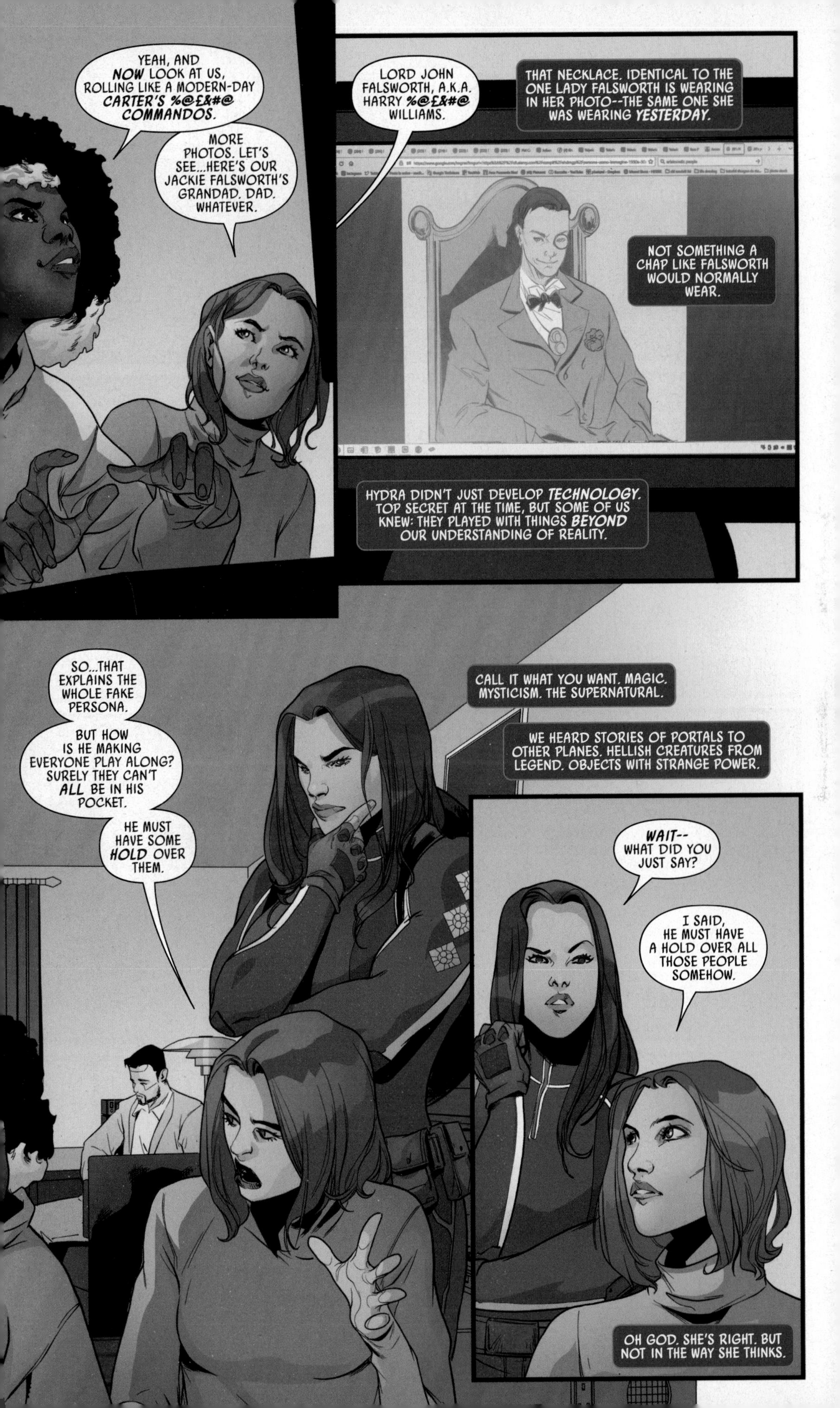
YEAH, AND NOW LOOK AT US, ROLLING LIKE A MODERN-DAY CARTER'S %@£&#@ COMMANDOS.
MORE PHOTOS. LET'S SEE...HERE'S OUR JACKIE FALSWORTH'S GRANDAD. DAD. WHATEVER.
LORD JOHN FALSWORTH, A.K.A. HARRY %@£&#@ WILLIAMS.
THAT NECKLACE. IDENTICAL TO THE ONE LADY FALSWORTH IS WEARING IN HER PHOTO--THE SAME ONE SHE WAS WEARING YESTERDAY.
NOT SOMETHING A CHAP LIKE FALSWORTH WOULD NORMALLY WEAR.
HYDRA DIDN'T JUST DEVELOP TECHNOLOGY. TOP SECRET AT THE TIME, BUT SOME OF US KNEW: THEY PLAYED WITH THINGS BEYOND OUR UNDERSTANDING OF REALITY.
SO...THAT EXPLAINS THE WHOLE FAKE PERSONA.
BUT HOW IS HE MAKING EVERYONE PLAY ALONG? SURELY THEY CAN'T ALL BE IN HIS POCKET.
HE MUST HAVE SOME HOLD OVER THEM.
CALL IT WHAT YOU WANT. MAGIC. MYSTICISM. THE SUPERNATURAL.
WE HEARD STORIES OF PORTALS TO OTHER PLANES. HELLISH CREATURES FROM LEGEND. OBJECTS WITH STRANGE POWER.
WAIT-- WHAT DID YOU JUST SAY?
I SAID, HE MUST HAVE A HOLD OVER ALL THOSE PEOPLE SOMEHOW.
OH GOD. SHE'S RIGHT. BUT NOT IN THE WAY SHE THINKS.

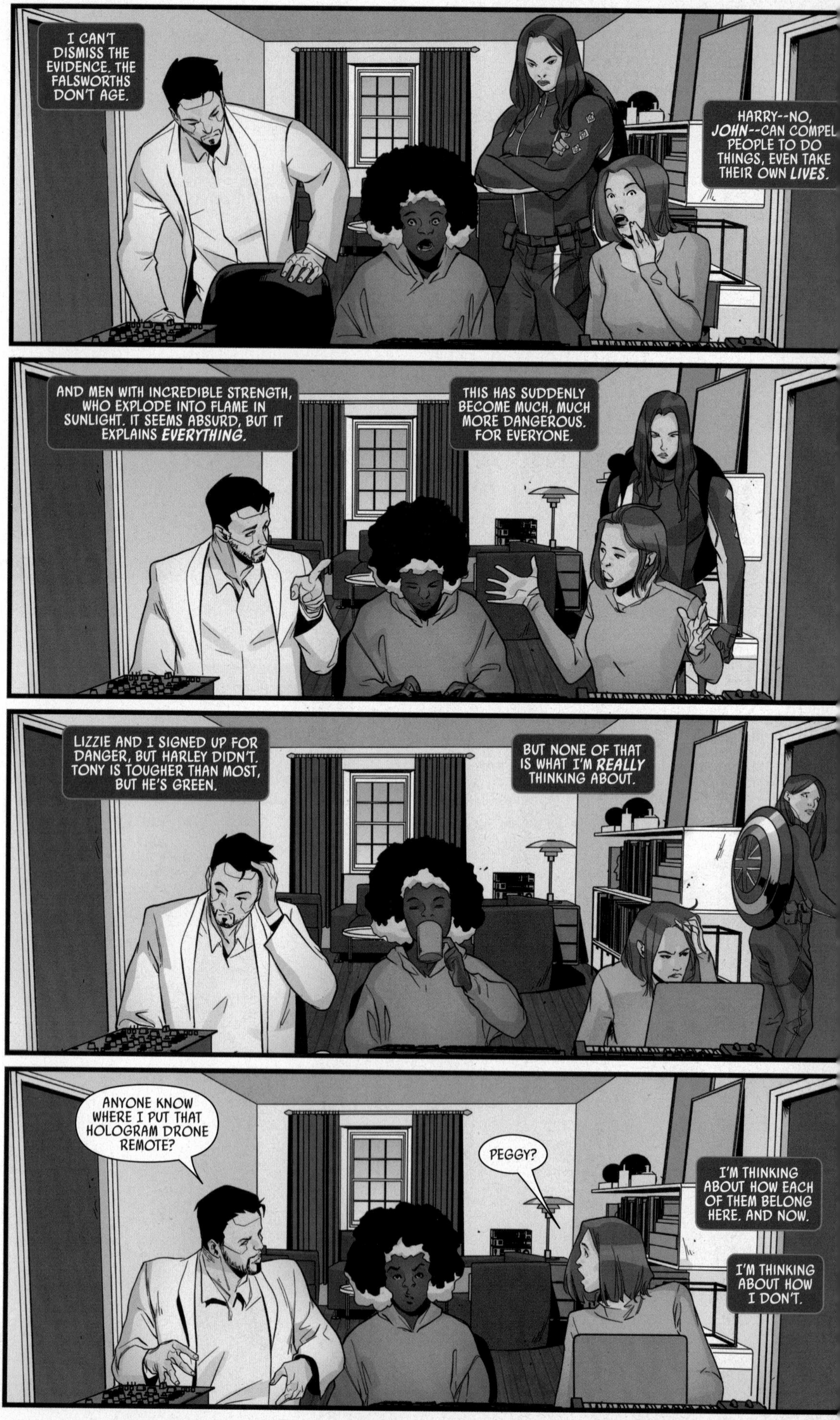
I CAN'T DISMISS THE EVIDENCE. THE FALSWORTHS DON'T AGE.
HARRY--NO, JOHN--CAN COMPEL PEOPLE TO DO THINGS, EVEN TAKE THEIR OWN LIVES.
AND MEN WITH INCREDIBLE STRENGTH, WHO EXPLODE INTO FLAME IN SUNLIGHT. IT SEEMS ABSURD, BUT IT EXPLAINS EVERYTHING.
THIS HAS SUDDENLY BECOME MUCH, MUCH MORE DANGEROUS. FOR EVERYONE.
LIZZIE AND I SIGNED UP FOR DANGER, BUT HARLEY DIDN'T. TONY IS TOUGHER THAN MOST, BUT HE'S GREEN.
BUT NONE OF THAT IS WHAT I'M REALLY THINKING ABOUT.
ANYONE KNOW WHERE I PUT THAT HOLOGRAM DRONE REMOTE?
PEGGY?
I'M THINKING ABOUT HOW EACH OF THEM BELONG HERE. AND NOW.
I'M THINKING ABOUT HOW I DON'T.

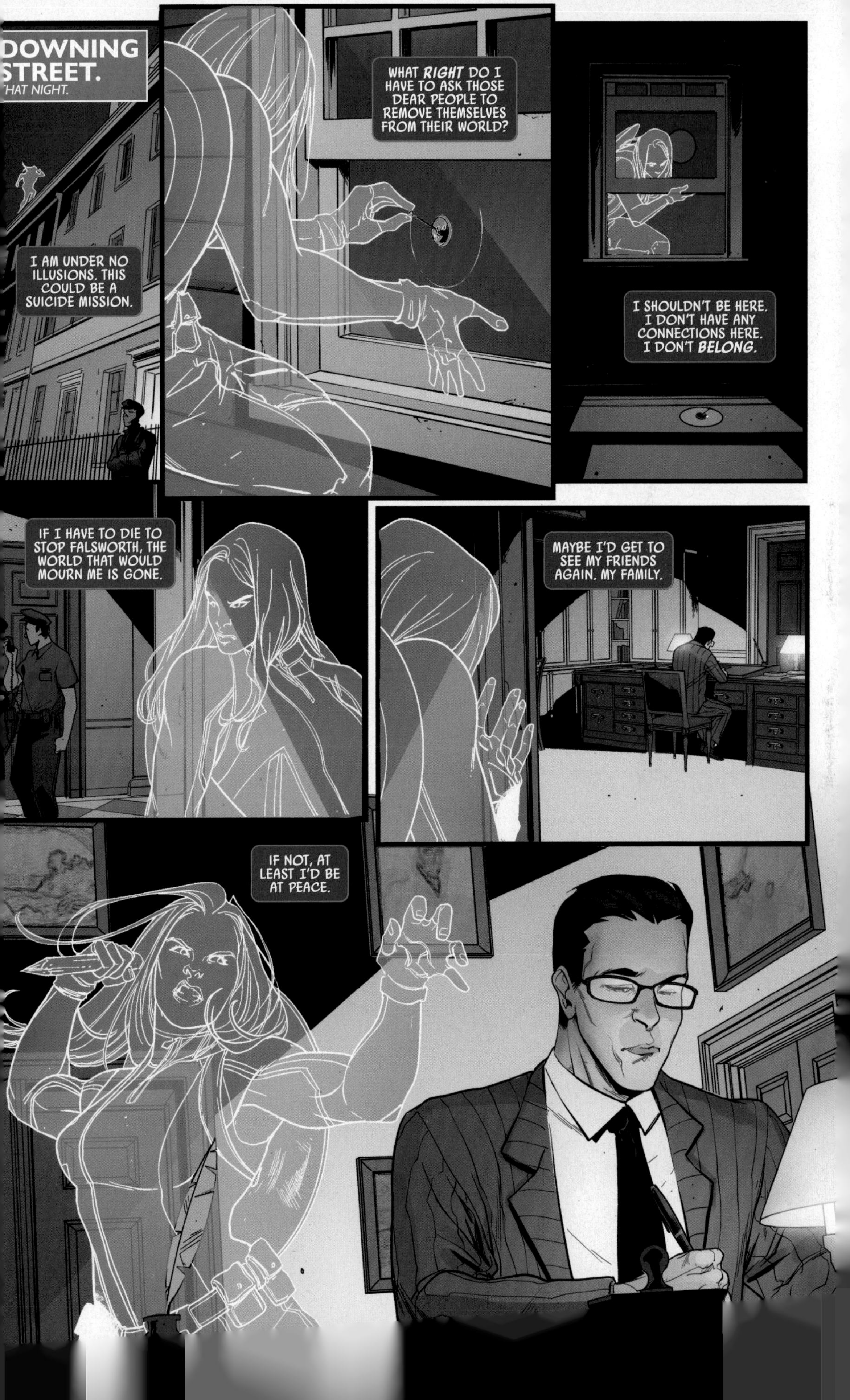
DOWNING STREET.
THAT NIGHT.
I AM UNDER NO ILLUSIONS. THIS COULD BE A SUICIDE MISSION.
WHAT RIGHT DO I HAVE TO ASK THOSE DEAR PEOPLE TO REMOVE THEMSELVES FROM THEIR WORLD?
I SHOULDN'T BE HERE. I DON'T HAVE ANY CONNECTIONS HERE. I DON'T BELONG.
IF I HAVE TO DIE TO STOP FALSWORTH, THE WORLD THAT WOULD MOURN ME IS GONE.
MAYBE I'D GET TO SEE MY FRIENDS AGAIN. MY FAMILY.
IF NOT, AT LEAST I'D BE AT PEACE.

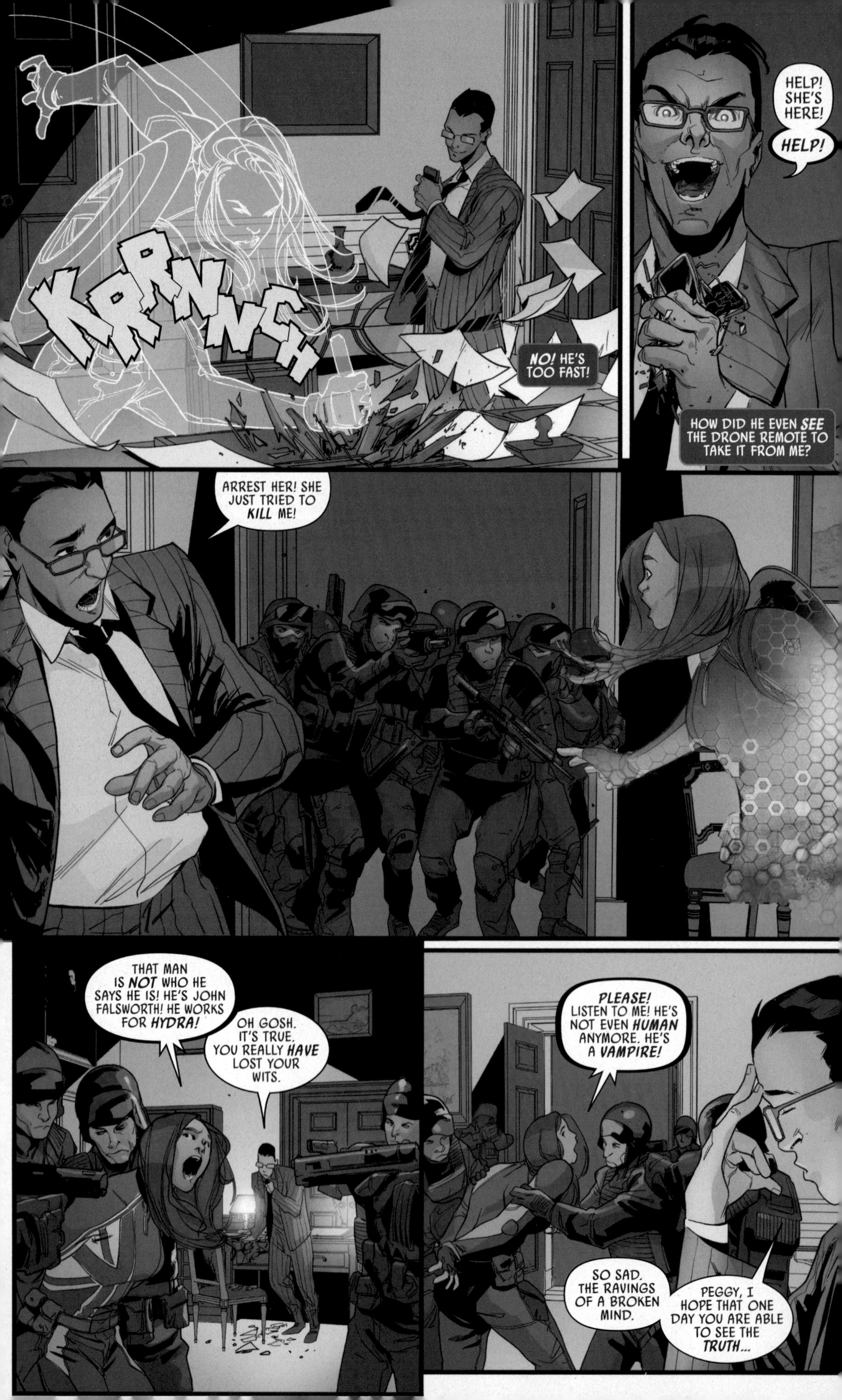
KRRNNCH
NO! HE'S TOO FAST!
HELP! SHE'S HERE! HELP!
HOW DID HE EVEN SEE THE DRONE REMOTE TO TAKE IT FROM ME?
ARREST HER! SHE JUST TRIED TO KILL ME!
THAT MAN IS NOT WHO HE SAYS HE IS! HE'S JOHN FALSWORTH! HE WORKS FOR HYDRA!
OH GOSH. IT'S TRUE. YOU REALLY HAVE LOST YOUR WITS.
PLEASE! LISTEN TO ME! HE'S NOT EVEN HUMAN ANYMORE. HE'S A VAMPIRE!
SO SAD. THE RAVINGS OF A BROKEN MIND.
PEGGY, I HOPE THAT ONE DAY YOU ARE ABLE TO SEE THE TRUTH...

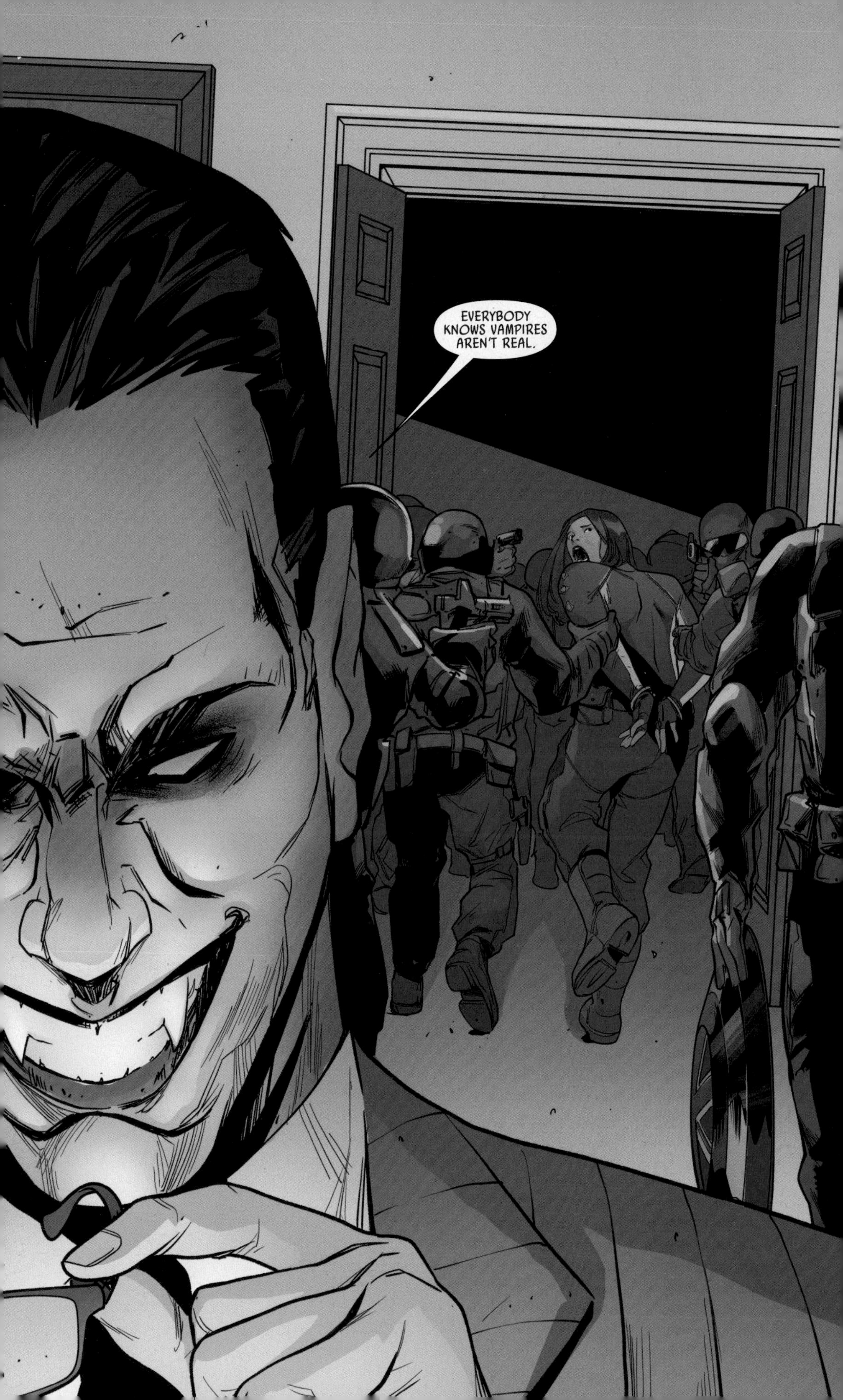
EVERYBODY KNOWS VAMPIRES AREN'T REAL.

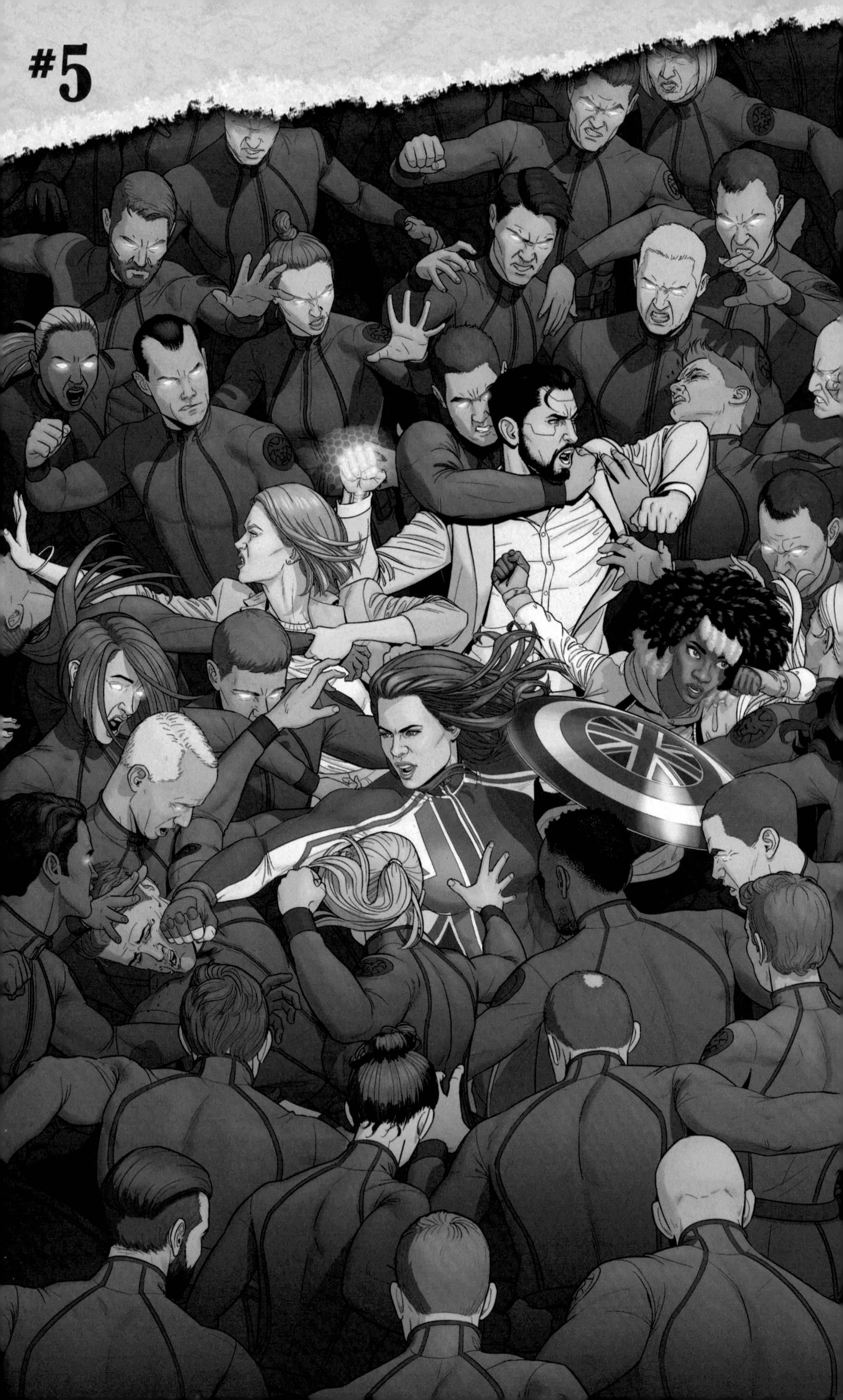
#5

LONDON
THE CAPITAL'S PREMIER FREE NEWSPAPER
OCK AS PRIME MINISTER SAYS PEGGY CARTER IS WANTED FOR MURDER

M:'CARTER
S HYDRA
TRAITOR'

Simon Williams
'Being a super hero is the greatest role of my career - so far' Page 21

Alice Hern Pymph
smartphone is their is it too small? Tech revie

The Morning Senti
Monday May 23 2022

Stark heir missing after ap
suicide during business me
Jeff Mitchell London

DAILY CORRESPONDENT
Daily Newspaper of the Decade
MONDAY, MAY 23, 2022
£1.20

Peggy Carter took advantage of our national pride and good faith to masquerade as a hero. After her merciful failure to assassinate the Prime Minister, there can be no doubt that she is, in truth, the...

ENEMY
OF THE
PEOPLE

HYDRA TERRORIST Peggy Carter was prevented from assassinating Prime Minister Harry Williams in his Downing Street flat by the brave officers of London Police in the early hours of Sunday morning.

Carter's attempt on the PM's life came mere hours after his shock press conference announcement that the former World War II Super-Soldier had aligned herself with the very hate group that she was supposed to protect the British people from.

By Charles St. John Political Editor

Just how the traitorous spy got past No. 10's heavy security measures is currently unknown, but the quick actions of the police detail assigned to protect the PM prevented her from doing him any serious harm.

The *Correspondent* understands Carter is being held at a top-secret location to prevent any attempts by Hydra terrorists to break their leader out of custody.

A government source has indicated to us that Carter's full list of despicable crimes will be made public in the coming days, once she is formally charged.

In a brief statement, Prime Minster Williams said: 'What makes this all the more sickening is that Britain is a fair and tolerant nation, and Peggy Carter abused those virtues to carry out her treasonous agenda.'

Turn to Page 2

TOP PEGGY

AILY
era
2022
Telling it like it i
TO KNOW WHY S.T.R.I.

OW
OU
THIS
HAP

Monday Ma

Morning Chronicle

BUSIN

anhunt launched for S.T.R.I.K.E.
ent accused of Carter conspir
Elizabeth Braddock is suspected of collaborati
orism as part of Hydra's campaign of viole

Stark accused
Missing biotech genius linked to Peggy Carter, says S.T.R.I.K.E. boss – PAGE 4

Prime Mini
Hydra bill
'Carter attack only prove

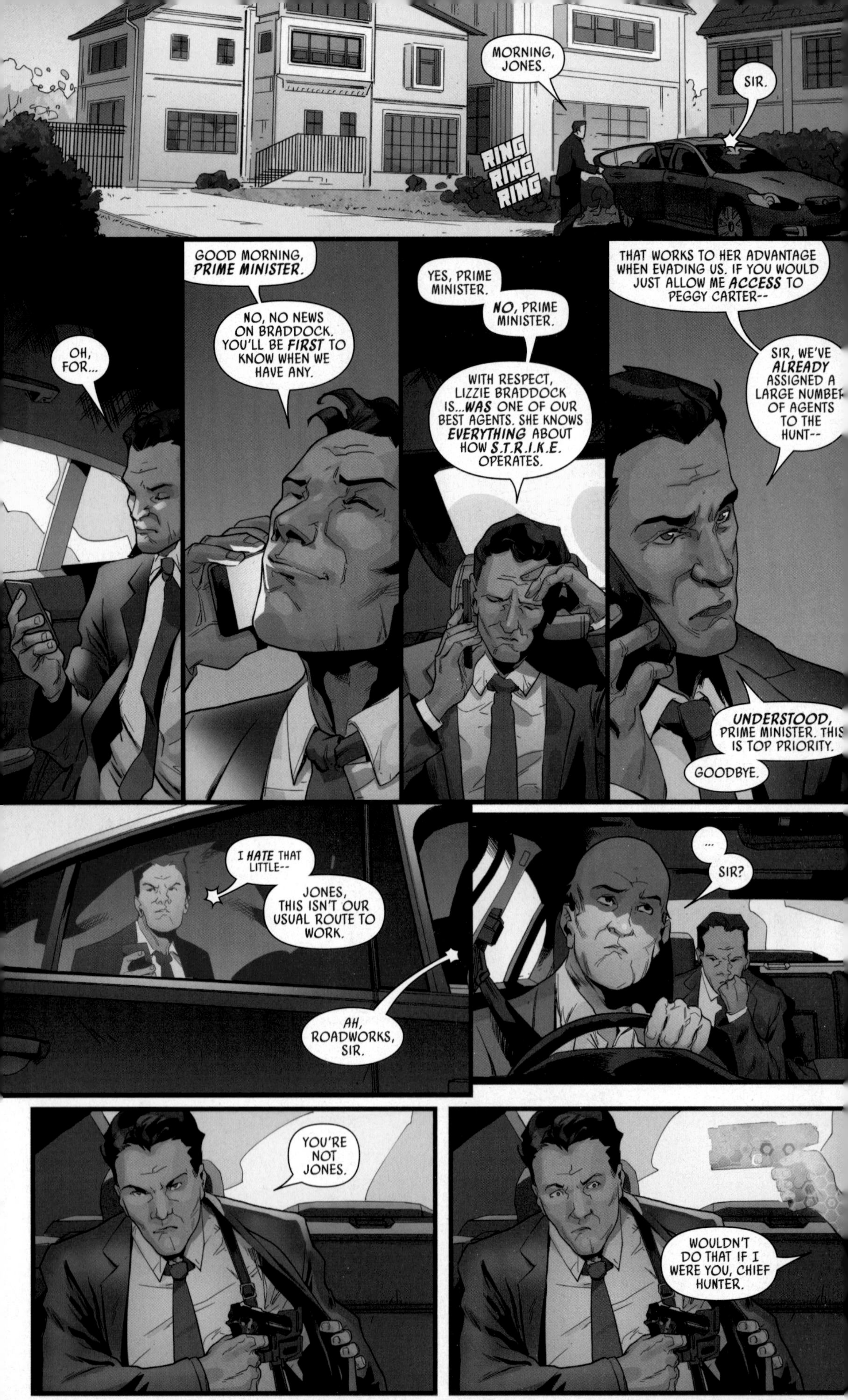
MORNING, JONES.
SIR.
RING RING RING
OH, FOR...
GOOD MORNING, PRIME MINISTER.
NO, NO NEWS ON BRADDOCK. YOU'LL BE FIRST TO KNOW WHEN WE HAVE ANY.
YES, PRIME MINISTER.
NO, PRIME MINISTER.
WITH RESPECT, LIZZIE BRADDOCK IS...WAS ONE OF OUR BEST AGENTS. SHE KNOWS EVERYTHING ABOUT HOW S.T.R.I.K.E. OPERATES.
THAT WORKS TO HER ADVANTAGE WHEN EVADING US. IF YOU WOULD JUST ALLOW ME ACCESS TO PEGGY CARTER--
SIR, WE'VE ALREADY ASSIGNED A LARGE NUMBER OF AGENTS TO THE HUNT--
UNDERSTOOD, PRIME MINISTER. THIS IS TOP PRIORITY.
GOODBYE.
I HATE THAT LITTLE--
JONES, THIS ISN'T OUR USUAL ROUTE TO WORK.
AH, ROADWORKS, SIR.
...
SIR?
YOU'RE NOT JONES.
WOULDN'T DO THAT IF I WERE YOU, CHIEF HUNTER.

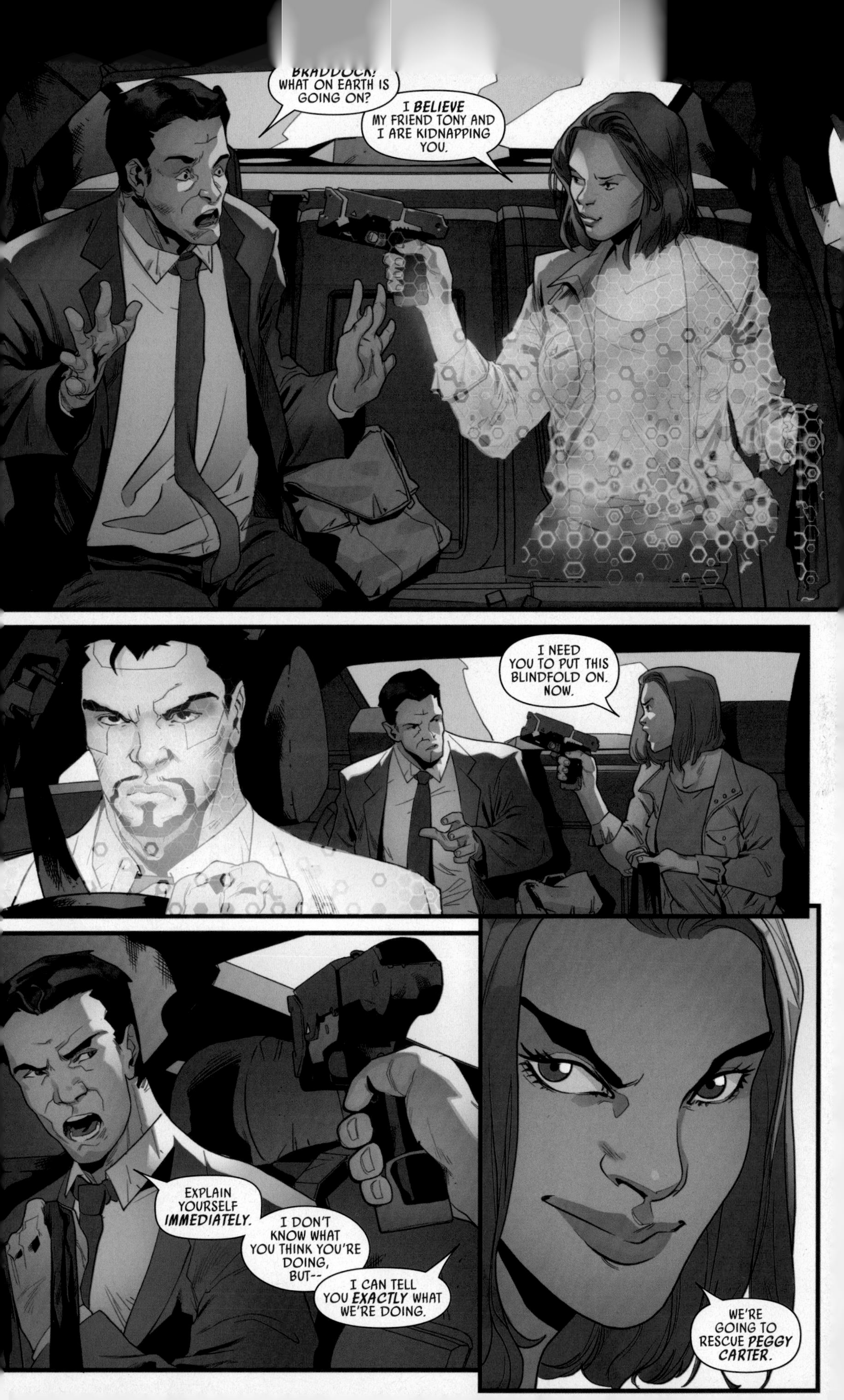
BRADDOCK! WHAT ON EARTH IS GOING ON?
I BELIEVE MY FRIEND TONY AND I ARE KIDNAPPING YOU.
I NEED YOU TO PUT THIS BLINDFOLD ON. NOW.
EXPLAIN YOURSELF IMMEDIATELY.
I DON'T KNOW WHAT YOU THINK YOU'RE DOING, BUT--
I CAN TELL YOU EXACTLY WHAT WE'RE DOING.
WE'RE GOING TO RESCUE PEGGY CARTER.

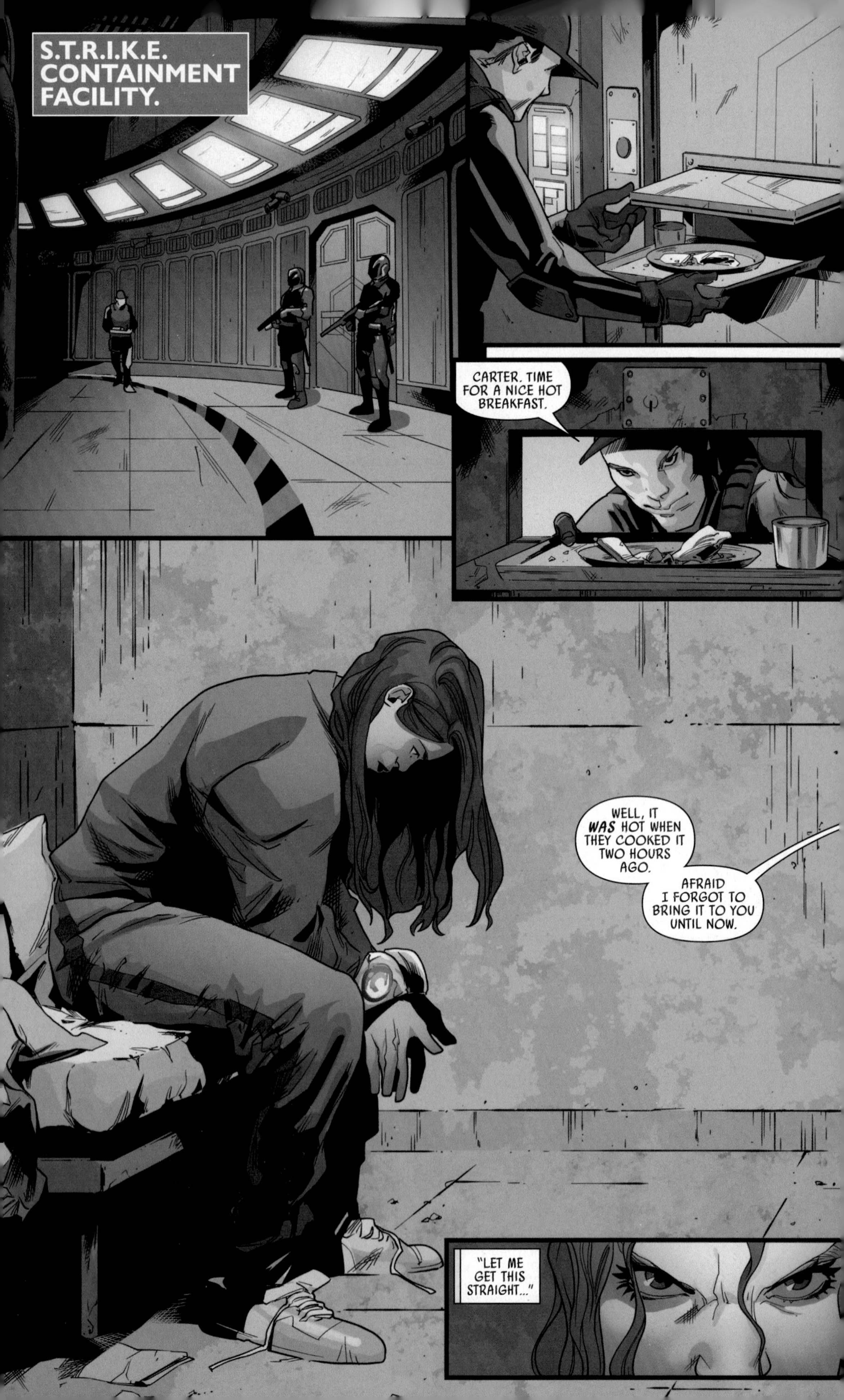
S.T.R.I.K.E. CONTAINMENT FACILITY.
CARTER. TIME FOR A NICE HOT BREAKFAST.
WELL, IT *WAS* HOT WHEN THEY COOKED IT TWO HOURS AGO.
AFRAID I FORGOT TO BRING IT TO YOU UNTIL NOW.
"LET ME GET THIS STRAIGHT..."

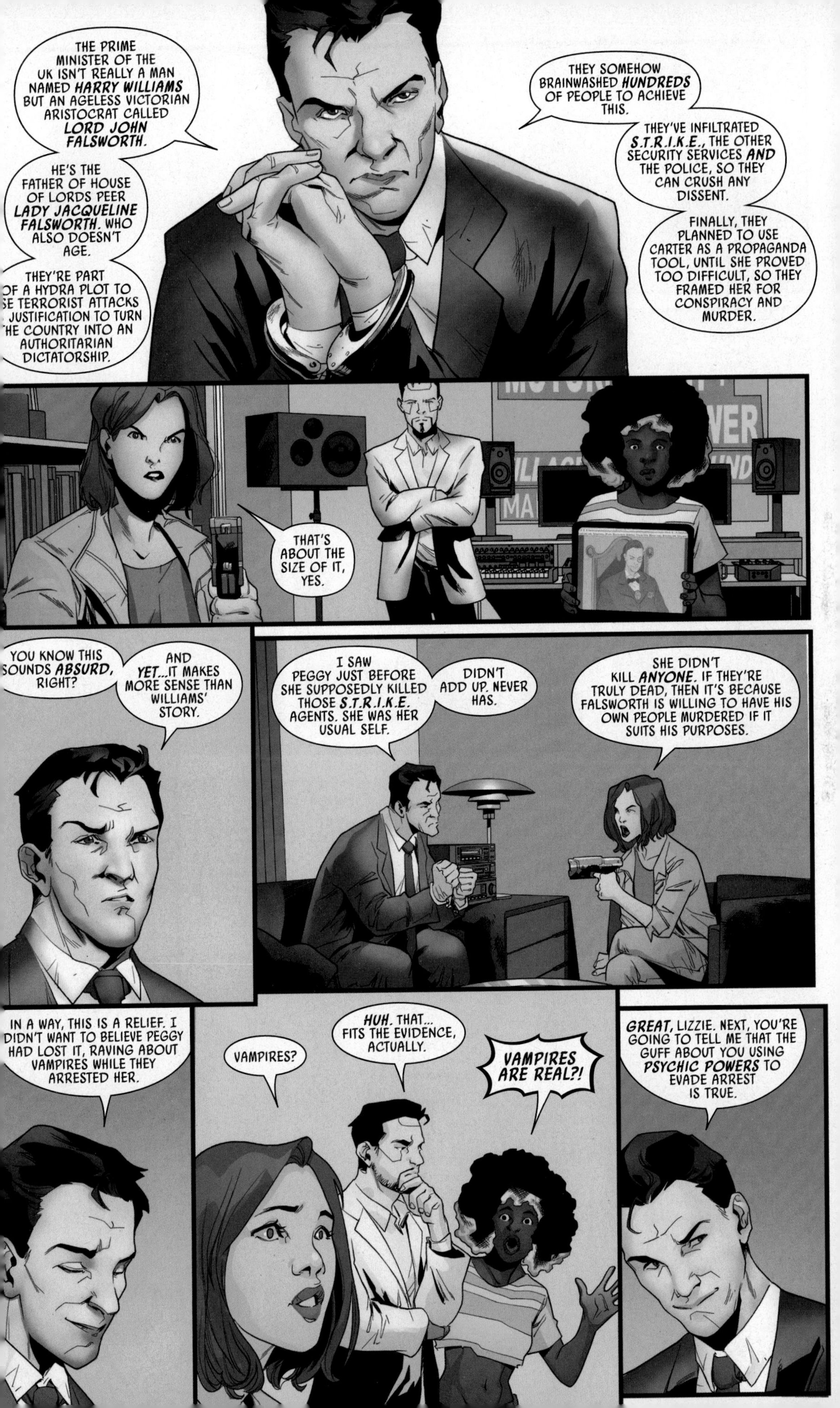
THE PRIME MINISTER OF THE UK ISN'T REALLY A MAN NAMED HARRY WILLIAMS BUT AN AGELESS VICTORIAN ARISTOCRAT CALLED LORD JOHN FALSWORTH.
HE'S THE FATHER OF HOUSE OF LORDS PEER LADY JACQUELINE FALSWORTH. WHO ALSO DOESN'T AGE.
THEY'RE PART OF A HYDRA PLOT TO SE TERRORIST ATTACKS JUSTIFICATION TO TURN HE COUNTRY INTO AN AUTHORITARIAN DICTATORSHIP.
THEY SOMEHOW BRAINWASHED HUNDREDS OF PEOPLE TO ACHIEVE THIS.
THEY'VE INFILTRATED S.T.R.I.K.E., THE OTHER SECURITY SERVICES AND THE POLICE, SO THEY CAN CRUSH ANY DISSENT.
FINALLY, THEY PLANNED TO USE CARTER AS A PROPAGANDA TOOL, UNTIL SHE PROVED TOO DIFFICULT, SO THEY FRAMED HER FOR CONSPIRACY AND MURDER.
THAT'S ABOUT THE SIZE OF IT, YES.
YOU KNOW THIS SOUNDS ABSURD, RIGHT?
AND YET...IT MAKES MORE SENSE THAN WILLIAMS' STORY.
I SAW PEGGY JUST BEFORE SHE SUPPOSEDLY KILLED THOSE S.T.R.I.K.E. AGENTS. SHE WAS HER USUAL SELF.
DIDN'T ADD UP. NEVER HAS.
SHE DIDN'T KILL ANYONE. IF THEY'RE TRULY DEAD, THEN IT'S BECAUSE FALSWORTH IS WILLING TO HAVE HIS OWN PEOPLE MURDERED IF IT SUITS HIS PURPOSES.
IN A WAY, THIS IS A RELIEF. I DIDN'T WANT TO BELIEVE PEGGY HAD LOST IT, RAVING ABOUT VAMPIRES WHILE THEY ARRESTED HER.
VAMPIRES?
HUH. THAT... FITS THE EVIDENCE, ACTUALLY.
VAMPIRES ARE REAL?!
GREAT, LIZZIE. NEXT, YOU'RE GOING TO TELL ME THAT THE GUFF ABOUT YOU USING PSYCHIC POWERS TO EVADE ARREST IS TRUE.

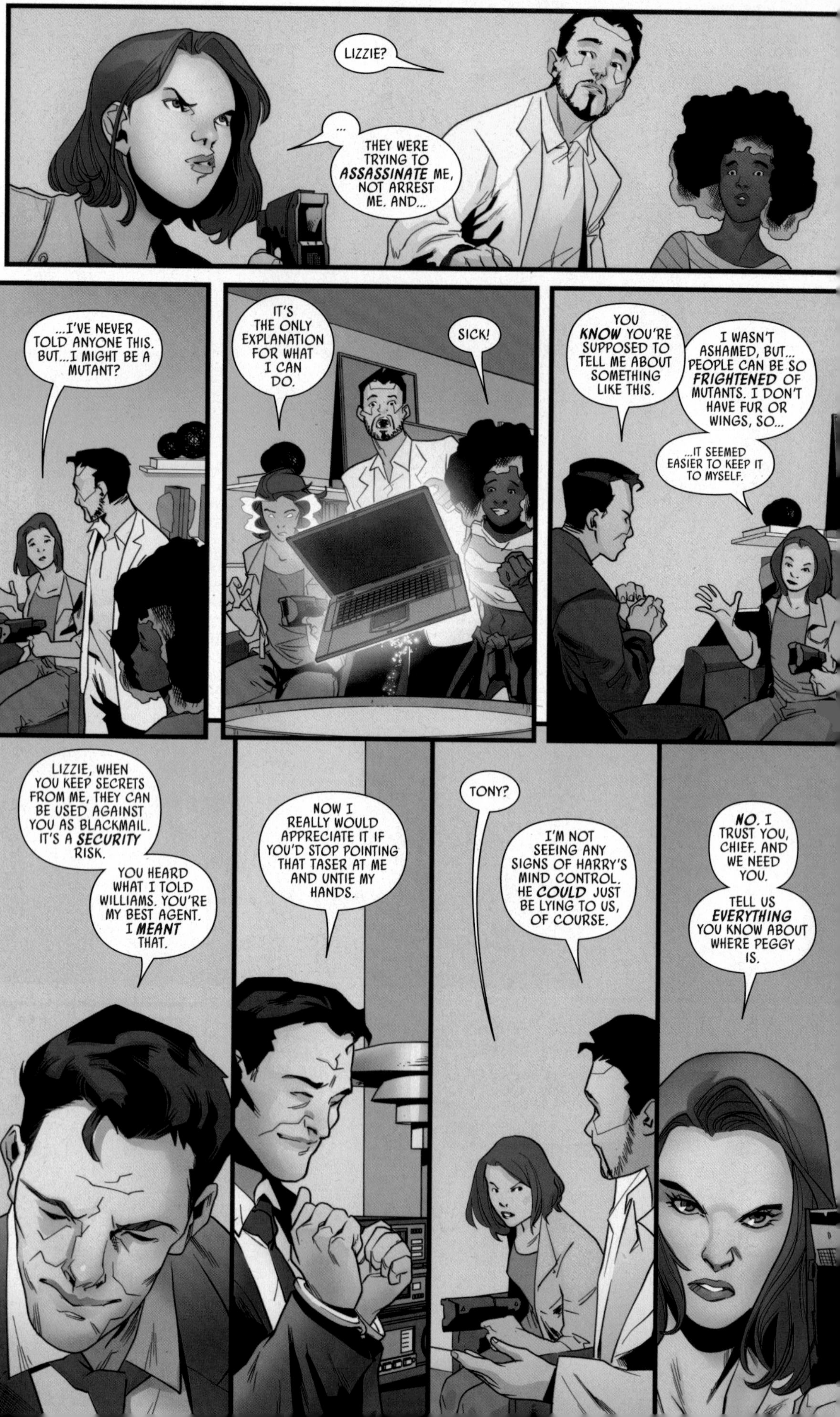
LIZZIE?
... THEY WERE TRYING TO ASSASSINATE ME, NOT ARREST ME. AND...
...I'VE NEVER TOLD ANYONE THIS. BUT...I MIGHT BE A MUTANT?
IT'S THE ONLY EXPLANATION FOR WHAT I CAN DO.
SICK!
YOU KNOW YOU'RE SUPPOSED TO TELL ME ABOUT SOMETHING LIKE THIS.
I WASN'T ASHAMED, BUT... PEOPLE CAN BE SO FRIGHTENED OF MUTANTS. I DON'T HAVE FUR OR WINGS, SO...
...IT SEEMED EASIER TO KEEP IT TO MYSELF.
LIZZIE, WHEN YOU KEEP SECRETS FROM ME, THEY CAN BE USED AGAINST YOU AS BLACKMAIL. IT'S A SECURITY RISK.
YOU HEARD WHAT I TOLD WILLIAMS. YOU'RE MY BEST AGENT. I MEANT THAT.
NOW I REALLY WOULD APPRECIATE IT IF YOU'D STOP POINTING THAT TASER AT ME AND UNTIE MY HANDS.
TONY?
I'M NOT SEEING ANY SIGNS OF HARRY'S MIND CONTROL. HE COULD JUST BE LYING TO US, OF COURSE.
NO. I TRUST YOU, CHIEF. AND WE NEED YOU.
TELL US EVERYTHING YOU KNOW ABOUT WHERE PEGGY IS.

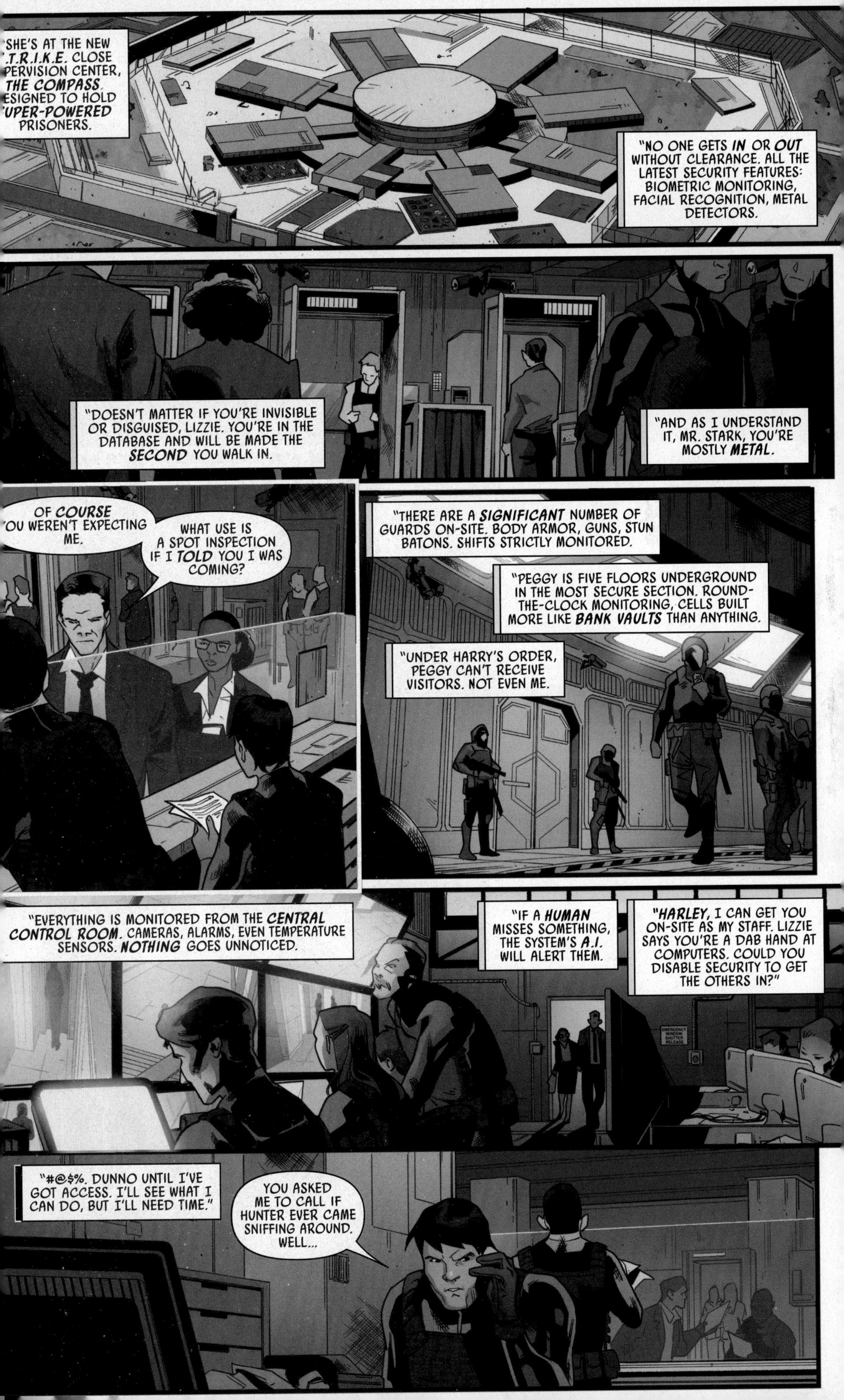

"SHE'S AT THE NEW S.T.R.I.K.E. CLOSE SUPERVISION CENTER, THE COMPASS. DESIGNED TO HOLD SUPER-POWERED PRISONERS.
"NO ONE GETS IN OR OUT WITHOUT CLEARANCE. ALL THE LATEST SECURITY FEATURES: BIOMETRIC MONITORING, FACIAL RECOGNITION, METAL DETECTORS.
"DOESN'T MATTER IF YOU'RE INVISIBLE OR DISGUISED, LIZZIE. YOU'RE IN THE DATABASE AND WILL BE MADE THE SECOND YOU WALK IN.
"AND AS I UNDERSTAND IT, MR. STARK, YOU'RE MOSTLY METAL.
OF COURSE YOU WEREN'T EXPECTING ME.
WHAT USE IS A SPOT INSPECTION IF I TOLD YOU I WAS COMING?
"THERE ARE A SIGNIFICANT NUMBER OF GUARDS ON-SITE. BODY ARMOR, GUNS, STUN BATONS. SHIFTS STRICTLY MONITORED.
"PEGGY IS FIVE FLOORS UNDERGROUND IN THE MOST SECURE SECTION. ROUND-THE-CLOCK MONITORING, CELLS BUILT MORE LIKE BANK VAULTS THAN ANYTHING.
"UNDER HARRY'S ORDER, PEGGY CAN'T RECEIVE VISITORS. NOT EVEN ME.
"EVERYTHING IS MONITORED FROM THE CENTRAL CONTROL ROOM. CAMERAS, ALARMS, EVEN TEMPERATURE SENSORS. NOTHING GOES UNNOTICED.
"IF A HUMAN MISSES SOMETHING, THE SYSTEM'S A.I. WILL ALERT THEM.
"HARLEY, I CAN GET YOU ON-SITE AS MY STAFF. LIZZIE SAYS YOU'RE A DAB HAND AT COMPUTERS. COULD YOU DISABLE SECURITY TO GET THE OTHERS IN?"
"#@$%. DUNNO UNTIL I'VE GOT ACCESS. I'LL SEE WHAT I CAN DO, BUT I'LL NEED TIME."
YOU ASKED ME TO CALL IF HUNTER EVER CAME SNIFFING AROUND. WELL...

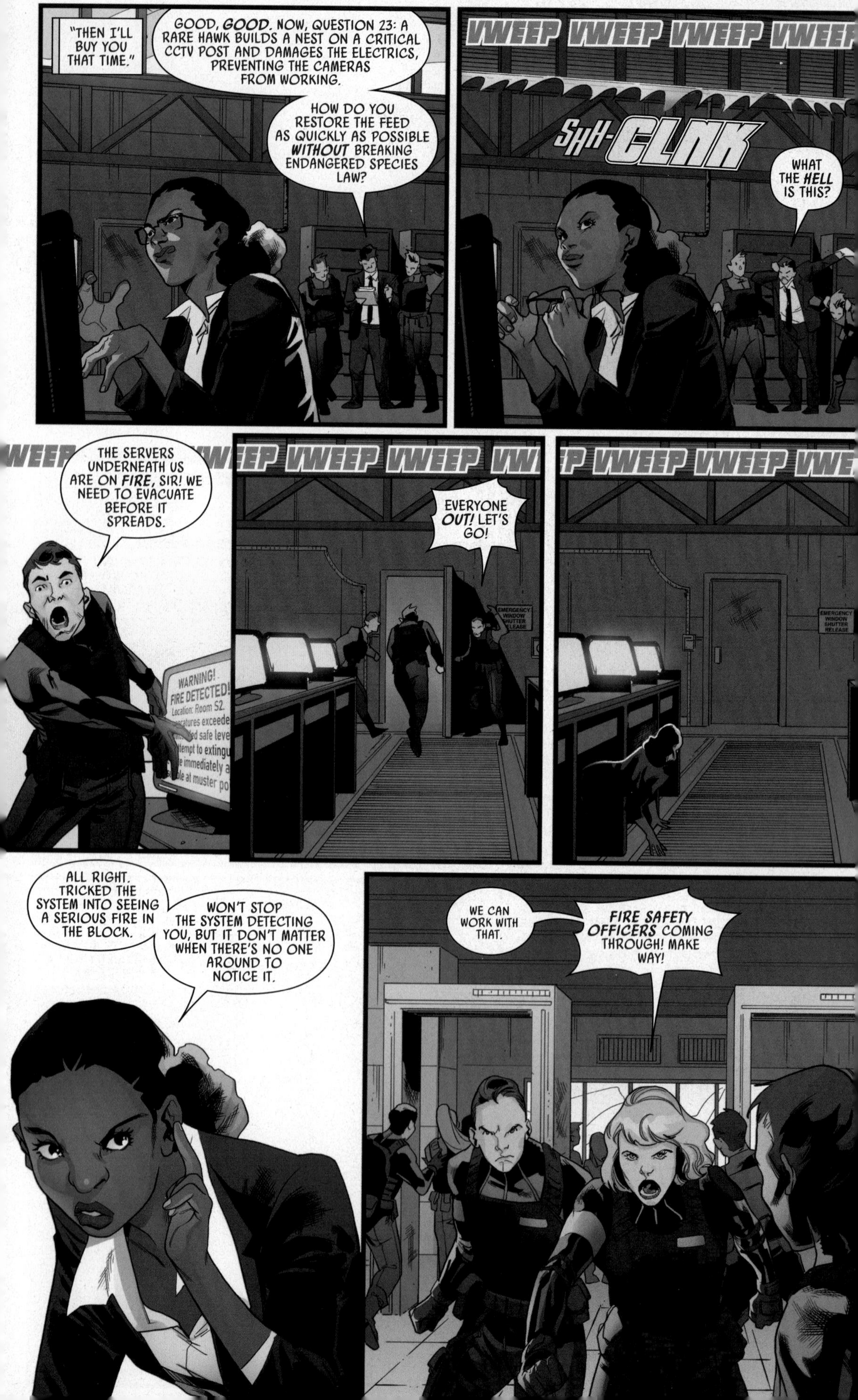
"THEN I'LL BUY YOU THAT TIME."
GOOD, GOOD. NOW, QUESTION 23: A RARE HAWK BUILDS A NEST ON A CRITICAL CCTV POST AND DAMAGES THE ELECTRICS, PREVENTING THE CAMERAS FROM WORKING.
HOW DO YOU RESTORE THE FEED AS QUICKLY AS POSSIBLE WITHOUT BREAKING ENDANGERED SPECIES LAW?
VWEEP VWEEP VWEEP VWEEP
SHH-CLNK
WHAT THE HELL IS THIS?
THE SERVERS UNDERNEATH US ARE ON FIRE, SIR! WE NEED TO EVACUATE BEFORE IT SPREADS.
WARNING! FIRE DETECTED! Location: Room S2.
VWEEP VWEEP VWEEP
EVERYONE OUT! LET'S GO!
EMERGENCY WINDOW SHUTTER RELEASE
VWEEP VWEEP VWEEP
EMERGENCY WINDOW SHUTTER RELEASE
ALL RIGHT. TRICKED THE SYSTEM INTO SEEING A SERIOUS FIRE IN THE BLOCK.
WON'T STOP THE SYSTEM DETECTING YOU, BUT IT DON'T MATTER WHEN THERE'S NO ONE AROUND TO NOTICE IT.
WE CAN WORK WITH THAT.
FIRE SAFETY OFFICERS COMING THROUGH! MAKE WAY!

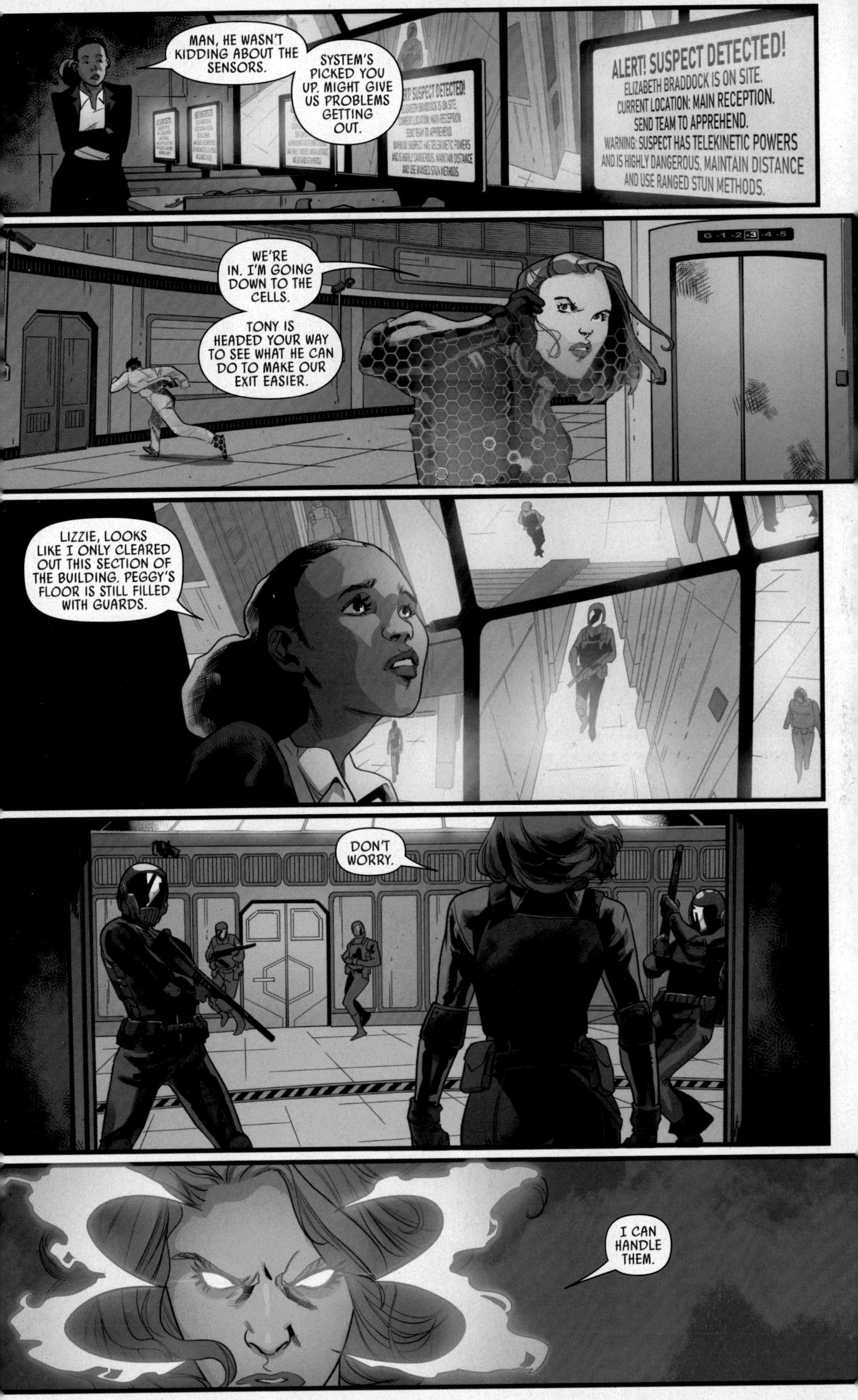
MAN, HE WASN'T KIDDING ABOUT THE SENSORS.
SYSTEM'S PICKED YOU UP. MIGHT GIVE US PROBLEMS GETTING OUT.
ALERT! SUSPECT DETECTED!
ELIZABETH BRADDOCK IS ON SITE.
CURRENT LOCATION: MAIN RECEPTION.
SEND TEAM TO APPREHEND.
WARNING: SUSPECT HAS TELEKINETIC POWERS AND IS HIGHLY DANGEROUS. MAINTAIN DISTANCE AND USE RANGED STUN METHODS.
G -1 -2 -3 -4 -5
WE'RE IN. I'M GOING DOWN TO THE CELLS.
TONY IS HEADED YOUR WAY TO SEE WHAT HE CAN DO TO MAKE OUR EXIT EASIER.
LIZZIE, LOOKS LIKE I ONLY CLEARED OUT THIS SECTION OF THE BUILDING. PEGGY'S FLOOR IS STILL FILLED WITH GUARDS.
DON'T WORRY.
I CAN HANDLE THEM.

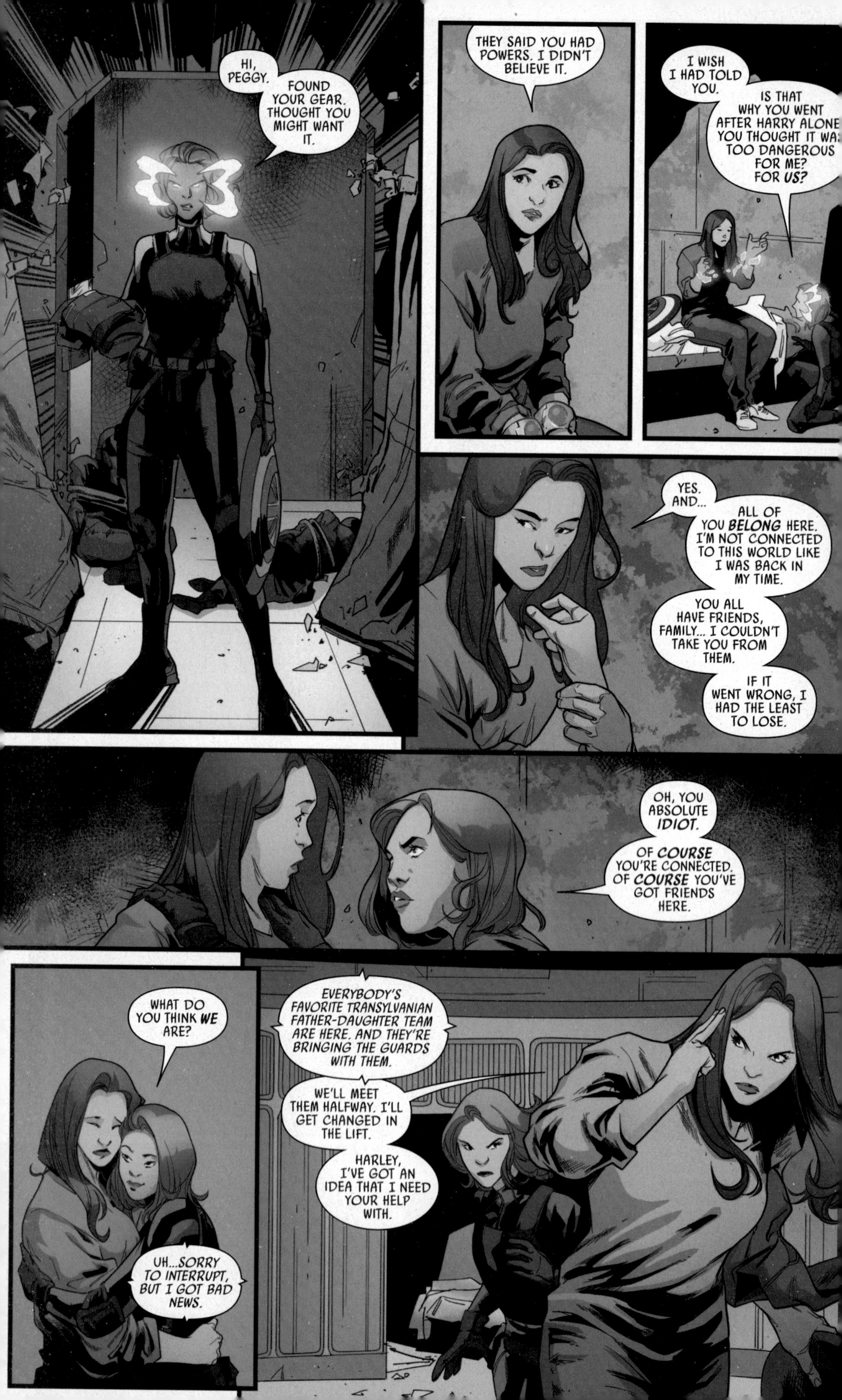

HI, PEGGY.
FOUND YOUR GEAR. THOUGHT YOU MIGHT WANT IT.
THEY SAID YOU HAD POWERS. I DIDN'T BELIEVE IT.
I WISH I HAD TOLD YOU.
IS THAT WHY YOU WENT AFTER HARRY ALONE? YOU THOUGHT IT WAS TOO DANGEROUS FOR ME? FOR US?
YES. AND...
ALL OF YOU BELONG HERE. I'M NOT CONNECTED TO THIS WORLD LIKE I WAS BACK IN MY TIME.
YOU ALL HAVE FRIENDS, FAMILY... I COULDN'T TAKE YOU FROM THEM.
IF IT WENT WRONG, I HAD THE LEAST TO LOSE.
OH, YOU ABSOLUTE IDIOT.
OF COURSE YOU'RE CONNECTED. OF COURSE YOU'VE GOT FRIENDS HERE.
WHAT DO YOU THINK WE ARE?
UH...SORRY TO INTERRUPT, BUT I GOT BAD NEWS.
EVERYBODY'S FAVORITE TRANSYLVANIAN FATHER-DAUGHTER TEAM ARE HERE. AND THEY'RE BRINGING THE GUARDS WITH THEM.
WE'LL MEET THEM HALFWAY. I'LL GET CHANGED IN THE LIFT.
HARLEY, I'VE GOT AN IDEA THAT I NEED YOUR HELP WITH.

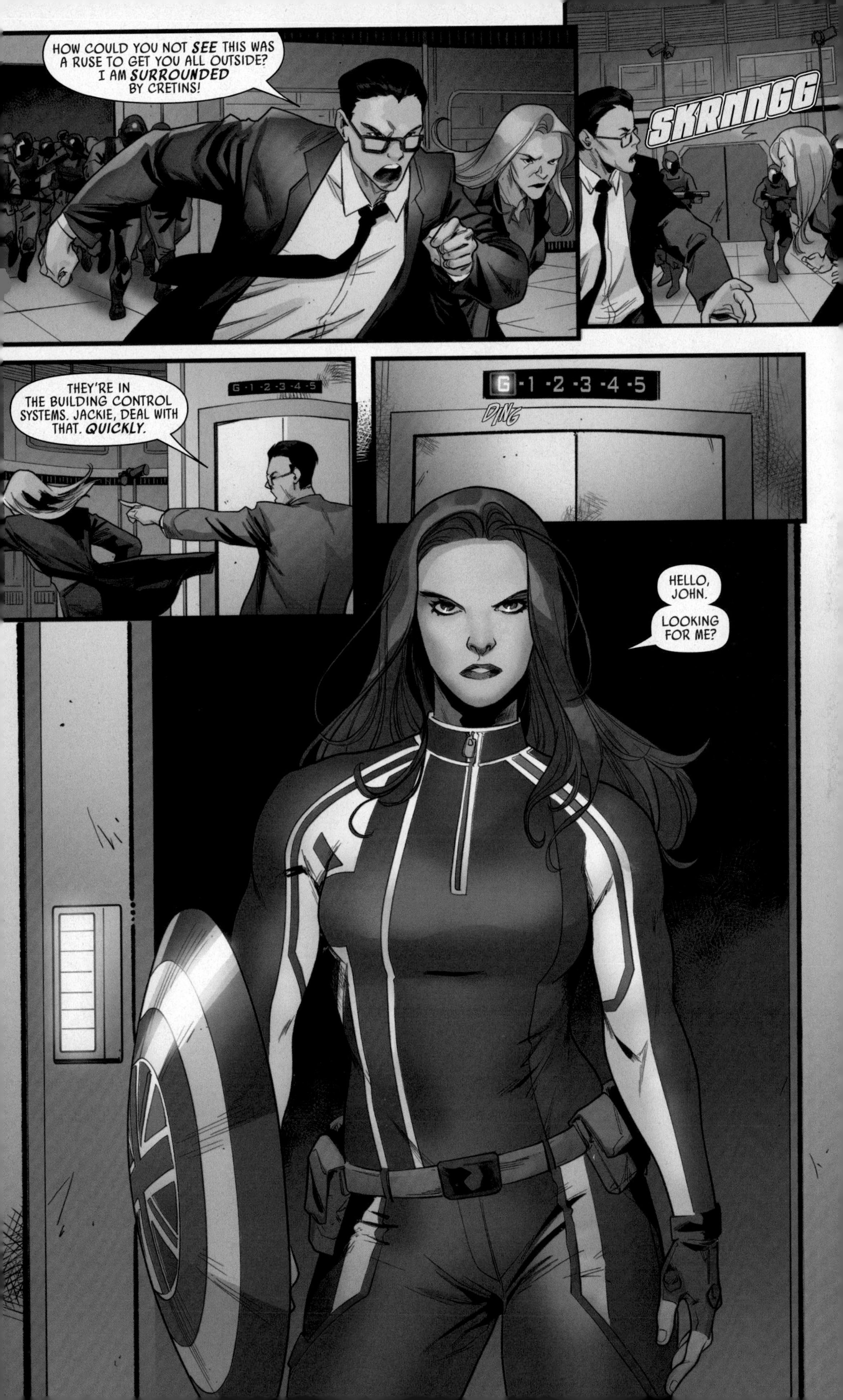
HOW COULD YOU NOT SEE THIS WAS A RUSE TO GET YOU ALL OUTSIDE? I AM SURROUNDED BY CRETINS!
SKRNNGG
THEY'RE IN THE BUILDING CONTROL SYSTEMS. JACKIE, DEAL WITH THAT. QUICKLY.
G-1-2-3-4-5
G-1-2-3-4-5
DING
HELLO, JOHN.
LOOKING FOR ME?

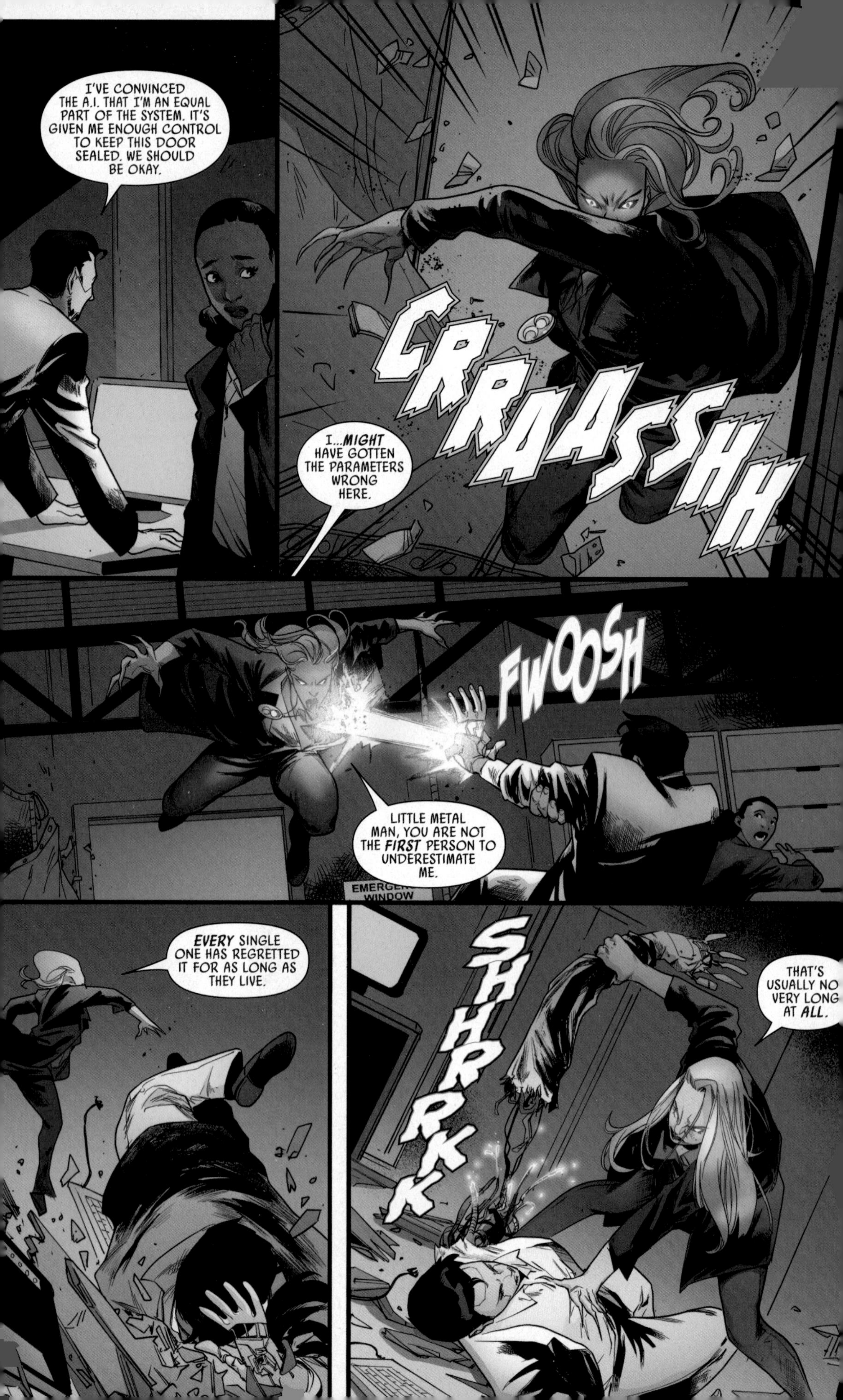
I'VE CONVINCED THE A.I. THAT I'M AN EQUAL PART OF THE SYSTEM. IT'S GIVEN ME ENOUGH CONTROL TO KEEP THIS DOOR SEALED. WE SHOULD BE OKAY.
CRRAASSHH
I...MIGHT HAVE GOTTEN THE PARAMETERS WRONG HERE.
FWOOSH
LITTLE METAL MAN, YOU ARE NOT THE FIRST PERSON TO UNDERESTIMATE ME.
EVERY SINGLE ONE HAS REGRETTED IT FOR AS LONG AS THEY LIVE.
SHHRRKK
THAT'S USUALLY NOT VERY LONG AT ALL.

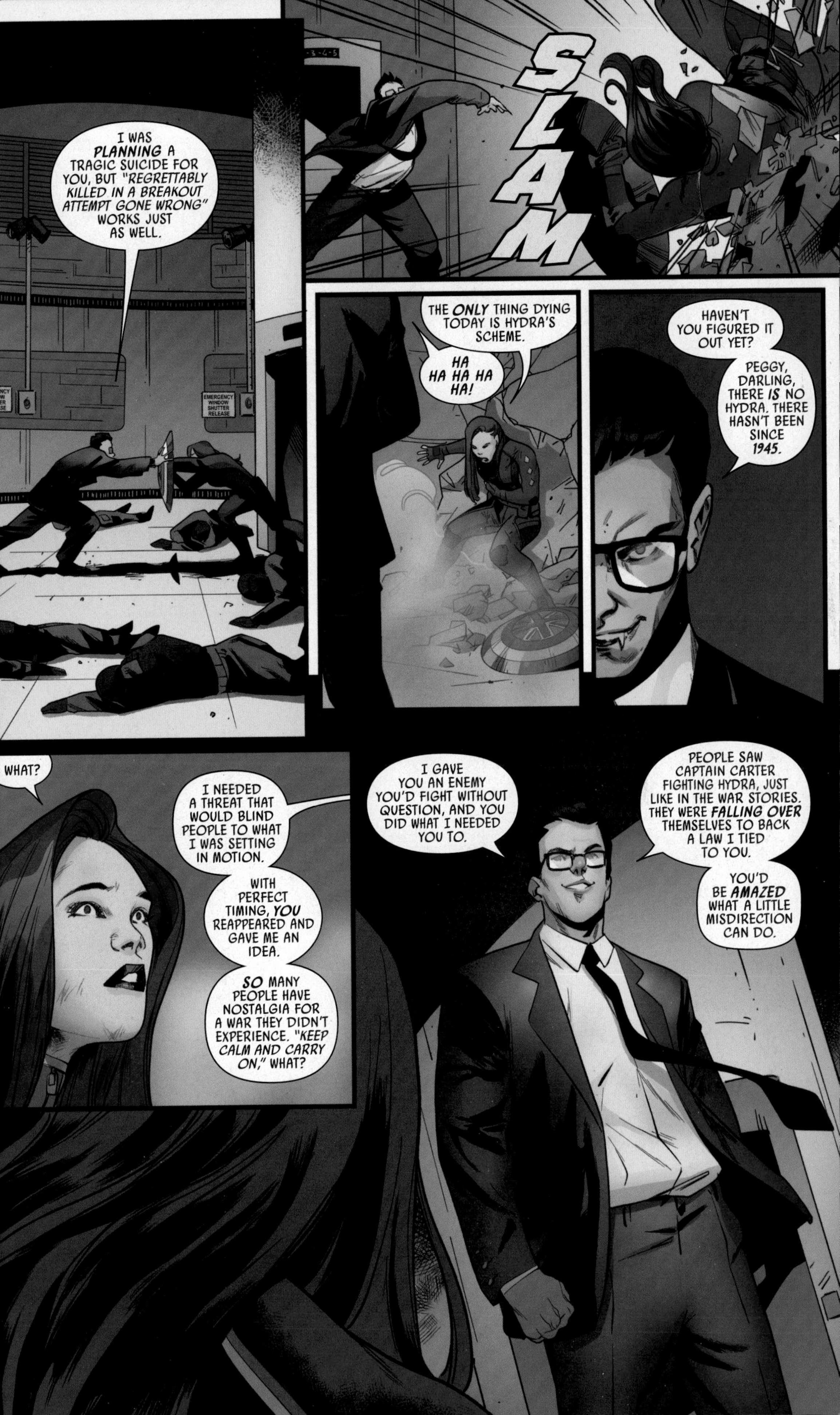

I WAS PLANNING A TRAGIC SUICIDE FOR YOU, BUT "REGRETTABLY KILLED IN A BREAKOUT ATTEMPT GONE WRONG" WORKS JUST AS WELL.
EMERGENCY WINDOW SHUTTER RELEASE
SLAM
THE ONLY THING DYING TODAY IS HYDRA'S SCHEME.
HA HA HA HA HA!
HAVEN'T YOU FIGURED IT OUT YET?
PEGGY, DARLING, THERE IS NO HYDRA. THERE HASN'T BEEN SINCE 1945.
WHAT?
I NEEDED A THREAT THAT WOULD BLIND PEOPLE TO WHAT I WAS SETTING IN MOTION.
WITH PERFECT TIMING, YOU REAPPEARED AND GAVE ME AN IDEA.
SO MANY PEOPLE HAVE NOSTALGIA FOR A WAR THEY DIDN'T EXPERIENCE. "KEEP CALM AND CARRY ON," WHAT?
I GAVE YOU AN ENEMY YOU'D FIGHT WITHOUT QUESTION, AND YOU DID WHAT I NEEDED YOU TO.
PEOPLE SAW CAPTAIN CARTER FIGHTING HYDRA, JUST LIKE IN THE WAR STORIES. THEY WERE FALLING OVER THEMSELVES TO BACK A LAW I TIED TO YOU.
YOU'D BE AMAZED WHAT A LITTLE MISDIRECTION CAN DO.

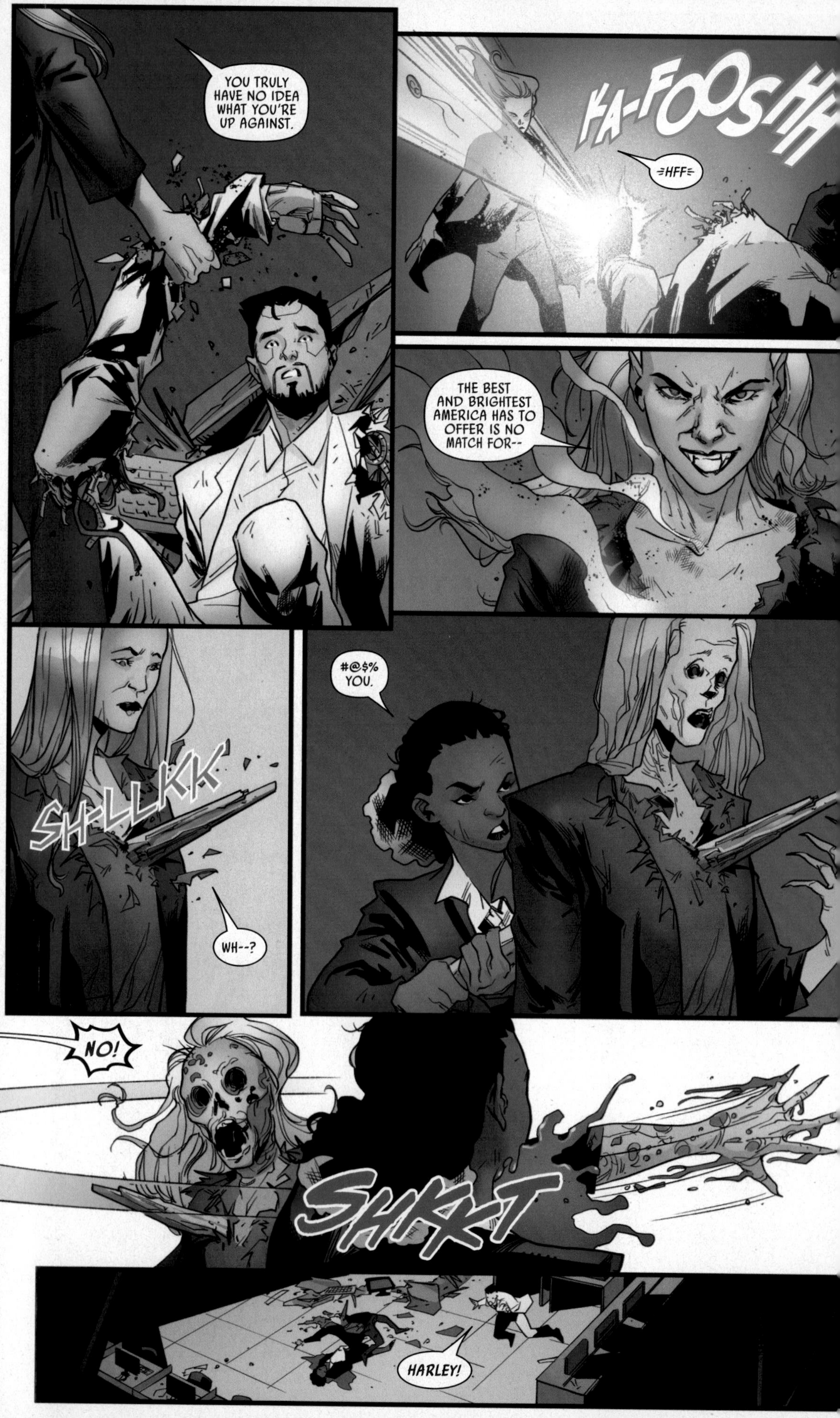
YOU TRULY HAVE NO IDEA WHAT YOU'RE UP AGAINST.
K'A-FOOSHH
=HFF=
THE BEST AND BRIGHTEST AMERICA HAS TO OFFER IS NO MATCH FOR--
SH-LLKK
WH--?
#@$% YOU.
NO!
SHKKT
HARLEY!

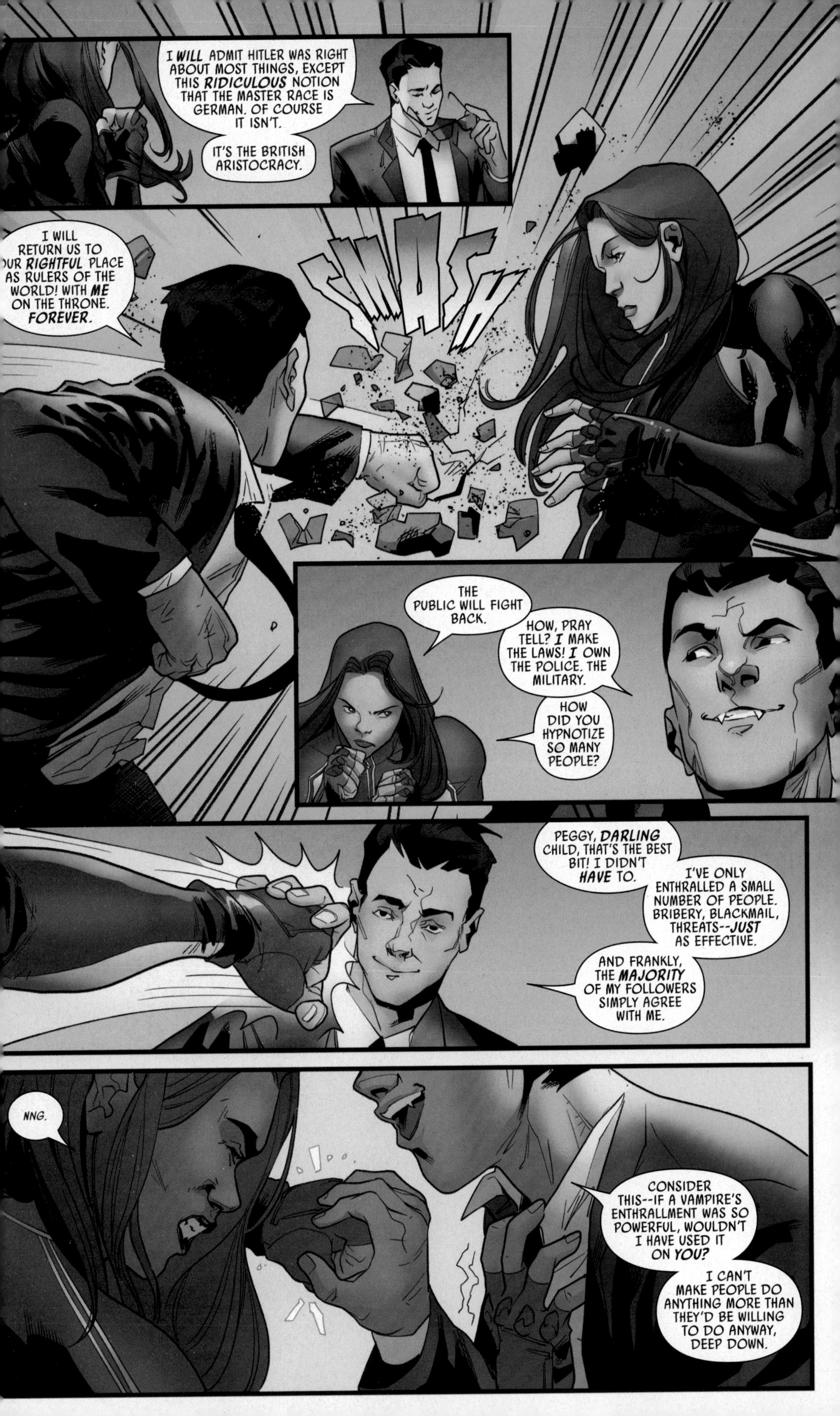
I WILL ADMIT HITLER WAS RIGHT ABOUT MOST THINGS, EXCEPT THIS RIDICULOUS NOTION THAT THE MASTER RACE IS GERMAN. OF COURSE IT ISN'T.
IT'S THE BRITISH ARISTOCRACY.
I WILL RETURN US TO OUR RIGHTFUL PLACE AS RULERS OF THE WORLD! WITH ME ON THE THRONE. FOREVER.
SMASH
THE PUBLIC WILL FIGHT BACK.
HOW, PRAY TELL? I MAKE THE LAWS! I OWN THE POLICE. THE MILITARY.
HOW DID YOU HYPNOTIZE SO MANY PEOPLE?
PEGGY, DARLING CHILD, THAT'S THE BEST BIT! I DIDN'T HAVE TO.
I'VE ONLY ENTHRALLED A SMALL NUMBER OF PEOPLE. BRIBERY, BLACKMAIL, THREATS--JUST AS EFFECTIVE.
AND FRANKLY, THE MAJORITY OF MY FOLLOWERS SIMPLY AGREE WITH ME.
NNG.
CONSIDER THIS--IF A VAMPIRE'S ENTHRALLMENT WAS SO POWERFUL, WOULDN'T I HAVE USED IT ON YOU?
I CAN'T MAKE PEOPLE DO ANYTHING MORE THAN THEY'D BE WILLING TO DO ANYWAY, DEEP DOWN.

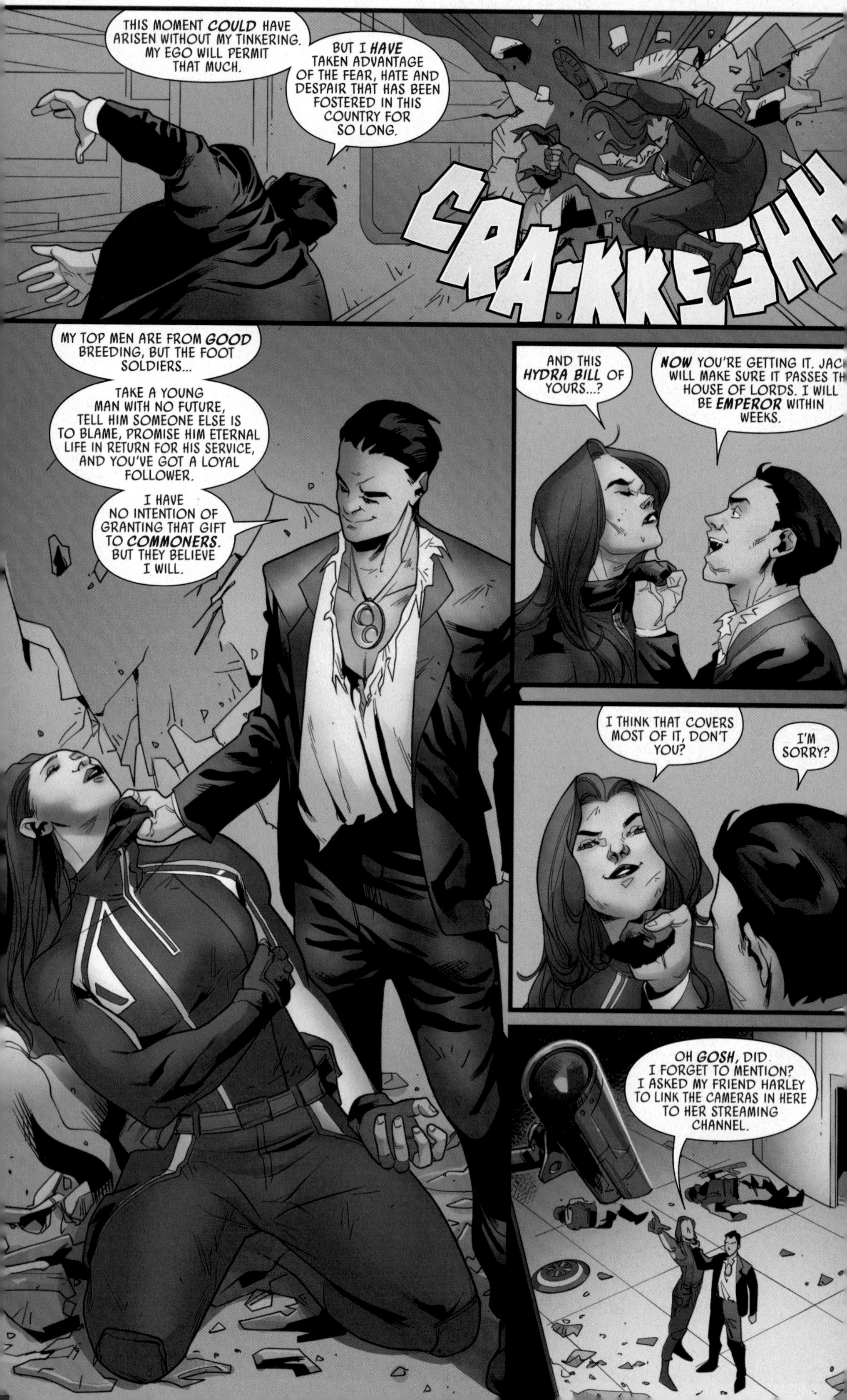

THIS MOMENT **COULD** HAVE ARISEN WITHOUT MY TINKERING. MY EGO WILL PERMIT THAT MUCH.
BUT I **HAVE** TAKEN ADVANTAGE OF THE FEAR, HATE AND DESPAIR THAT HAS BEEN FOSTERED IN THIS COUNTRY FOR SO LONG.
CRA-KKSSHH
MY TOP MEN ARE FROM **GOOD** BREEDING, BUT THE FOOT SOLDIERS...
TAKE A YOUNG MAN WITH NO FUTURE, TELL HIM SOMEONE ELSE IS TO BLAME, PROMISE HIM ETERNAL LIFE IN RETURN FOR HIS SERVICE, AND YOU'VE GOT A LOYAL FOLLOWER.
I HAVE NO INTENTION OF GRANTING THAT GIFT TO **COMMONERS.** BUT THEY BELIEVE I WILL.
AND THIS **HYDRA BILL** OF YOURS...?
NOW YOU'RE GETTING IT. JAC WILL MAKE SURE IT PASSES TH HOUSE OF LORDS. I WILL BE **EMPEROR** WITHIN WEEKS.
I THINK THAT COVERS MOST OF IT, DON'T YOU?
I'M SORRY?
OH **GOSH**, DID I FORGET TO MENTION? I ASKED MY FRIEND HARLEY TO LINK THE CAMERAS IN HERE TO HER STREAMING CHANNEL.

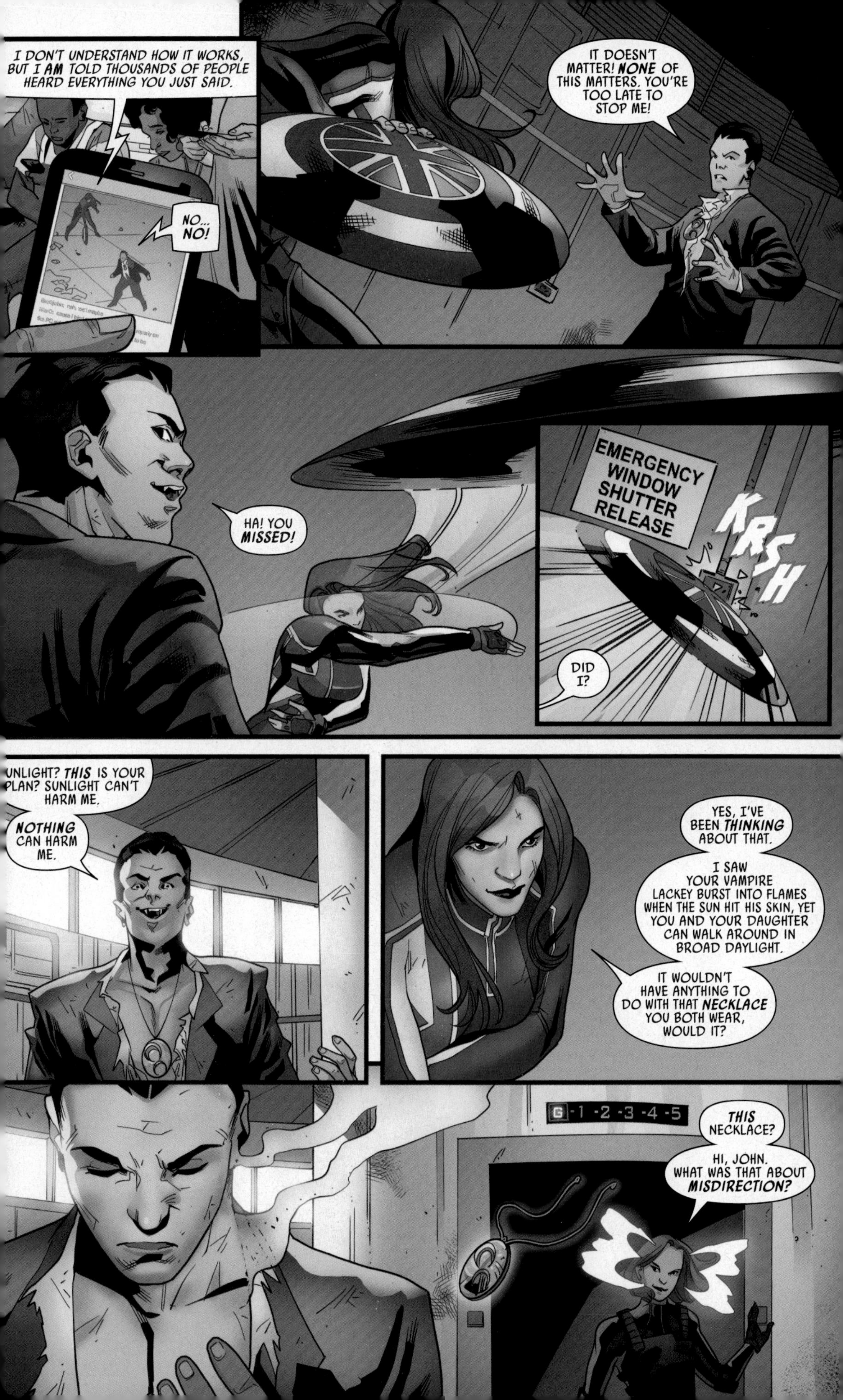
I DON'T UNDERSTAND HOW IT WORKS, BUT I AM TOLD THOUSANDS OF PEOPLE HEARD EVERYTHING YOU JUST SAID.
NO... NO!
IT DOESN'T MATTER! NONE OF THIS MATTERS. YOU'RE TOO LATE TO STOP ME!
HA! YOU MISSED!
EMERGENCY WINDOW SHUTTER RELEASE
KRSH
DID I?
UNLIGHT? THIS IS YOUR PLAN? SUNLIGHT CAN'T HARM ME.
NOTHING CAN HARM ME.
YES, I'VE BEEN THINKING ABOUT THAT.
I SAW YOUR VAMPIRE LACKEY BURST INTO FLAMES WHEN THE SUN HIT HIS SKIN, YET YOU AND YOUR DAUGHTER CAN WALK AROUND IN BROAD DAYLIGHT.
IT WOULDN'T HAVE ANYTHING TO DO WITH THAT NECKLACE YOU BOTH WEAR, WOULD IT?
G-1-2-3-4-5
THIS NECKLACE?
HI, JOHN. WHAT WAS THAT ABOUT MISDIRECTION?

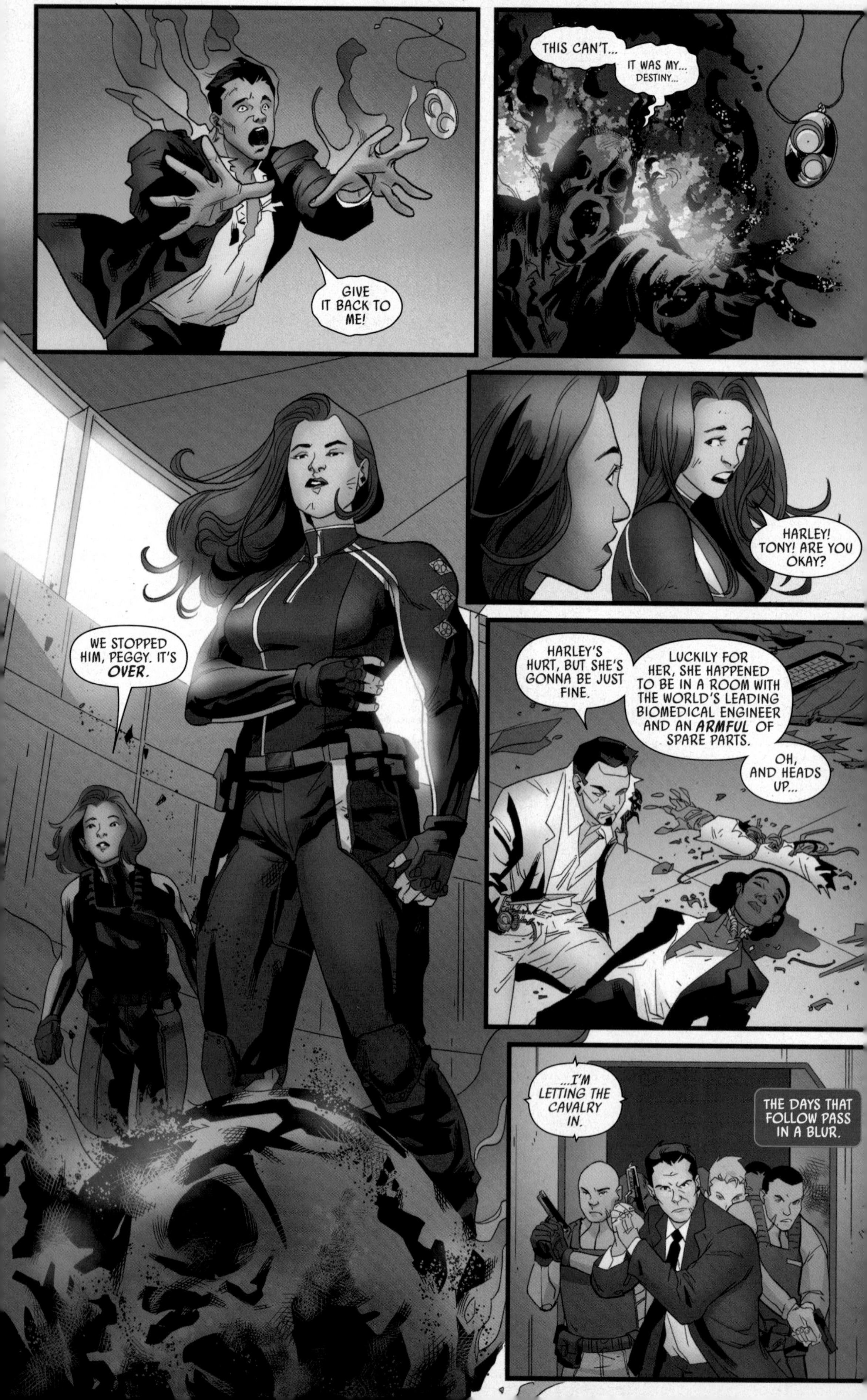
GIVE IT BACK TO ME!
THIS CAN'T...
IT WAS MY... DESTINY...
WE STOPPED HIM, PEGGY. IT'S OVER.
HARLEY! TONY! ARE YOU OKAY?
HARLEY'S HURT, BUT SHE'S GONNA BE JUST FINE.
LUCKILY FOR HER, SHE HAPPENED TO BE IN A ROOM WITH THE WORLD'S LEADING BIOMEDICAL ENGINEER AND AN ARMFUL OF SPARE PARTS.
OH, AND HEADS UP...
...I'M LETTING THE CAVALRY IN.
THE DAYS THAT FOLLOW PASS IN A BLUR.

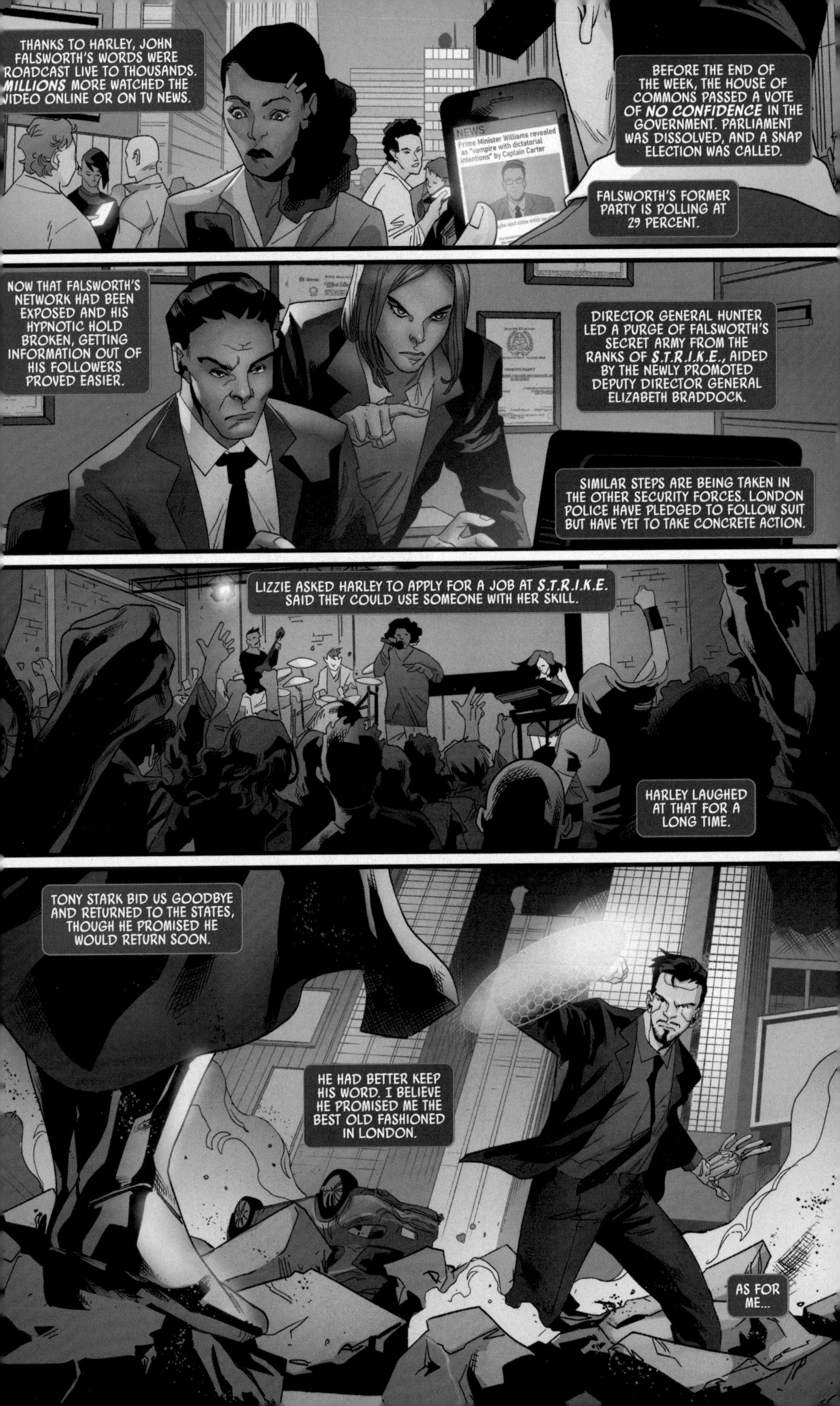
THANKS TO HARLEY, JOHN FALSWORTH'S WORDS WERE BROADCAST LIVE TO THOUSANDS. MILLIONS MORE WATCHED THE VIDEO ONLINE OR ON TV NEWS.
NEWS
Prime Minister Williams revealed as "vampire with dictatorial intentions" by Captain Carter
BEFORE THE END OF THE WEEK, THE HOUSE OF COMMONS PASSED A VOTE OF NO CONFIDENCE IN THE GOVERNMENT. PARLIAMENT WAS DISSOLVED, AND A SNAP ELECTION WAS CALLED.
FALSWORTH'S FORMER PARTY IS POLLING AT 29 PERCENT.
NOW THAT FALSWORTH'S NETWORK HAD BEEN EXPOSED AND HIS HYPNOTIC HOLD BROKEN, GETTING INFORMATION OUT OF HIS FOLLOWERS PROVED EASIER.
DIRECTOR GENERAL HUNTER LED A PURGE OF FALSWORTH'S SECRET ARMY FROM THE RANKS OF S.T.R.I.K.E., AIDED BY THE NEWLY PROMOTED DEPUTY DIRECTOR GENERAL ELIZABETH BRADDOCK.
SIMILAR STEPS ARE BEING TAKEN IN THE OTHER SECURITY FORCES. LONDON POLICE HAVE PLEDGED TO FOLLOW SUIT BUT HAVE YET TO TAKE CONCRETE ACTION.
LIZZIE ASKED HARLEY TO APPLY FOR A JOB AT S.T.R.I.K.E. SAID THEY COULD USE SOMEONE WITH HER SKILL.
HARLEY LAUGHED AT THAT FOR A LONG TIME.
TONY STARK BID US GOODBYE AND RETURNED TO THE STATES, THOUGH HE PROMISED HE WOULD RETURN SOON.
HE HAD BETTER KEEP HIS WORD. I BELIEVE HE PROMISED ME THE BEST OLD FASHIONED IN LONDON.
AS FOR ME...

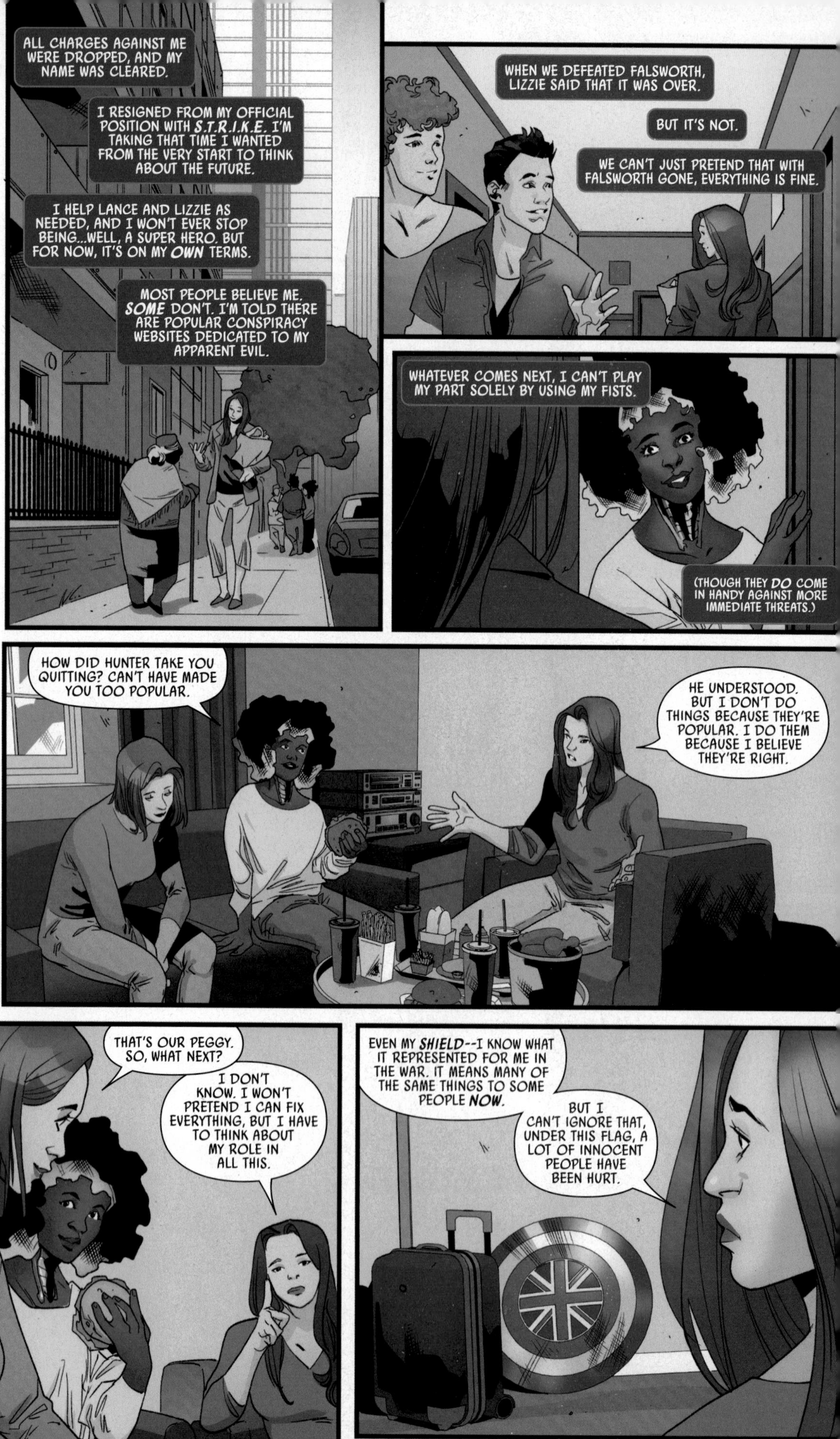

ALL CHARGES AGAINST ME WERE DROPPED, AND MY NAME WAS CLEARED.
I RESIGNED FROM MY OFFICIAL POSITION WITH S.T.R.I.K.E. I'M TAKING THAT TIME I WANTED FROM THE VERY START TO THINK ABOUT THE FUTURE.
I HELP LANCE AND LIZZIE AS NEEDED, AND I WON'T EVER STOP BEING...WELL, A SUPER HERO. BUT FOR NOW, IT'S ON MY OWN TERMS.
MOST PEOPLE BELIEVE ME. SOME DON'T. I'M TOLD THERE ARE POPULAR CONSPIRACY WEBSITES DEDICATED TO MY APPARENT EVIL.
WHEN WE DEFEATED FALSWORTH, LIZZIE SAID THAT IT WAS OVER.
BUT IT'S NOT.
WE CAN'T JUST PRETEND THAT WITH FALSWORTH GONE, EVERYTHING IS FINE.
WHATEVER COMES NEXT, I CAN'T PLAY MY PART SOLELY BY USING MY FISTS.
(THOUGH THEY DO COME IN HANDY AGAINST MORE IMMEDIATE THREATS.)
HOW DID HUNTER TAKE YOU QUITTING? CAN'T HAVE MADE YOU TOO POPULAR.
HE UNDERSTOOD. BUT I DON'T DO THINGS BECAUSE THEY'RE POPULAR. I DO THEM BECAUSE I BELIEVE THEY'RE RIGHT.
THAT'S OUR PEGGY. SO, WHAT NEXT?
I DON'T KNOW. I WON'T PRETEND I CAN FIX EVERYTHING, BUT I HAVE TO THINK ABOUT MY ROLE IN ALL THIS.
EVEN MY SHIELD--I KNOW WHAT IT REPRESENTED FOR ME IN THE WAR. IT MEANS MANY OF THE SAME THINGS TO SOME PEOPLE NOW.
BUT I CAN'T IGNORE THAT, UNDER THIS FLAG, A LOT OF INNOCENT PEOPLE HAVE BEEN HURT.

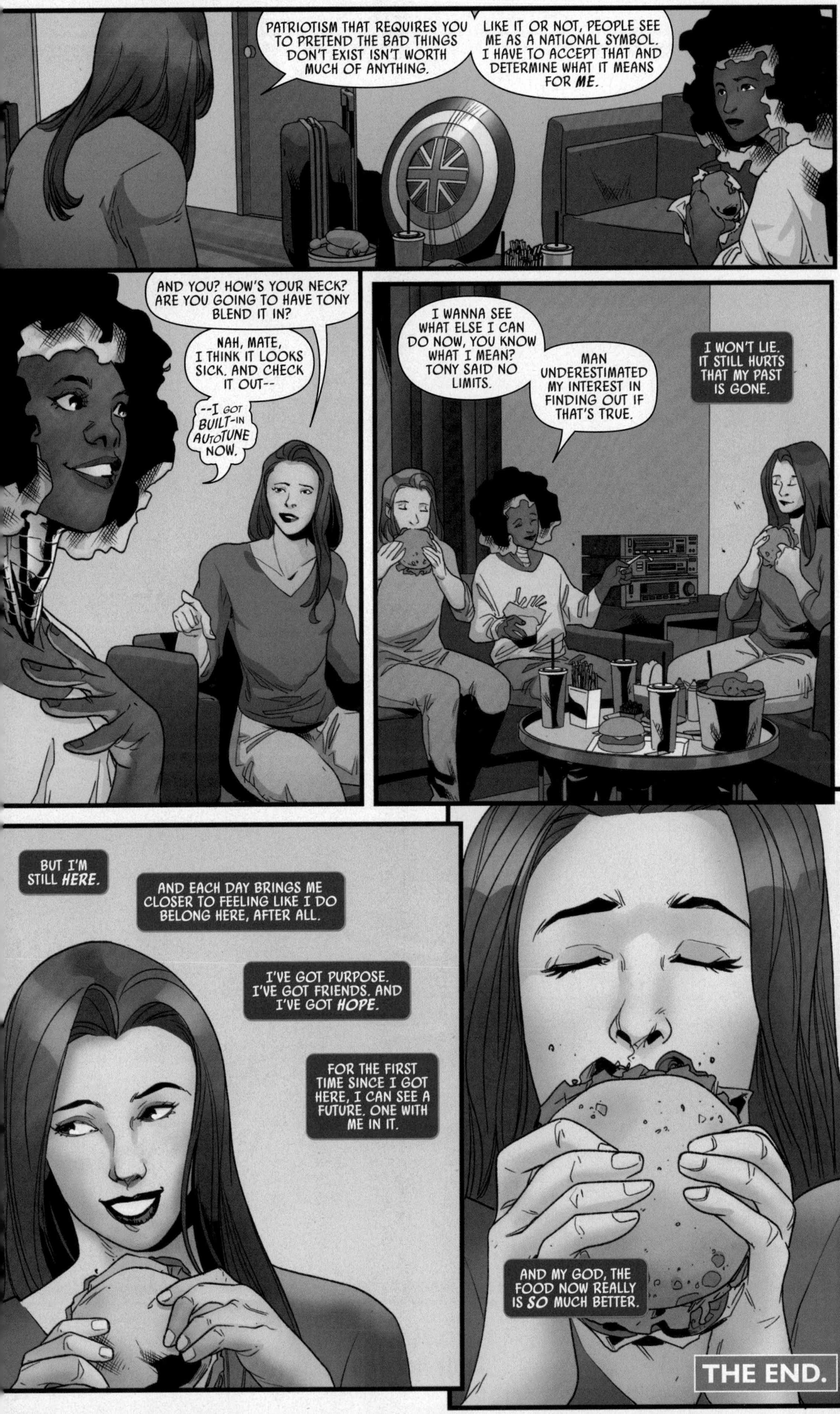
PATRIOTISM THAT REQUIRES YOU TO PRETEND THE BAD THINGS DON'T EXIST ISN'T WORTH MUCH OF ANYTHING.
LIKE IT OR NOT, PEOPLE SEE ME AS A NATIONAL SYMBOL. I HAVE TO ACCEPT THAT AND DETERMINE WHAT IT MEANS FOR ME.
AND YOU? HOW'S YOUR NECK? ARE YOU GOING TO HAVE TONY BLEND IT IN?
NAH, MATE, I THINK IT LOOKS SICK. AND CHECK IT OUT--
--I GOT BUILT-IN AUTOTUNE NOW.
I WANNA SEE WHAT ELSE I CAN DO NOW, YOU KNOW WHAT I MEAN? TONY SAID NO LIMITS.
MAN UNDERESTIMATED MY INTEREST IN FINDING OUT IF THAT'S TRUE.
I WON'T LIE. IT STILL HURTS THAT MY PAST IS GONE.
BUT I'M STILL HERE.
AND EACH DAY BRINGS ME CLOSER TO FEELING LIKE I DO BELONG HERE, AFTER ALL.
I'VE GOT PURPOSE. I'VE GOT FRIENDS. AND I'VE GOT HOPE.
FOR THE FIRST TIME SINCE I GOT HERE, I CAN SEE A FUTURE. ONE WITH ME IN IT.
AND MY GOD, THE FOOD NOW REALLY IS SO MUCH BETTER.
THE END.

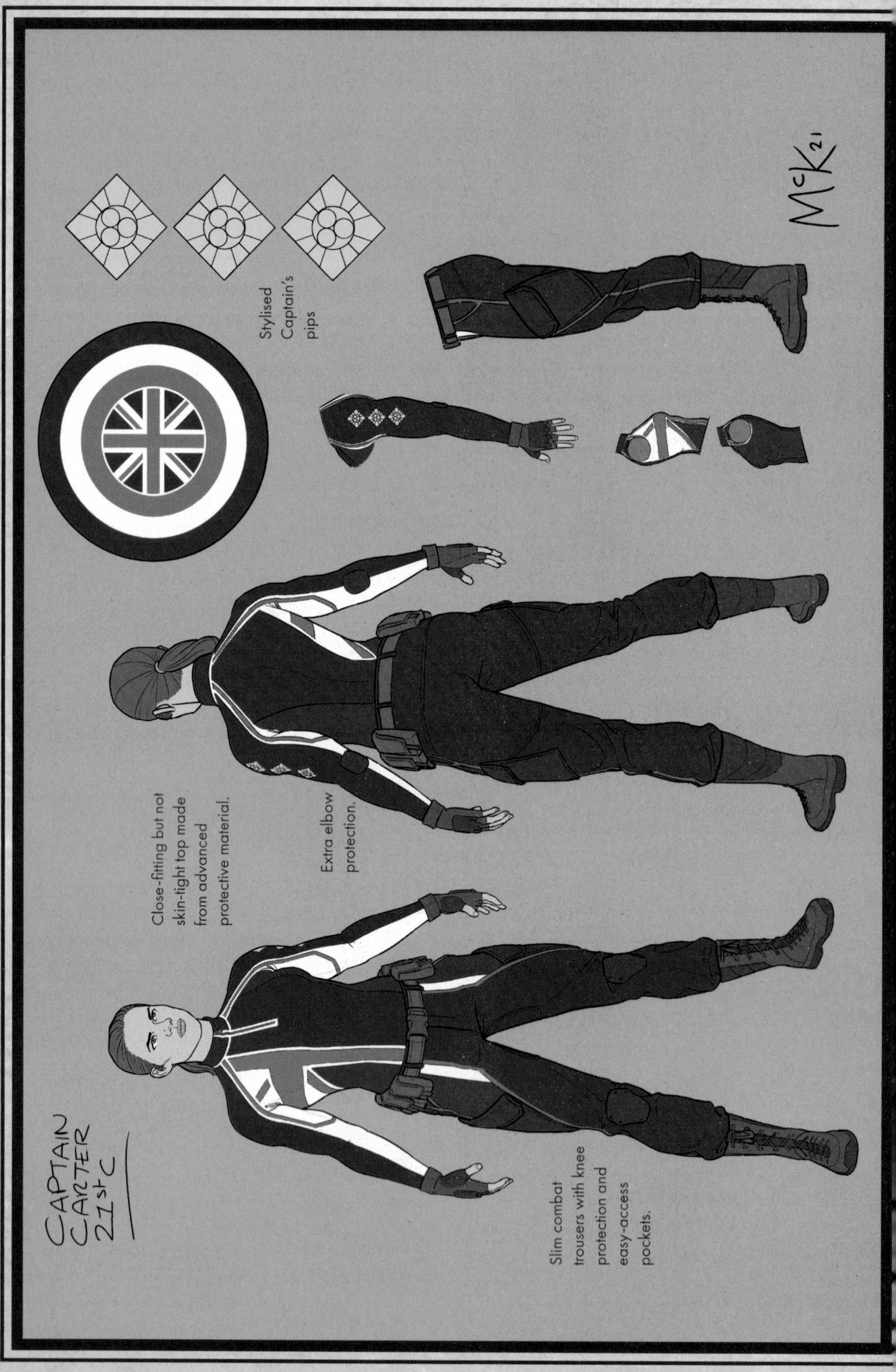

CAPTAIN CARTER 21st C
Slim combat trousers with knee protection and easy-access pockets.
Close-fitting but not skin-tight top made from advanced protective material.
Extra elbow protection.
Stylised Captain's pips
McK 21

#1 DESIGN VARIANT BY
JAMIE McKELVIE

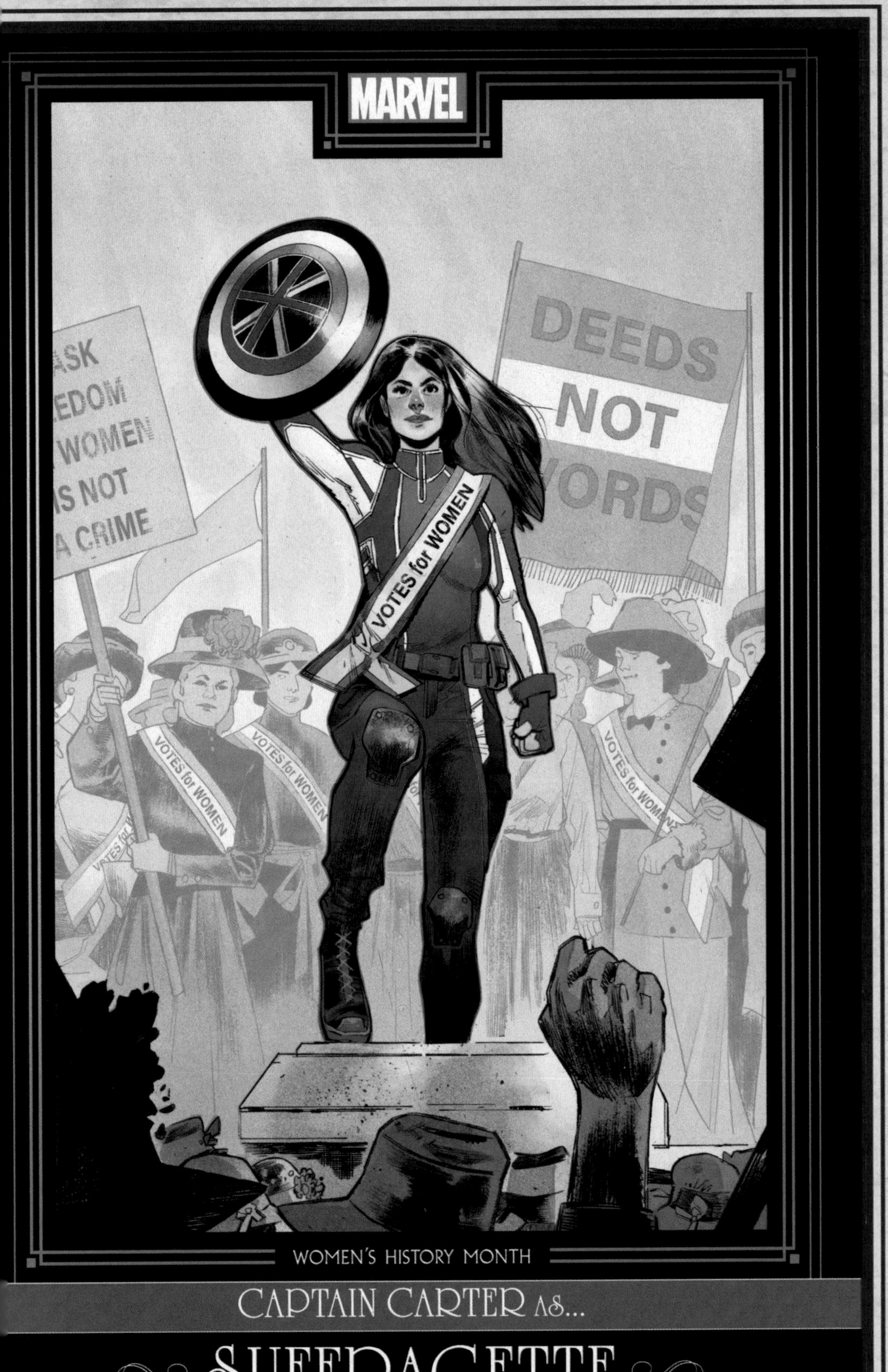
MARVEL
DEEDS
NOT
VOTES for WOMEN
WOMEN'S HISTORY MONTH
CAPTAIN CARTER AS...
SUFFRAGETTE

#1 WOMEN'S HISTORY MONTH VARIANT BY
SARA PICHELLI & MATTHEW WILSON

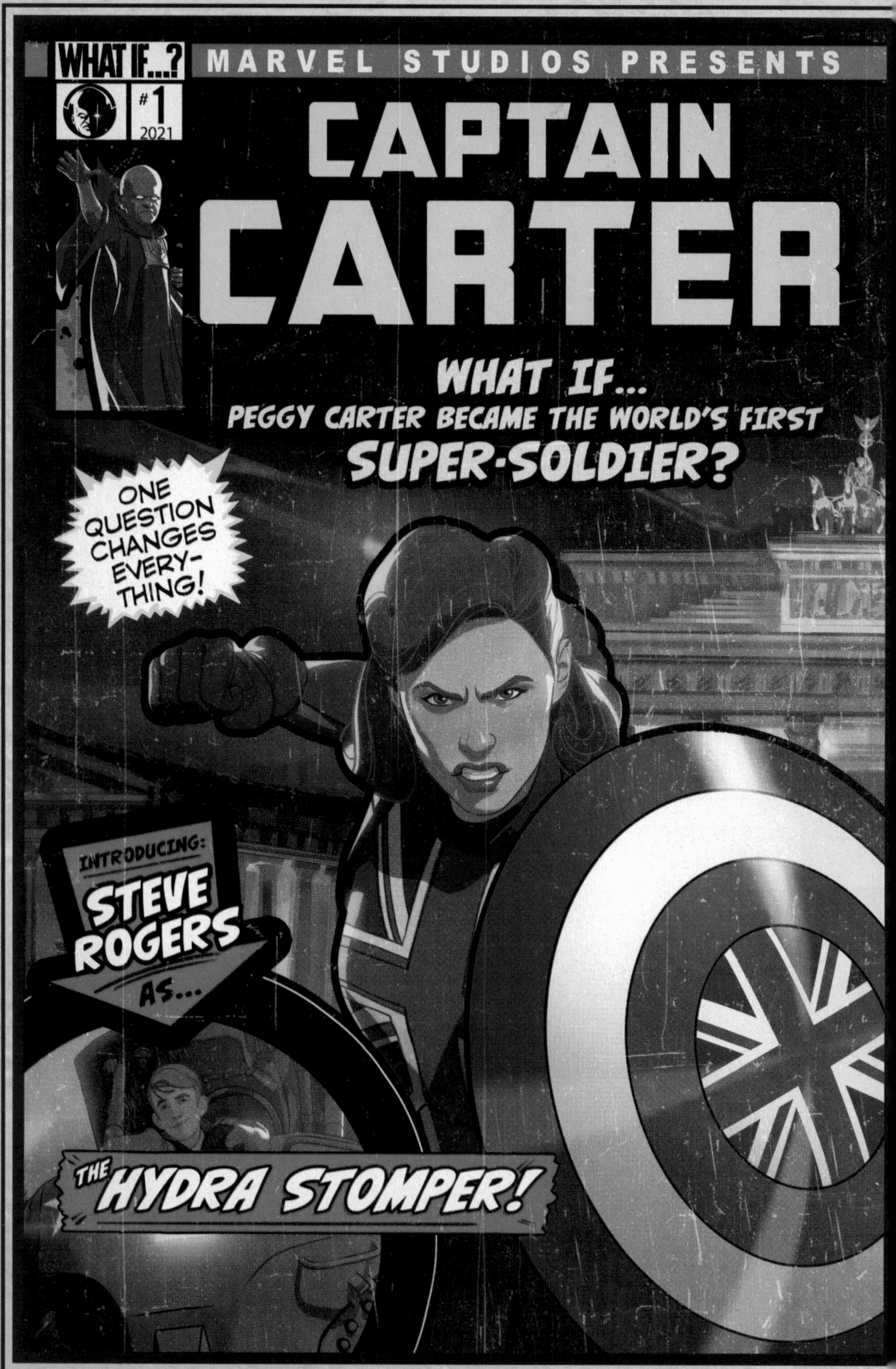
WHAT IF...?
MARVEL STUDIOS PRESENTS
#1
2021
CAPTAIN CARTER
WHAT IF...
PEGGY CARTER BECAME THE WORLD'S FIRST
SUPER-SOLDIER?
ONE QUESTION CHANGES EVERY-THING!
INTRODUCING:
STEVE ROGERS
AS...
THE HYDRA STOMPER!

#1 ANIMATION VARIANT BY
MARVEL STUDIOS

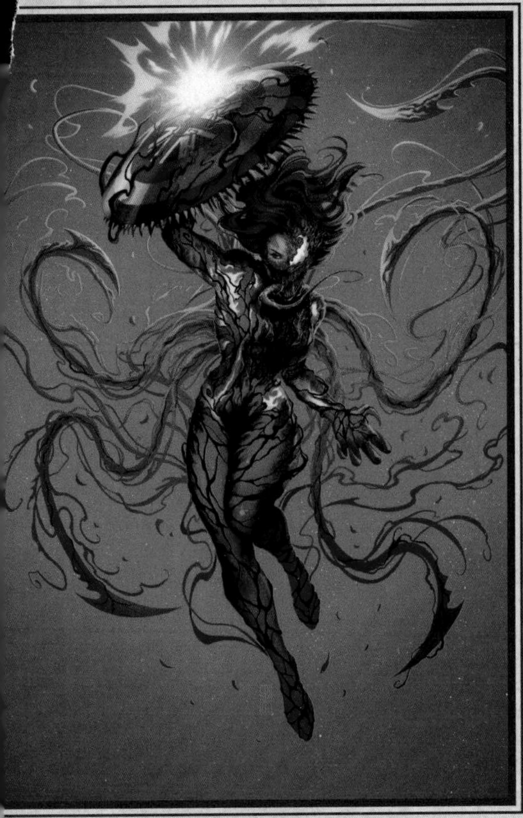

#1 CARNAGE FOREVER VARIANT BY
JEN BARTEL

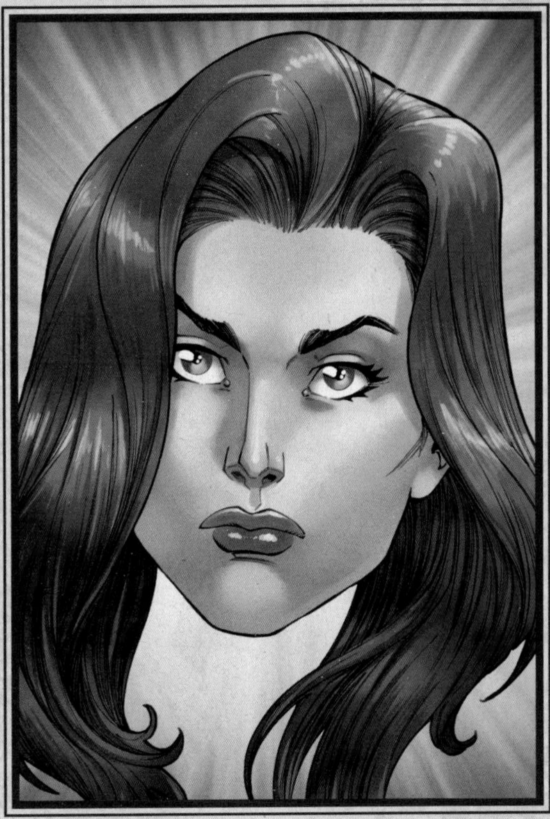

#1 HEADSHOT VARIANT BY
TODD NAUCK & RACHELLE ROSENBERG

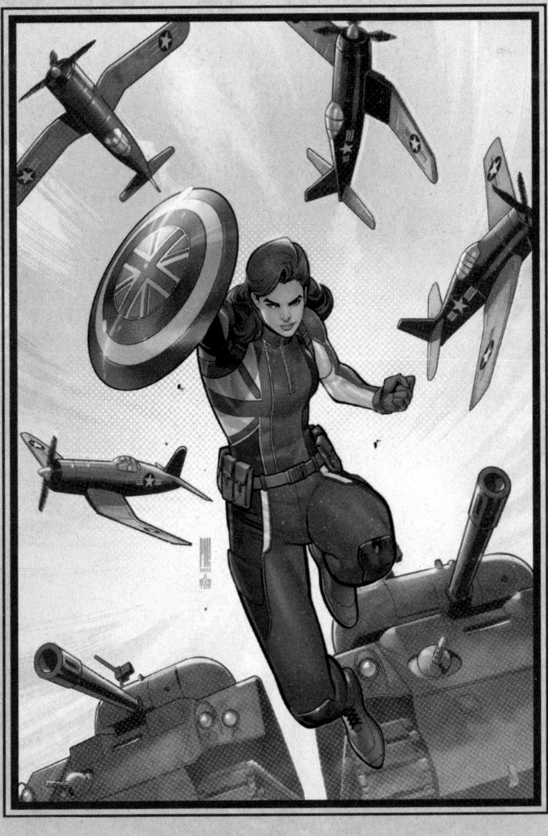

#1 2ND PRINTING VARIANT BY
PACO MEDINA & JESUS ABURTOV

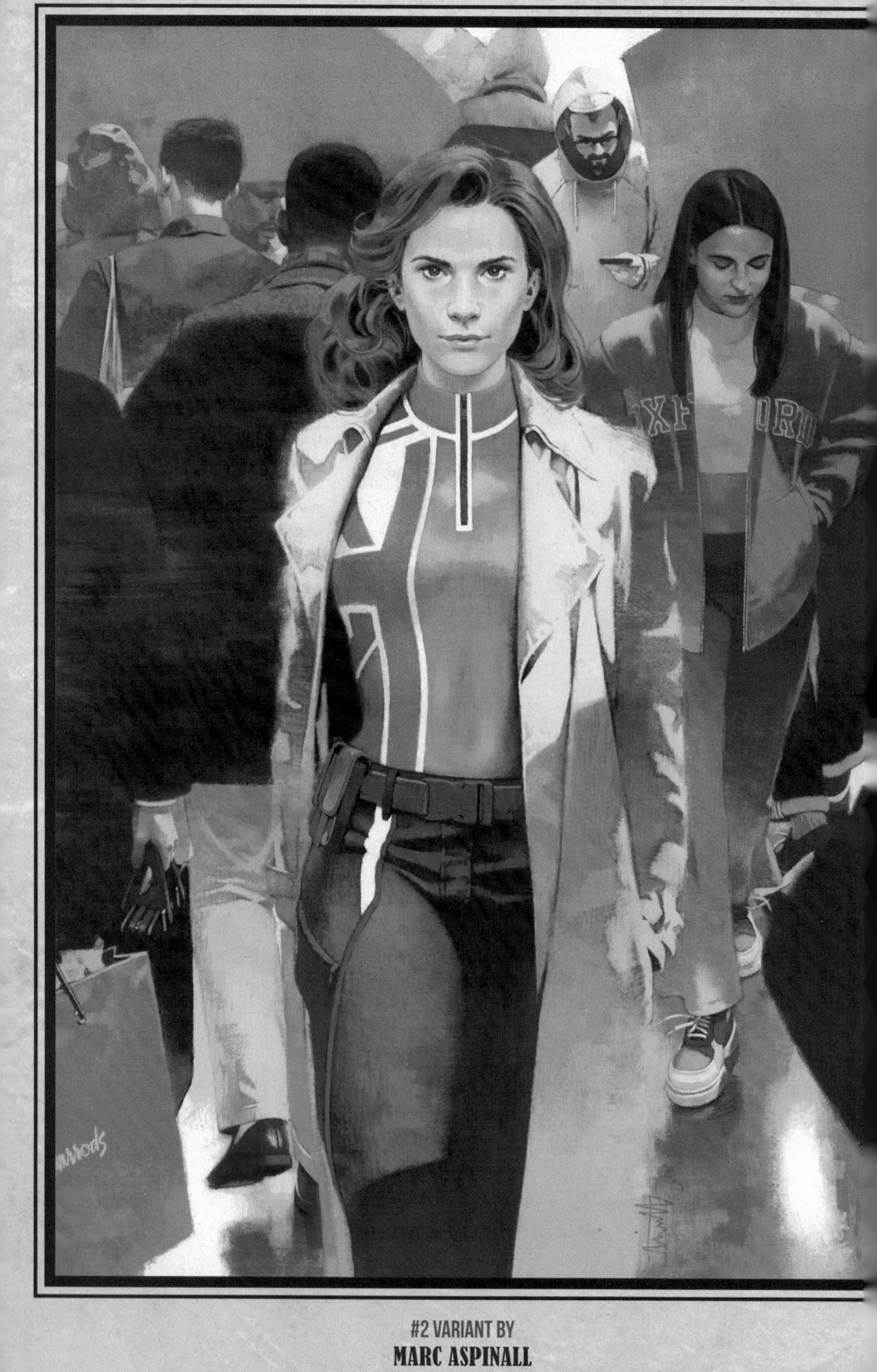

#2 VARIANT BY
MARC ASPINALL

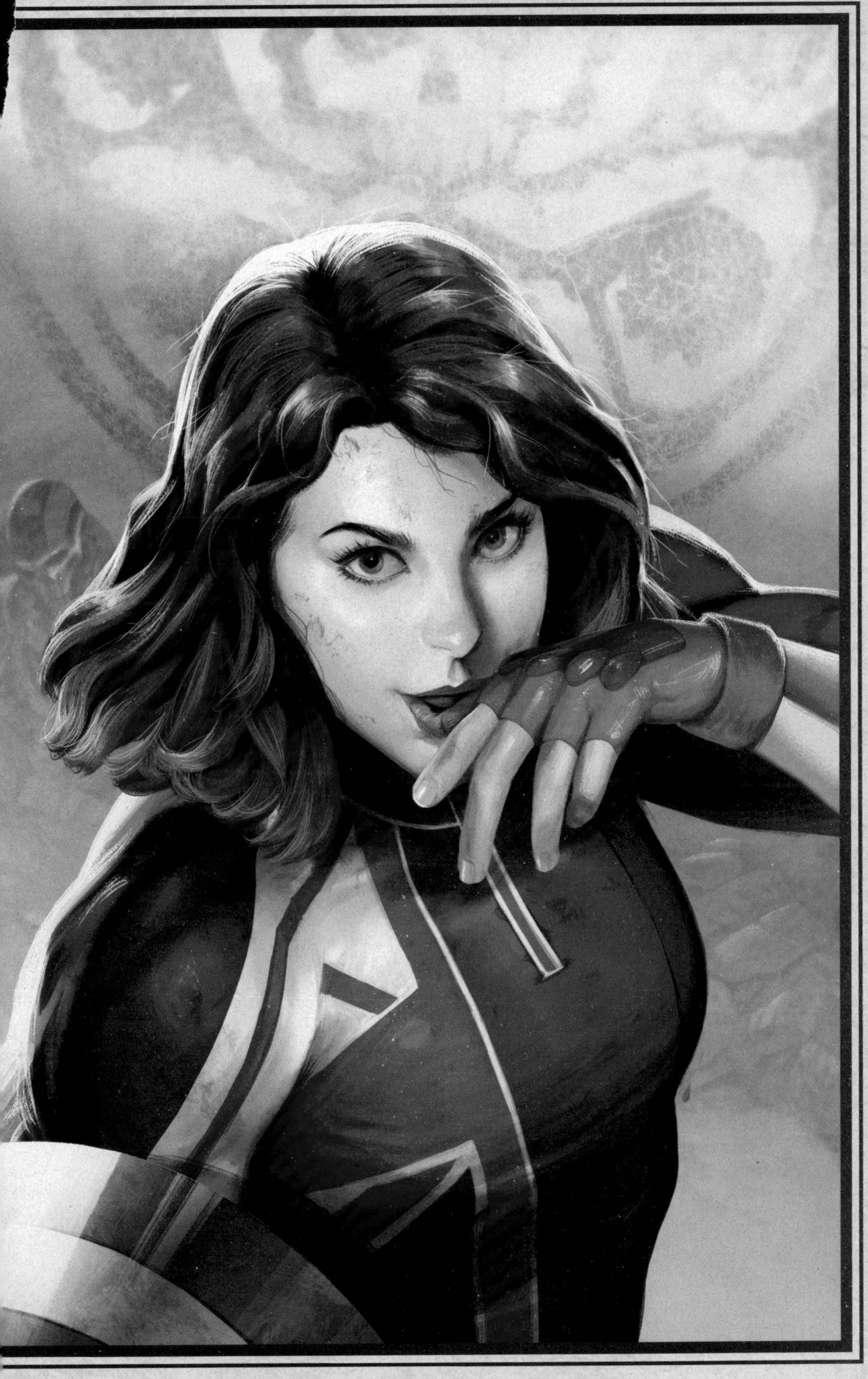

#3 VARIANT BY
ASHLEY WITTER

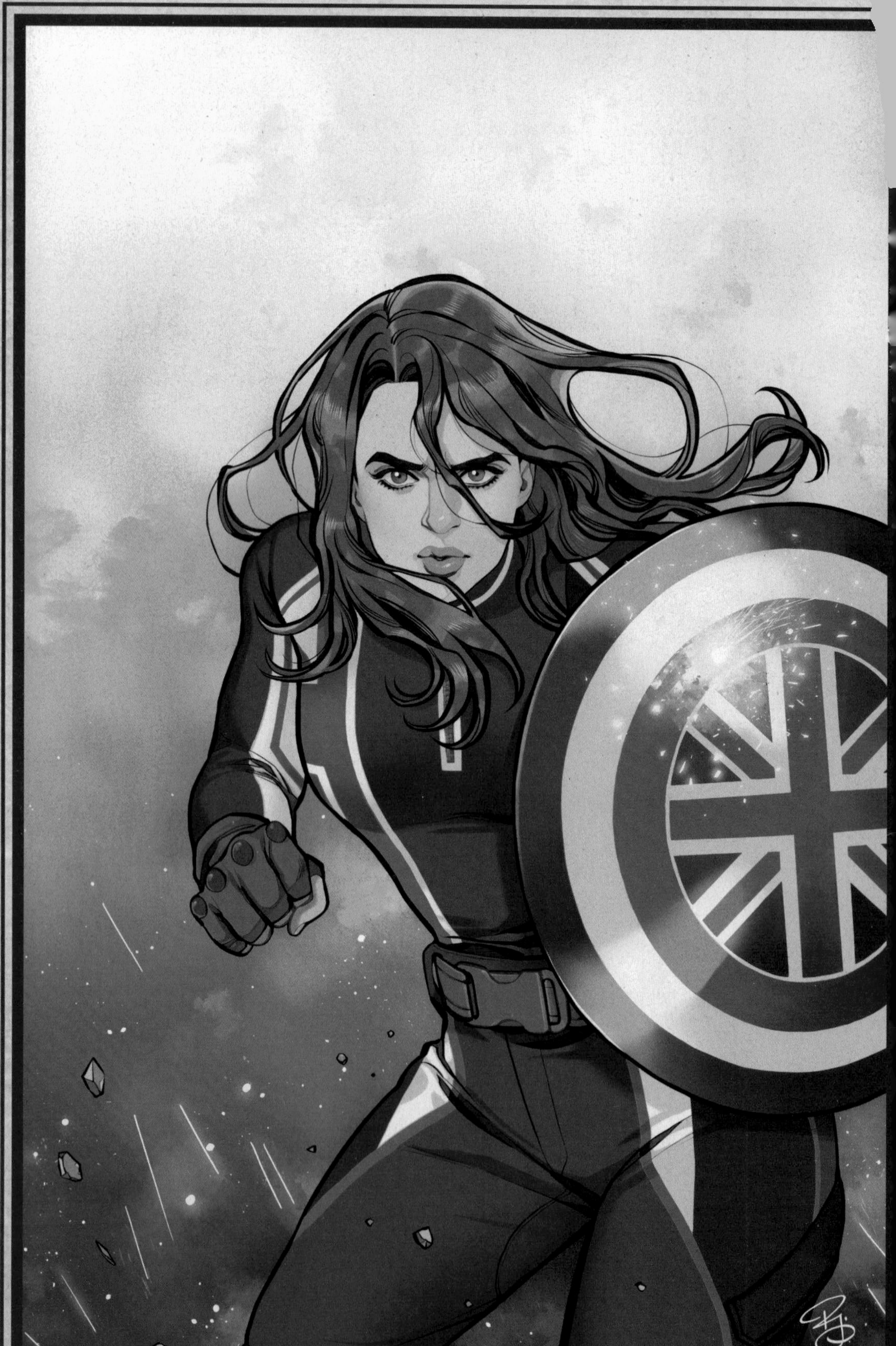

#4 VARIANT BY
ROMY JONES